CW00621228

* - A UU...
DEPARTED
(1095)
HONG KONG

DEPARTMENT OF IMMIGRATION
PERMITTED TO ENTER
AUSTRALIA.
on 24 APR 1986
For stay of 12 Month
SYDNEY AIRPORT 56

IMMIGRATION DIVISION BANGKOK THAILAND
A
72
DEPARTED
-9 FEB 1987
SIGNED

IMMIGRATION & ETHNIC AFFAIRS
............Person
30 OCT 1989
DEPARTED
AUSTRALIA
SYDNEY 32

TRAVELER'S
HONG KONG
COMPANION

中华人民共和国
东省公安厅

上陸許可
ADMITTED
15. FEB. 1986
4
Status: 4-1-
Duration: 90 days
NARITA(N)
№ 011278 Immigration Inspector
日本国

ADMITTED
20 OCT. 1988
Status: 4-1-16
Duration 180 days
Port: HANEDA
Signature

THE UNITED STATES
OF AMERICA
NONIMMIGRANT VISA
ISSUED AT
PASSED Air Port

HONG KONG
(1038)
-7 JUN 1998
IMMIGRATION
OFFICER

U.S. IMMIGRATION
170 HHW 1710
JUL 20 1998

The 1998–1999 Traveler's Companions

ARGENTINA • AUSTRALIA • BALI • CALIFORNIA • CANADA • CHINA • COSTA RICA • CUBA • EASTERN CANADA • ECUADOR • FLORIDA • HAWAII • HONG KONG • INDIA • INDONESIA • JAPAN • KENYA • MALAYSIA & SINGAPORE • MEDITERRANEAN FRANCE • MEXICO • NEPAL • NEW ENGLAND • NEW ZEALAND • PERU • PHILIPPINES • PORTUGAL • RUSSIA • SPAIN • THAILAND • TURKEY • VENEZUELA • VIETNAM, LAOS AND CAMBODIA • WESTERN CANADA

Traveler's HONG KONG Companion
First Published 1998

World Leisure Marketing Limited
9 Downing Road, West Meadows Industrial Estate
Derby, DE21 6HA, England
Web Site: http://www.map-world.co.uk
Published by arrangement with Kümmerly+Frey AG, Switzerland

ISBN: 1 84006 059 X

© 1998 Kümmerly+Frey AG, Switzerland

Created, edited and produced by
Allan Amsel Publishing, 53 rue Beaudouin,
27700 Les Andelys, France. E-mail: aamsel@aol.com
Editor in Chief: Allan Amsel
Editors: Fiona Nichols and Julia Wilkinson
Original design concept: Hon Bing-wah
Picture editor and designer: Chan Sio Man

Printed by Samhwa Printing Company Limited, Seoul, Korea

TRAVELER'S
HONG KONG
COMPANION

by Derek Maitland

Photographed by Nik Wheeler

Kümmerly+Frey

Contents

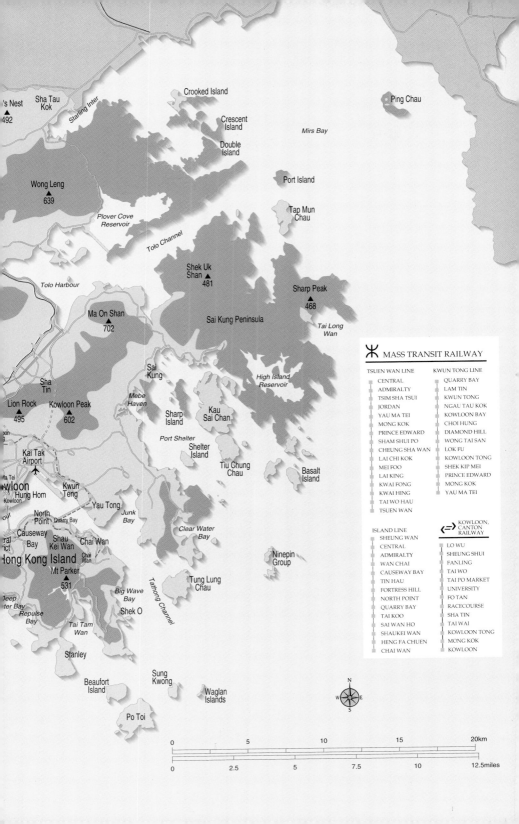

TOP SPOTS

province), imperial Peking banquets (don't miss a taste of Peking duck), the famous hairy crabs of Shanghai, spicey and sizzling Sichuan dishes, and fiery Hunan fare (the province's most famous son, Mao Zedong, claimed the more chillies you ate the more revolutionary you became). Check the GALLOPING GOURMETS chapter for some suggestions of where to find the best restaurants, or pick up a copy of the Hong Kong Tourist Association's (HKTA) *Official Dining and Entertainment Guide.* If you manage to sample a little of every Chinese cuisine represented here you'll begin to understand what makes the Hong Kong people tick.

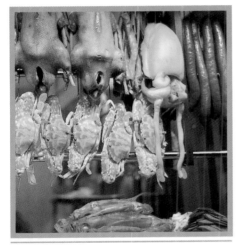

Taste the World's Finest Chinese Food

IT'S OFTEN SAID THAT THE FINEST CHINESE FOOD IN THE WORLD ISN'T NECESSARILY FOUND IN MAINLAND CHINA ITSELF but in places where emigrant Chinese have established successful restaurants and can afford to import the best quality ingredients for their discerning clientele. Chinatowns all over Europe and North America offer some excellent places to sample Chinese fare, but for mind-boggling choice, variety of cuisines, freshness of ingredients and some sumptuous dining experiences right at the frontier of the "new" China, you can't beat Hong Kong's culinary scene.

After you've sampled Cantonese cuisine try exploring some of the other regional tastes: there's rich Chiu Chow cuisine (from eastern Guangdong

The Shoppers' Dream

YES, IT'S TRUE: HONG KONG IS STILL A SHOPPER'S DREAM COME TRUE, with an extraordinary number of shops cramming the streets, duty-free competitive prices and opening hours so long you wonder how the shopkeepers ever find time to replenish the shelves. Be warned, though: you'll be hard pushed to find any real bargains here any more or a guarantee of polite service. Hong Kong shoppers themselves can be almost as aggressive as the sales staff. So unless you're a hardened shopper, you may find the

OPPOSITE: Lavish display of specialties including Peking Duck as the centerpiece at a Central District restaurant. ABOVE: Duck, crab, squid and sausage, Chiu Chow-style.

Hong Kong shopping experience a real strain on the nerves. Take the advice of those in the know: browse briefly, rest often and compare several shop prices before buying.

If you've got something particular in mind you'd be wise to choose a shop recommended by the Tourist Association (and listed in their *Official Shopping Guide*). Prices may be a little higher than a place in the back-of-beyond but service should be more reliable. The only exceptions to this rule are the fantastic street markets

(for instance, in Mongkok's **Fa Yuen Street**, Jordan's **Temple Street** at night or Central's **Li Yuen Streets East and West**) where you can pick up cheap clothing and fake name-brand accessories for a song; and the computer and software emporium of the Golden Shopping Arcade where you'll be right in thinking the goods can't possibly be the real thing for the price offered.

For my money, though, the stores specializing in Chinese or Asian goods are the most rewarding: I've been buying Christmas presents for years at the **Chinese Arts & Crafts** stores (especially noted for its enamel jewelry and exquisite embroidered cotton and silk items) and at the Chinese Emporiums or Products stores where you can find everything from cheap toys and decorations to exotic Chinese musical instruments and calligraphy equipment. Another little-known gem is the **Mountain Folkcraft** shop in Central which has annoyingly attentive sales staff but some fabulous (and reasonably priced) traditional handicrafts from China. The SHOP TILL YOU DROP section (see page 62) offers more tips and suggestions on where to enjoy spending your dollars and cents.

Gambling Galore

NEXT TO EATING, HONG KONG CHINESE LOVE MAKING MONEY ESPECIALLY IF THEY CAN WIN IT ON THE GAMBLING TABLES OR AT THE RACES. In fact, Hong Kong's passion for punting produces the world's highest per capita horse race betting turnover: in 1995, over 3.25 million punters laid more than US$10 billion in bets during the September to June racing season.

To get into the Hong Kong gambling spirit, follow the punters to the two **racecourses** operated by the Hong Kong Jockey Club: one is in Happy Valley on Hong Kong island and the other at Shatin in the New Territories (easily accessible by train). Although the original Happy Valley course has recently been enlarged, the newer 100-hectare (247-acre) Shatin course is still the more impressive of the two, with state-of-the-art facilities and a capacity for 83,000 visitors. If you prefer, you can simply lay a bet at one of the 125 off-course betting shops (a HK$20 computerized ticket even saves you the hassle of picking a particular horse) or join the special tour organized for visitors by the Hong Kong Tourist Association

which gives you access to the exclusive Members' Enclosure.

Macau is even more obsessed with gambling. Hundreds of Hong Kong punters make the one-hour jetfoil ride to Macau every weekend to lay bets at the **casino** in the Lisboa Hotel, the most popular of Macau's half dozen casinos. Almost every game known to gamblers can be found in Macau — from slot machines (known locally as "hungry tigers") to roulette, blackjack to baccarat. There are also a couple of Chinese games you may not have encountered before: *Dai-Siu* ("big and small") and *Fan Tan*. Stakes at most tables start at a minimum of 10 patacas (about US$1.50), although VIP gamblers in private rooms will have to shell out as much as US$250 to start the game rolling. If your gambling fancies prefer outdoor pursuits, Macau can also offer horse-racing (at the Macau Jockey Club on Taipa island) and greyhound racing (at the Canidrome).

OPPOSITE TOP: Pseudo-traditional decor at Hollywood Road where antique shops abound above Central District. OPPOSITE BOTTOM: Chinese Silk is a good buy in Hong Kong. ABOVE: On-course crowd at Shatin race-track.

See the World's Biggest Outdoor Buddha

LANTAU ISLAND — THE LARGEST OF KONG KONG'S 235 OUTLYING ISLANDS AND ONLY AN HOUR'S FERRY RIDE FROM THE CENTRAL DISTRICT — HAS LONG BEEN A HAVEN FOR BUDDHIST RETREATS. Tucked away in the island's central range of hills are several nunneries and monasteries. The most famous of them all is **Po Lin (Precious Lotus) Monastery**, situated high on Ngong Ping mountain. Po Lin was first established in 1905 but it has been considerably renovated and extended since then. The latest addition to today's huge complex of temples, halls and dormitories is a huge 34-m- (113-ft)-high Buddha statue — the world's largest seated outdoor bronze Buddha — which dominates the complex from an adjacent plateau. Forged in China and funded by wealthy Hong Kong Buddhists, it was opened to the public at the end of 1993 and has become a big attraction for the thousands of visitors who now flock to Po Lin. At weekends, when the souvenir stalls around the statue do a roaring trade in Buddhist trinkets, medallions and photos, the place feels dangerously like a theme park rather than a place of worship but come here during the week and you'll still be able to catch a sense of Po Lin's grandeur and majestic, scenic setting.

If the weather is fine I can recommend making it the start of a grand day's outing: after the bus from the Mui Wo ferry pier has whisked you directly up to Po Lin and you've visited the Buddha and perhaps had a vegetarian lunch in the complex below (the monastery serves these lunches daily), strike out west towards the coastal village of Tai O. The downhill walk along the mountain ridge passes several other smaller monasteries and finally brings you to Tai O where you can pick up a bus for the 45-minute run back to Mui Wo.

Have Your Face and Fortune Told

YOU'VE GOT FOUR CHOICES WHEN IT COMES TO CHOOSING A METHOD OF FORTUNE-TELLING IN HONG KONG: PALM, FACE, CARDS OR STICKS. Five, actually, if you count the budgies. Fortune tellers of all varieties can be found in many of Hong Kong's temples (their fees help with the temple upkeep) and their services are widely sought after, even by the younger generation of Hong Kong Chinese who may be more highly educated than their parents but are often just as superstitious.

OPPOSITE: The world's biggest outdoor Buddha, Po Lin Monastery, Lantau island. Two faces of Hong Kong spiritualism: Fortune teller ABOVE awaits clients and palmist RIGHT reads hands in Temple Street night market in Kowloon.

Of all the techniques practiced in Hong Kong, the "budgie" technique (often found in the night-time Temple Street market) is probably the jokiest and least reliable: the bird (a budgie, small parakeet or finch) picks out a card from those displayed by his master and this is then "interpreted" appropriately. I've never heard a bad omen from the budgie so in some ways it can be highly recommended.

More popular — especially among the fortune-tellers which line the route to Wong Tai Sin Temple and operate from Yaumatei's Tin Hau Temple — are the card-, palm- and face-readers. There's a venerable Chinese tome about the "right" and "wrong" face shapes but unfortunately Western features (such as big eyes and noses) aren't included in the lexicon so you should probably be a little suspicious about the face-readers' prognosis, though they do the best they can. I was once told, for instance, that my straight nose meant I would make a good spouse but that my small ear-lobes meant I'd never have any money (well, he was right on that count, anyway). Palm readers are on safer ground, of course, though you should be careful if they also ask about your date of birth: not only do Chinese fortune-tellers usually require the exact hour you were born but they also calculate a person's age from the moment of conception, so that a day-old baby is already considered one year old. Choose an English-speaking fortune teller if you can (there are several at Wong Tai Sin Temple) so you can be sure of getting the information correct to start with.

The most widely practiced method of Chinese fortune-telling is the one that's the noisiest and most fun and takes place in temples all over the territory: it involves kneeling before the temple god and shaking a bamboo container of numbered "fortune sticks' (called *chim*) until one falls out. The number corresponds to a book of fortunes which the resident fortune-teller (often just the temple caretaker) will interpret. Often three sticks are shaken out to be sure of getting a full interpretation. There's no set fee for using the *chim* in the temple but you should leave the caretaker

a small donation. And if you get really hooked on the practice, you can even buy your own set of *chim* (complete with instructions in English) for around US$12 from places such as the China Arts & Crafts Store (several locations) or Welfare Handicraft shop in the Basement of Jardine House (next to the HKTA Information & Gift Centre).

Hike the Trails of Hidden Hong Kong

HONG KONG'S ISN'T ALL TRAFFIC AND CONCRETE, SKYSCRAPERS AND TOWER BLOCKS. In fact, over 70 percent of all Hong Kong's territory is rural or country park land, left untouched by the developers thanks to its remoteness from the city or its mountainous, rugged terrain. Since the 1970s, about 30 percent of Kong's land has been classified into 21 Country Parks or specially protected areas. Clearly marked trails wriggle their way across many of the parks, up hill and dale, past reservoirs and woodlands, along

coastlines and beaches. Many of them have sections which would challenge the most determined hiker (and there are designated camping sites if you're keen to do an overnight stint) but there are also shorter, gentler "family walks" at many of the parks' entrances if you only want a simple stroll.

The most easily accessible trail is the **Hong Kong Trail** on Hong Kong island: it starts at The Peak and ends at Shek O, right at the other side of the island, though a couple of hours downhill to Aberdeen is usually enough for most people. For a sense of real countryside, though, I'd recommend heading out to Lantau island to tackle a bit of the 70-km (44-mile) **Lantau Trail**. The mountaintop trail doubles back along the coast so you've got a choice of uphill but scenically splendid climbs up peaks such as Lantau and Sunset Peaks or a coastal dawdle along Lantau's southern coast to Tai O.

One of my own favorite trails which isn't too demanding is along the northern coast, from Tung Chung (accessible by bus from the ferry terminal of Mui Wo)

westwards to Tai O — a four-hour walk which can be done in either direction, though the bus connections at the end of the day (and the restaurant choices) are best at Tai O. Tung Chung is right opposite the new Chek Lap Kok Airport so the trip also gives you a fascinating comparison between the new Hong Kong and the old, with Tai O still surprisingly unspoilt by the nearby development.

For a hike to really make those leg muscles ache, consider the 100-km (63-mile) **Maclehose Trail** in the New Territories or the newest and perhaps toughest trail of all, the 78-km (49-mile) **Wilson Trail** which, unique among Hong Kong's trails, runs south to north (across Hong Kong island into the New Territories) instead of east to west. For details of trails, see THE GREAT OUTDOORS, page 25.

Don't be deceived by the easy accessibility of most of these trails: once you're out on a blustery peak or deserted beach, the sense of remoteness is very real

ABOVE: Hiking and camping in Sai Kung.

indeed. Be sure to take a map (excellent ones are available at the Government Publications Centre in Queensway, Central) and plenty of water. And be prepared for the shock of returning to the noise and crowds of the city after the birdsong, breezes and wilderness of Hong Kong's hidden hills.

Bar-Hop in Suzy Wong's New Wanchai

IN THE 1950S AND 60S, THE WANCHAI DISTRICT IMMEDIATELY EAST OF CENTRAL ON HONG KONG ISLAND WAS NOTORIOUS AS THE NAUGHTIEST BIT OF HONG KONG, FULL OF BROTHELS AND TOPLESS BARS, TATTOO ARTISTS AND DUBIOUS DIVES. This was the playground of American sailors on their R&R from Vietnam, and where Richard Mason's 1957 best-seller, *The World of Suzy Wong*, and the film of the same name was set. The book is still a great read, but you won't find Wanchai anything like as raunchy these days. Instead of brothels there are office blocks, and in place of

ABOVE: Wanchai's strip of hostess bars and discos. OPPOSITE: Dancing lion "walk the plank" at a temple in Shaukeiwan at Tin Hau Festival.

the topless bars stand art galleries, conference centers and five-star hotels. True, there's still a scattering of garish neon on Lockhart Road and Fenwick Street advertising topless entertainment and some suitably seedy pick-up joints like the New Makati or New Pussy Cat bars, but you'll find that the real new beats on Wanchai are a lot more up-market and in tune with Hong Kong's glitzy international 1990s image.

To see how the tide has turned, first pop into **Delaney's**, an Irish-style pub at 18 Luard Road with Guinness on tap, live Irish music on Tuesdays, Fridays and Saturdays and Irish stews on the menu. What's more, the clientele on weekdays is predominantly Suits (the territory's successful young businessmen seem to be everywhere these days), who don't think twice about paying over the odds for Delaney's exclusive "designer" ale, specially brewed for the pub by Hong Kong's very own micro-brewery. Another yuppie haunt (and yes, it's got its designer brew, too, including a sweet lemongrass variety) is **BB's Bar & Brasserie** at 114 Lockhart Road, as slick an operation as the many hotel bars in the area. Try the New World Harbour View's **Lobby**

Lounge, for instance, which really does have a terrific harbor view and decent live music. Of course, if you're really trying to impress, you can't beat the Grand Hyatt Hotel's glamorous **Champagne Bar** if anything states Wanchai's new image, this does.

But that's not to say that the "Wanch" as it's still affectionately called, can't provide some good old-fashioned fun, too. Many bars and clubs here have fantastic DJs and dancing music, especially at weekends. Some of the best include the always-crowded **Big Apple Pub & Disco** at 20 Luard Road; the "rock-around-the-clock" **Carnegie's** at 53 Lockhart Road; the tiny, long-established **The Wanch** at 54 Jaffe Road which has live rock and folk music nightly and a decor of Hong Kong memorabilia; or the New World Harbour View's funky **Westworld** with its strobe lights, smoke machines and techno-pop sounds. Bravely upholding Wanchai's reputation for notoriety is **Joe Bananas** at 23 Luard Road, which has a happy hour lasting an incredible 11 hours (from 11 AM to 10 PM daily) and a crowd of inebriated dancers packing the place every weekend.

But the last word in Wanchai entertainment still goes to the new image crowd, and to the Grand Hyatt Hotel's immensely popular (and expensive) **JJ's.** You won't even get past the door of this ostentatious bar-disco if you're dressed in T-shirt and shorts, sports shoes or torn jeans, which gives you an idea of the class of the place. People do come here for the great live bands (the best in town, it's said) but mostly they come here to be seen — preferably by the paparazzi. So forget Suzy Wong, and her seedy Wanchai bar: the like of JJ's is the future of Wanchai, all glitz and glamor and the flash of sequins and dollars.

Catch a Lion Dance

NOTHING CAPTURES THE ESSENCE OF HONG KONG'S CHINESENESS WITH AS MUCH COLOR, NOISE AND ATMOSPHERE AS A LION DANCE DURING ONE OF ITS TRADITIONAL TOP SPOTS

CHINESE FESTIVALS. No-one really knows how the lion dance originated — the Chinese lion is a mythical creature and has never been native to the country — but it has been practiced for centuries in China, in various forms, and nearly always occurs to accompany a major festival since it's believed to ward off evil spirits. Unfortunately, you are unlikely to catch sight of the more dramatic dragon dance (performed to assure prosperity) since it needs so many performers and a very expensive length of silk costume.

But if you're in Hong Kong during Chinese New Year, or at the time of the Tin Hau Festival or Cheung Chau Bun Festival (see FESTIVE FLINGS on page 78) you're bound to encounter at least one lion dance. An essential accompaniment to the ritual performance is a great deal of noise from drums and cymbals, enthusiastically performed by members of the lion dance troupe. This troupe is usually composed of young lads who are probably keen martial arts practitioners, too, since the dance itself requires a good deal of stamina from its duo of dancers (one operating the head of the lion, and the other the body). The most experienced lion dancers can perform formidable acrobatics — balancing on high poles, jumping from table-tops, rolling on the ground and prancing in mock-combat with "rival" lions or unicorns (spot the horn to tell the difference). During Cheung Chau's Bun Festival, almost every street association has its own lion dance troupe and the clamor when they encounter one another in the village's narrow streets has to be heard to be believed. This festival is also an ideal time to see the different kinds of lions in action: the shaggy yellow lion originates from north China while the black, yellow or multi-colored lion is a southern beast.

During Chinese New Year, the lion dance is performed not only as part of the public festivities (check with the Hong Kong Tourist Association on likely times and venues) but also to enact a ritual of good-luck blessings on various offices and organizations (who have paid for this service, naturally). You'll see the lion bowing before the doorway to the rumble of rolling drums and then jumping up to grab a hanging offering of oranges and lettuce leaves (which have symbolic significance). Lion dancers often perform this service at the opening of new buildings or offices or at the start of an important public event to exorcise any lingering evil spirits and soothe everyone's superstitions. VIP government officials are usually called in at these times to "dot the eyes" of the dragon and symbolically give it life — another curious ritual which is still faithfully followed, revealing Hong Kong's tenacious grip on Chinese tradition.

Take a Trip on Asia's First Funicular Tram

IN 1885, WHEN THE HONOURABLE PHINEAS KYRIE AND WILLIAM KERFOOT HUGHES ANNOUNCED THAT THEY INTENDED TO BUILD A TRAMWAY TO THE TOP OF VICTORIA PEAK — THE EXCLUSIVE RESIDENTIAL AREA FOR COLONIAL BRITS IN HONG KONG'S EARLY DAYS — THEY WERE COMPLETELY RIDICULED. No-one, it was thought, could possibly engineer a tram to tackle the steep and forested 554-m- (1,817-ft)-high peak on Hong Kong Island. Indeed, no-one anywhere in the region had ever attempted such a thing. Sedan chairs were considered the only form of transport possible to this elite eyrie. But three years later, the plan became reality and a tram (strictly speaking, it's a funicular railway) started trundling up The Peak, starting from Garden Road and finishing 373 m (1,223 ft) higher, just below the summit of The Peak.

The Peak Tram has been going strong ever since (though today's carriages are modern versions dating from 1989 and both terminals have been repeatedly

OPPOSITE: The peak tram affords a panoramic view of Hong Kong Island and Kowloon.

renovated, the one at the top most recently in 1996). But fundamentally, the operating system and the route itself haven't changed. And the only times the tram has stopped service are during World War II and during a ferocious 1966 typhoon which washed away some of the hillside. Today's passengers are mostly tourists (Peak residents tend to prefer their chauffeur-driven limousines), although many Mid-level residents (those living in the lower reaches of The Peak) still use it to commute to and from work: the four stops en route are at Kennedy, Macdonnell, May and Barker roads.

If you're traveling the Tram for the first time, though, don't even think about getting off before reaching the top: assuming you've chosen a clear day, the eight-minute journey is one of the most remarkable you'll make in Hong Kong. Pick a right-hand seat when you board and you'll be rewarded with some fantastic views as the tram slowly glides uphill: the tower blocks of Central and Mid-levels far below, the rooftop penthouses and swimming pools, and the stunning harbor beyond. Nearby, almost close enough to touch, the untamed greenery and banyan creepers are full of chittering birds. Keep an eye out when you start for some of Hong Kong's older buildings — the white-washed Helena May boarding house and St Paul's Church. As the gradient increases, the buildings below seem to tilt and you'll find yourself clutching the handrail in front of you anxiously.

At the top, you'll be greeted by the stunning new Peak Tower, a seven-story extravaganza which opened in 1997. It incorporates not only the tram terminus but also shops, restaurants and entertainment including a motion-simulated ride called the Peak Explorer and a dark computer-operated ride, the Rise of the Dragon, which takes you through the history of Hong Kong. There's even a Ripley's Believe it or Not! Museum here, with 500 oddities from around the world.

But escape from all these distractions for a while, to take in The Peak's

spectacular views (that's the fundamental attraction here, after all). Laid out below you is Hong Kong Island from Central to Quarry Bay, the harbor, Kowloon and many of the outlying islands. It's hard to say which is the more dramatic time to be up here — at night or day — but if you've got the weather on your side you should try and do both at least once.

And it's not only views that The Peak offers. Opposite the terminus, Harlech and Lugard Roads provide a delightful one-hour walk encircling The Peak, a cool escape in summer and great for jogging at any time. And when you're ready for a bite to eat, you can return to the Peak Tower or the adjacent Peak Galleria which has three floors of shops and restaurants,

including the exquisite Café Deco Bar & Grill, a must for art deco buffs. As you gaze out at the view (trams run until midnight so you can linger over that meal), raise a glass in honor of those Honourable and determined Gentlemen, Mr Kyrie and Mr Hughes, without whom The Peak might never have gained so many admirers.

Meet East and West in Macau

AN HOUR'S JETFOIL RIDE WEST OF HONG KONG LIES THE OLDEST EUROPEAN SETTLEMENT IN CHINA: MACAU. Established by Portuguese traders in 1557, this

Portuguese-administered territory (which is due to return to Chinese rule in 1999) has long been famous not only for its casinos but also for the escape it has offered to Hong Kong expats homesick for some European fare and ambiance. In the past decade, much to the despair of the nostalgic expats, Macau has been swept up in a frenzy of mainly Chinese-funded development that almost matches the pace of concrete construction in Hong Kong itself. An international airport has opened, office blocks and hotels sprung up, and a massive reclamation project started off the once-sleepy waterfront Praia Grande.

ABOVE: A-Ma Temple in Macau.

But there is a marked difference: in Macau, unlike Hong Kong, there has been considerable success in preserving and restoring much of the fine old European architecture that marks Macau's heritage. And curiously, despite growing Chinese influence and increasing modernization, there are more excellent Portuguese restaurants here than ever before, providing a cuisine and ambiance so utterly Portuguese (and often to a clientele almost entirely Portuguese) that it comes as a shock to step outside after your meal and realize you're on China's doorstep.

This, then, is the place to come to find out how East meets West. And to truly embrace the experience, you should really stay in the finest "colonial-era" hotel in town, the exclusive eight-room **Bela Vista** which has overlooked the harbor for over a century. Unfortunately, recent renovations, while enhancing its majestic appeal, have also turned it into the most expensive place in town (around US$250 a night) but the restaurant and, best of all, the almost wrap-around veranda is still the most traditionally romantic nook in Macau (the darkness helpfully obliterates the sight of the harborfront development). An alternative historic hostelry is the **Pousada de Sao Tiago**, which is built around an old castle and is slightly more affordable, at around US$150 a night.

But if these are beyond your budget, you'll find plenty of East-meets-West styles of rendezvous on the restaurant scene. Macau's outlying islands of Taipa and Coloane (joined to the mainland by bridges and a causeway) have become famous for their typical Portuguese fare: try the popular Fernando's in Coloane where **Fernando** is well known for dispensing with the menu to personally order you a feast of clams, sardines and salads, matched with a perfect Portuguese wine. When I first started coming here, some 15 years ago, the restaurant was a simple beach-side café with graffiti on the walls. The café is still here, but the main restaurant has expanded behind to cater to the growing band of visitors

and Fernando-fans. Inevitably, it has lost some of its ambiance in the process, which is why my favorite island haunt is now **Os Santos** on neighboring Taipa. A tiny, simple place run by Senor Santos himself (an ex-mariner who speaks only Portuguese) it's a lunchtime favorite for resident Portuguese (get here by 11.30 AM or you won't find a table) and provides the most enormous servings of homely Portuguese food. At the opposite extreme in terms of decor and price is the exquisite **Clube Militar**, near the Lisboa Hotel on the mainland. The Military Club's restaurant is the most elegant East-meets-West setting in Macau you'll find, with beautiful mahogany Chinese furniture, Portuguese paintings and colonial-style ceiling fans. The mainly Portuguese and Macanese menu is surprisingly reasonable, too, with a daily lunchtime buffet for around US$20.

To jolt yourself back into your true whereabouts, you only have to visit the Lisboa Hotel casino, packed with visiting Hong Kong Chinese, or the famous A-Ma Temple, thick with joss-offering crowds. The ruins of **St Paul's Cathedral** are the most obvious Portuguese counterpart. But my own favorite, the delightful **Lou Lim Ioc Gardens**, has perhaps the last word in this bi-cultural tour: here you'll find a charming combination of classic Chinese gardens set around a colonial, Western-style villa. Despite Macau's modernization, the unique old-fashioned lure of a place like this never fails to work.

OPPOSITE: The ruins of the famous St. Paul's Cathedral, Macau.

YOUR CHOICE

The Great Outdoors

I'm standing at dawn at the summit of a 934-m- (3,063 ft)-high peak and watching the mist slowly lift to reveal a landscape of hills as far as the eye can see. When the sun starts to blaze, the view is tremendous: far below are lush valleys, resonant with birdsong, while in the distance is the sparkling sea. There's not a car or building in sight, nor even a road or village. If it wasn't for the sub-tropical heat, you might think you were in the remoter corners of Scotland. But welcome, instead, to Hong Kong's biggest surprise: its wilderness.

Lantau island's Fung Wong Shan (more commonly called **Lantau Peak**) is Hong Kong's second highest after the 958-m (3,142-ft) Tai Mo Shan in the New Territories and is one of the most popular

peaks to climb in the territory, largely because of its accessibility from the Po Lin Monastery at Ngong Ping (see TOP SPOTS page 13). You'd need to spend a spartan night at the nearby youth hostel, however, if you wanted to get to the summit at sunrise. Many do, since such outdoor adventures have become increasingly popular in recent years with Hong Kong's young generation: so much so that you'd be wise to avoid weekends when sunrise on Lantau Peak can become something of a camera-clicking circus. But on weekdays you can have much of Lantau's wilderness to yourself and that's only one of the outdoor options available in Hong Kong.

An astonishing 70 percent of Hong Kong's 1,070 sq km (414 sq miles) is rural land, a dramatic combination of wild granite peaks and grassy slopes, bamboo forests and lush, river-fed lowlands. If you find that statistic hard to believe especially as you stand in the noisy, smog-ridden streets of Tsimshatsui or Central pop into the nearest bookshop to take a look at a couple of photographic books that tell it all: *The Green Dragon* by Martin Williams, with photographs by wildlife cameraman Michael Pitts, and *Hong Kong's Wild Places* by Edward Stokes (see BIBLIOGRAPHY at the end of this book).

Into the arms of mother nature. OPPOSITE: Lamma Island. ABOVE It is not difficult to get away from it all in a junk.

Most of their photographs were taken in Hong Kong's 21 **Country Parks** whose 41,000 hectares (101,270 acres) comprise 40 percent of Hong Kong's land. Five of these parks can be found on Hong Kong Island, two on Lantau, and 14 in the New Territories. Most are natural wildernesses, although some are forested "green belts", classified as Country Parks to protect Hong Kong's 17 fresh water supplies and reservoirs. Threading their way through these parks are ancient village trails, linked by new Country Park pathways and **nature trails**. The latter are mostly short, easy rambles (less than five or six kilometers long) geared for families or school groups, with interpretation signplates giving information on local plants, animals or geographical features. The trails are easily accessible by public transport.

But if you're a serious hiker — and determined to discover the real wilderness areas of Hong Kong — you'll need more challenge than this. Consider, instead, Hong Kong's four **long-distance trails** which have been designed in stages (most accessible by public transport) so each stage can be completed in a day. The **Country Parks Authority** (2733-2176, 12th Floor, 393 Canton Road, Kowloon, have detailed leaflets and 1:10,000 scale maps for each trail, with information on how to get to the trails' various stages by public transport and where to find campsites and youth hostels en route. It's also worth buying the excellent Countryside Series maps, available (as are some of the Country Park Authority's information) at the Government Publications Centre, Low Block Government Offices, 66 Queensway, Admiralty.

Choosing your trail depends on your energy levels. The easiest and shortest is the 50-km (31-mile) **Hong Kong Trail** which traverses the Island's high-level Country Parks, from Victoria Park all the way to Shek O in the southeast of the Island. It's a grand walk for city and seascape panoramas, with views out across Victoria Harbour and the outlying islands.

The **Lantau Trail** is considerably more demanding. Stretching for a circular 70 km (42 mile), it runs along the majestic mountainous ridge of the island and then loops back along the southern coast. Technically, you could cover it in 24-hours (without stops), though few are so foolish as to try. Instead, pick a section that takes your fancy — the shortest of the stages is just over a couple of kilometers, the longest over 10 km, and all except one can be reached by bus. For lung-bursting, leg-aching panoramic rewards, the 17.5-km (11-mile) stretch from Ngong Ping's Po Lin Monastery over the island's two highest peaks, Lantau and Sunset and all the way down back to the ferry terminal at Mui Wo, is an unbeatable challenge. It's officially estimated to take at least seven hours, though I've found the Parks' estimates to be on the cautious side.

For a slightly shorter and all-flat coastal walk, get off the bus at Shek Pik and walk round the southern coast to Tai O. I love this less popular route — not only because you can go for hours without seeing anyone but because it has a sense of history: the ruins of the 1,300-year-old Fan Lau fort lie on the southwesternmost headland, near to the remains of a mysterious (perhaps Bronze Age) stone circle. Hong Kong's two newest trails, named after former British Governors, offer some of the territory's most challenging and rewarding hikes. The 100-km (60-mile) **MacLehose Trail**, which has been described as "the quintessential Hong Kong outdoor experience", crosses the New Territories in ten stages, from Pak Tam Chung in the Sai Kung Country Park west to Tuen Mun. Seven of the stages are accessible by public transport. The trail passes through eight Country Parks which include some of the grandest mountain scenery in Hong Kong including the highest peak of all, the 958-m (3,142-ft) Tai Mo Shan. All along the route, you'll be treated to some stunning views of the Kowloon Peninsula and Hong Kong Island — not exactly wilderness views, it's true, but mesmerising nonetheless.

As with the other trails, the stages vary: the easiest is just 4.6 km (less than three miles) and takes less than two hours, while you'll need at least five hours for the longest stages. The Gurkhas and other marathon-fit runners have taken as little as 16 hours to complete this trail in a grueling annual race but ordinary hiking mortals should consider 30 to 40 hours the minimum to complete the entire length, and that's pushing it. Just one or two sections of the trail is enough for most people.

Opened in 1995, the 78-km (24-mile) **Wilson Trail** is the only one of the trails to run vertically up the entire Territory, from Stanley on the south side of Hong Kong Island, up to Nam Chung in the northern New Territories. It's the only one to entail an MTR link, too, to enable hikers to cross the harbor! The trail incorporates the glorious Pat Sin Leng range in the northeast New Territories — a series of eight successive peaks which delight in continually challenging your leg muscles. I particularly remember the well-named Needle Hill. Specific information about the MacLehose Trail is available from Friends of the Country Parks (2377-2967, Room 701, Ocean Centre.

If you're hooked enough on this wilderness scene to want to extend the experience for several days, you'll have to resort to campsites or youth hostels as there's little else out there on the trail (thank goodness). There are six campsites on the Lantau Trail, and 11 on the MacLehose, plus a couple of youth hostels on each. One of the best places to stock up on camping and hiking supplies is the Mountaineer Shop (2397-0585, 395 Portland Street, Kowloon (open 12.30 to 10 PM on weekdays and until 7 PM on Saturdays). The campsites are simple but usually well-maintained and often with excellent washing facilities. But again, avoid weekends if you want to stay clear of the music-playing, barbecue gangs.

So what are you likely to encounter on the trail of Hong Kong's great outdoors? Not much in the way of wild animals,

sadly, since Hong Kong's forests were cleared by early settlers centuries ago. But the flora, bird and insect life is remarkable. Keen botanists will find booklets on everything from ferns and seaweed to lichen and shrubs at the Government Publications Centre. Ornithologists might also want to pick up a copy of *Hong Kong Birds* by Karen Phillips & Clive Viney to take along on their hikes. And they'll certainly want to try and visit Hong Kong's most famous bird site — the Mai Po Marshes Nature Reserve, part of one of east Asia's most important wetlands.

Recently listed under the Ramsar Convention on Wetlands of International Importance, **Mai Po Marshes** cover over 300 hectares (741 acres) of shrimp and fish ponds, mudflats and mangrove plants in the northwest corner of Hong Kong, next to the shallow (despite its name) Deep Bay and the mainland Chinese border. One of over 40 Sites of Special Scientific Interest in Hong Kong, Mai Po is the only extensive area of wetland left in the territory. It's fighting a tough battle against encroaching development and worsening pollution but it's still one of Asia's most extraordinary bird-watching sites.

Over half of the 400 species currently known in Hong Kong can be spotted here, including a thriving colony of egrets and herons. Dozens of other species use Mai Po as a vital resting and feeding haven on their migrations between wintering grounds to the south and breeding areas to the north. Among the rarest of Mai Po's visitors are the Saunders' gulls, Black-faced spoonbills, Nordmann's greenshanks and Oriental white storks — you'll be lucky indeed to spot these — but especially during the winter and spring you'll have a wealth of other birds to spot, including flocks of ducks and sandpipers, buntings, cormorants and black kites.

Since 1981 Mai Po has been managed and funded by the World Wide Fund for Nature (WWF) Hong Kong which has built an excellent Wildlife Education Centre on the site for visitors and school groups and published guides to the marshes' plants and birdlife. Unfortunately for tourists, the WWF's necessarily strict protection of the site means that on-the-spot visits are impossible: you have to book and pay for a place on their four daily guided tours in advance (HK$70 per person) and since the tours only take place at weekends and on public holidays you may find they're booked up weeks or months ahead. Still, it's always worth giving **WWF** (2526-4473 a call or popping into their office at 1 Tramway Path, Central (next to the Peak Tram entrance) to see if a last-minute space is available.

While the birds of Mai Po are flying into an uncertain future as their habitat is eaten up by development, the **Chinese white dolphins** in Hong Kong's western waters are facing an even more desperate situation. Often called pink dolphins since they are usually more pink than white, there are thought to be no more than 140 or so of this Indo-Pacific humpback breed, the *Sousa chinensis*, in the waters around northern Lantau and the mouth of the Pearl River.

Although historical references to Chinese white dolphins date back several centuries, their existence in Hong Kong wasn't known about until quite recently. And now it's probably too late to save them. Their numbers — possibly as many as 400 at the beginning of the decade — are rapidly being decimated by sewage and pesticides washed down the Pearl River estuary (DDT — not banned in China as in other countries — has been found in higher levels in dolphin corpses than among any other cetaceans anywhere), by drastically declining food supplies due to the dredging and construction work for the new Chek Lap Kok Airport, and by the increasingly heavy traffic of trawlers, oil tankers and dredgers.

Stirred by growing public outcry, the Hong Kong government finally declared a 12 sq km (130 sq mile) dolphin sanctuary — the Lung Kwu Chau and Sha Chau Marine Park — in late 1996.

But though this will keep out trawlers and recreational watersports it is not spared from the pollution of the nearby underwater contaminated waste disposal pits, the construction of the Aviation Fuel Receiving Facility or the off-loading of oil tankers.

Hongkong Dolphinwatch, a private organization set up in 1995 to raise awareness of the threats the dolphins face, is the organization to contact if you want to see the dolphins for yourself and contribute to their cause: the organization runs day-long cruises (including lunch) to the dolphins' usual haunt on Wednesdays, Fridays and Sundays for HK$400 per person (HK$200 per child), during which

You don't have to go out of your way to enjoy windsurfing and sightseeing. The two combines well at Repulse Bay Beach on Hong Kong Island.

you can learn all about their sorry fate. Call (2984-1414 for bookings, or check their web site for more information: http//www.zianet.com/dolphins.

Sporting Spree

Hong Kong people may be workaholics but they've always made time for some physical exercise, whether it's half-an-hour of *tai chi* ("shadow boxing") in a park at dawn before going to work, a game of basketball in the local playground or simply a Sunday stroll with the wife and kids.

In recent years, there's been a growing interest in all kinds of "Western" sports, especially **windsurfing**, which encouraged

a host of ambitious novices after local girl, Lee Lai Shan, won the Olympic gold medal (Hong Kong's first) in 1996.

The place where San San (as she's affectionately called) made her first wobbly moves to windsurfing fame is off her home island of Cheung Chau. Her uncle's Windsurfing Centre (2981-8316 or FAX 2981-5063, on Tung Wan beach, is now one of the most popular in Hong Kong. Combined with a very pleasant open-air café where you can sit and watch the windsurfers race by, it's a popular weekend spot. It costs around HK$60 (US$8) an hour to rent a board here (or HK$250 a day) or around HK$550 (US$70) for a one-day tuition course. Kayaks are also available for rent.

Other good windsurfing spots are Sai Kung in the New Territories — check out the Windsurfing Centre (2792-5605, at nearby Sha Ha (best if the wind is from north) — and Stanley's Windsurfing Promotions Centre (2813-2372, on Hong Kong Island (best when there's an easterly or northeasterly wind blowing). Stanley is also where the Hong Kong Open Windsurfing Championship takes place every December (September to December is the ideal windsurfing period), organized by the Windsurfing Association of Hong Kong (2504-8255 FAX 2577-7529. Incidentally, boardsailors will find Hong Kong a great place to buy sail supplies since two of the world's leading sail manufacturers are based here.

For faster (and costlier) thrills, there's always **waterskiing**. The Deep Water Bay Speedboat Company (2812-0391, on the south side of Hong Kong Island, rents out a boat with driver and skis for about HK$520 an hour.

A long-established watersport in Hong Kong is, of course, **sailing**. The Hong Kong Yacht Club (2832-2817 FAX 2572-5399, based in Causeway Bay, is the biggest of the expatriate yachting organizations and can offer temporary membership if you already belong to a sailing club at home. For details, contact HKYC, Kellet Island, Causeway Bay. Other major yacht clubs are based at Aberdeen ((2552-8182), Hebe Haven in the New Territories ((2719-9682), and Discovery Bay on Lantau ((2987-9591). For learning to sail or chartering your own yacht, contact Blue Surround (2872-8060 FAX 2817-0426, homepage:

ABOVE: The open-air swimming pool at the Kowloon Park.

http://www.thcpress.com/bluesurr, or visit them at Rutonjee Centre, 11 Duddell Street, Central.

If there's a group of you, a cheaper option for taking to the seas and exploring some of Hong Kong's distant hidden bays and beaches is to **rent a junk** for the day a very popular pastime among local expats. A medium-sized junk, able to take up to 35 people, costs from HK$2,500 for eight hours (more during summer and on weekends). Contact Charterboats (2555-7349 FAX 2555-7340, Aberdeen Marina Tower, 8 Shum Wan Road, Aberdeen.

Swimming is another pastime that's grown tremendously popular here recently. But although Hong Kong has many charming beaches, several of them are now quite dangerously polluted, in particular the beaches between Tsuen Wan and Tuen Mun and Silvermine Bay on Lantau. The cleanest beaches are those on the south side of Hong Kong Island and in Sai Kung and Clearwater Bay — although the latter are also occasionally favored by sharks. After a spate of sightings (and a couple of attacks) during 1995 and 1996, special shark nets were installed at many beaches for the safety of swimmers. Warning flags are raised if sharks are seen in the area. Sharks have rarely been spotted in Hong Kong's western waters.

If you're concerned about pollution levels, check with the HKTA about the current situation or find the signboards that are at many of the 42 gazetted public beaches controlled by the Urban Council or Urban Services Department and that indicate the level of pollution for the day. Not that danger levels seem to put local people off very much. At weekends and on public holidays during the "official" swimming season (April 1st to October 31st) the most popular beaches (such as at Stanley on Hong Kong Island) are packed with swimmers and sunbathers. There are good facilities at these major beaches — lifeguards, warning flags for rough seas, changing rooms and toilets and sometimes even beachside cafés or snack stalls. The

biggest and most glorious stretch of beach in Hong Kong is Cheung Sha on Lantau; there are facilities at both ends of the beach, with a couple of Chinese restaurants at its easternmost end (Lower Cheung Sha).

If you prefer to stick to swimming pools, you'll find over a dozen well-maintained pools operated by the Urban and Regional Councils. These tend to be packed during school holidays but practically deserted on weekdays during school time. Two of the most conveniently located are the open-air pool in Victoria Park, Causeway Bay (2578-8903 and that of Kowloon Park, Tsimshatsui (2724-3577. There's also the indoor pool at Morrison Hill in Wanchai (2893-4933. Opening hours at all of them are from 7 AM to 9 PM daily.

For deeper dives than the pools can ever offer, you could try **scuba-diving**. True, the water quality in Hong Kong is hardly crystal-clear and you're never going to find the kind of spectacular coral reefs that exist elsewhere in Asia, but the sport is nevertheless thriving in Hong Kong, with several diving centers offering PADI or NAUI courses. Dive trips take place most weekends to the Sai Kung and Clearwater Bay areas, especially Little Beach and Town Island (popular for novices) and Breakers Reef in Mirs Bay (for experienced divers). For more information, call the Underwater Association (2572-3792, in Queen Elizabeth Stadium, or contact the following dive centers: Pro-Dive USA (2890-5634 FAX 2577-3400; The Dive Shop HK (2397-6222 FAX 2398-3199; or the Scuba Centre (2887-7922 FAX 2887-8680.

A useful source of information about scuba diving in the Asia region is the excellent *Action Asia magazine* (2865-5880 FAX 2529-5488, or check into their website: www.ActionAsia.com, which is packed with all kinds of sporting tips, feature articles and superb photographs. It's available at most bookstores.

Landlubbers will find plenty of sporting options in Hong Kong.

There are some excellent **golf** courses and facilities at Hong Kong's private clubs (open to visitors on weekdays only). The most popular is the three-course layout of the Hong Kong Golf Club (HKGC) (2670-1211, at Fanling in the New Territories. The green fees for 18 holes cost HK$1,400. The club also has a cheaper nine-hole course at Deep Water Bay (2812-7070 on Hong Kong Island. There's another course (27-hole) high above the Discovery Bay residential development on Lantau Island. Ferries run frequently from Central, and there's a bus to take you up to the course. To check in advance, call the Discovery Bay Golf Club on (2987-7271. The Clearwater Bay Golf & Country Club (2719-5936 in Sai Kung charges similar fees as the HKGC for its 18-hole championship course which stretches down to the edge of the ocean. The Hong Kong Tourist Association has a special tour package to the club which includes reduced green fees. Call (2807-6390 for details. If you just want to keep your hand in at a driving range, head for the new 91-bay Tuen Mun Golf Centre (2466-2600 near the Tuen Mun pier. It's open daily from 8 AM to 10 PM (except Monday and Thursday when it's open from 1 PM to 10 PM). Costs are around HK$33 an hour. Bring your passport to register.

Finding an available court for tennis, squash or badminton may not be so easy as these are very popular sports in the territory. Your best bet for **squash** is the Hong Kong Squash Centre (2521-5072, located at the entrance to Hong Kong Park, opposite the Peak Tram, at 23 Cotton Tree Drive in Central, but you could also try Queen Elizabeth Stadium (2591-1331 in Wanchai and in Kowloon, Kowloon Tsai Park (2336 7878 and Lai Chi Kok Indoor Games Sports Hall (2745-2796. For **tennis**, on the island, Victoria Park in Causeway Bay (2570-6186 and the Tennis Centre (2574-9122 at Wongneichong Gap Road; in Kowloon, King's Park (2385-8985. For **badminton**

The Hong Kong Golf Club at Fanling, New Territories.

and **table tennis,** try Queen Elizabeth Stadium, Sai Wan Ho Complex Indoor Games Hall (2569-7330, and the South China Athletic Association (2577-6932, at 88 Caroline Hill Road, Causeway Bay. For watching the pros, check with the Hong Kong Tennis Association (2890-1132, on the dates for the Hong Kong Open Tennis Championship, held every September.

Hong Kong's open countryside may seem ideal for exploring on **horseback** but unfortunately there are few opportunities. The Hong Kong Riding Union (2488-6886, at 76 Waterloo Road, Kowloon Tong, and the Tai Yuen Riding School (2471-8492 in Castle Peak Road, New Territories, have horses for hire (about HK$500 an hour), riding trails and lessons but you're unlikely to be able to go far beyond the school boundary. Simply for lessons, you can try the Pokfulam Public Riding School (2550-1359, on Hong Kong Island, and the Park Lodge Riding School (2607-3131, in Sha Tin.

Ice-skating enthusiasts should check out the Cityplaza Ice Palace (2885-4697 in the Cityplaza Shopping Centre, Taikoo Shing (take the E exit at the Taikoo MTR station). It's open from 9.30 AM to 10 PM on weekdays, from 7 AM to 10 PM on Saturday and from 12.30 PM to 10 PM on Sundays. The charge, including skates, is around HK$50 an hour. In Kowloon, there's the Whampoa Super Ice (2774-4899 in Whampoa Gardens shopping complex, Hunghom.

If you're interested in **martial arts,** the Hong Kong Chinese Martial Arts Association (2394-4803 will do their best to arrange a demonstration of *kung fu, tai chi chuan* (Chinese shadow boxing), Thai boxing and others, although you can easily see *tai chi* for yourself any early morning in places such as the Kowloon Park in Kowloon and the Chater Gardens and Victoria Park on Hong Kong Island.

Despite the heat and the urban crush, Hong Kong has a large army of joggers and a number of good **jogging** routes. A spectacular city route is along the waterfront promenade in Tsimshatsui.

On the island, popular routes are in Victoria Park, at the Happy Valley Racetrack and, best of all, along the scenic Bowen Road path in the Mid-Levels, which runs for several kilometers above Wanchai and around into Happy Valley to the roundabout at Stubbs and Tai Hang roads. The Hash House Harriers (2846-9522 sally forth on a hue and cry each week and are remarkable, aside from their stamina, for the considerable amounts of liquid replenishment that they take after each run.

Amateur **runners** are also welcome to take part in Hong Kong's three annual marathons, the Hong Kong to Shenzhen Marathon in February, the Coast of China Marathon on the first Sunday of March, and the International Marathon in Chinese New Year. For more information, contact the Hong Kong Amateur Athletics Association (2504-8215, the Athletic Veterans of Hong Kong (2818-4856, or the Hong Kong Tourist Association (2807-6177.

For something a little more adventurous, how about **rock climbing** or paragliding? Recreational climbing is a booming sport in Hong Kong. With its rocky islands and rugged, mountainous terrain, the territory has some ideal locations — most dramatically at the massive, 130-m (426-ft) granite crag of Lion Rock which now offers some 20 different recorded climbing routes; Kowloon Peak, with its overhangs and gullies and vast variety of crags; coastal Shek O, whose rocky point juts into the sea; and Tung Lung Island, south of Clearwater Bay, which perhaps offers the best sports climbing of all in Hong Kong with its many varied routes, from rock walls to 70-m- (230-ft)-high cliffs. If you're a novice and fancy getting your first step up the climbing scene, contact the Hong Kong Mountaineering Training Centre (2384-8190 FAX 2770-7110, which offers a day's beginner's course for around HK$250; or the Bureaux des Guides (2791-4269 which has one-day beginners' and advanced courses. Climbing is best done during the "dry" months between October and May. The only climbing wall that can be used by the public on a regular basis is at the Flora Ho Sports Centre (2904-9661 at the University of Hong Kong on Hong Kong Island.

Hong Kong's mountains and open ridges also offer great **paragliding** sport, with the reward of fantastic panoramas once you're airborne. You'd need to be here for several weeks during the dry season to participate in any serious training but if you're already an experienced flyer, contact the Hong Kong Paragliding Association (2543-2901 FAX 2541-7845 for free temporary membership, insurance, and details on where to fly and not to fly. The Ma On Shan ridge in the New Territories is a popular place for beginners, followed by the horseshoe ridge of Long Ke in Sai Kung, the steep-sided slopes of Lantau Island (especially Sunset Peak) and the dramatic Dragon's Back ridge overlooking Shek O on Hong Kong Island. There are powerful gusts and updrafts around, so be careful.

The Open Road

Here's the bad news for those of you who'd like to tour Hong Kong on your own in a hire car: it'll drive you mad. The traffic is too frenetic, the network of roads, tunnels and highways too confusing and parking spaces too frustratingly few. And you'll miss some of the territory's highlights — its outlying islands. The good news is that public transport is so efficient (and taxis so numerous), you won't regret for an instant being away from the wheel. As long as you're equipped with the relevant Hong Kong Tourist Association brochures, maps and information, you'll find getting around by bus, train, tram or boat easy and fun. (Just be sure to have plenty of change in your pocket for the fares).

For serious exploring, you'd be advised to pick up some of the detailed Countryside Series maps (in various scales covering the entire territory)

from the Government Publications Centre, Government Offices Low Block, 66 Queensway, Admiralty, on Hong Kong Island.

So where's the best place to go touring for a day, away from the city center and immediately obvious tourist haunts such as Stanley Market? If it's the remoter reaches of Hong Kong Island you fancy exploring, I'd recommend striking out to the far southeast village resort of Shek O.

Shek O, a former fishing village is now one of the swankiest residential areas in Hong Kong, although very discreetly so. It's got a fine beach (behind the car park and not to be confused with the polluted Rocky Bay beach north of the headland), a golf course and a couple of great restaurants that are popular with the weekend expat crowd. The most well-known of all is the **Chinese–Thai Seafood** (2809-4426, serving standard Thai favorites with speed and smiles. You'll find it near the bus stop, at 303 Shek O Village. At N° 452, you will find the **Black Sheep** (2809-2021, a charmingly homey place with the menu is handwritten on a disposable plate. It serves imaginative international fare in a relaxed atmosphere.

But it's not just the food that makes a trip to Shek O worthwhile. The walk through the village (and, yes, it still feels like a village) gives you a sense for the laidback atmosphere of the place while the Shek O Headland provides intoxicating panoramas of the coastline and South China Sea. A half-hour's pleasant walk to the north brings you to Big Wave Bay, which has another good beach (less crowded than Shek O's beach on weekends). There are bikes to rent (from the car park) if you want to explore even further afield.

To get to Shek O, take the MTR to Shau Kei Wan and then a N° 9 bus to the end of the line: try and get an upper-deck seat as the views en route are splendid. If you've got the time, consider taking a tram back to Central from Shau Kei Wan: it's one of the most relaxing ways to view the passing urban scene.

An alternative route from Shaukeiwan is directly south to **Stanley**. Bus N° 14 from the Shaukeiwan terminal will take you there, over the high hills and past the reservoir of Tai Tam Country Park, swooping down to Turtle Cove with its pretty little beach, before reaching Stanley itself. There are plenty of restaurants and cafés here (and, of course, the popular tourist market, see page 200). Express buses leave frequently for the 45-minute run back to Central. Or you can hop on a N° 73 bus and head west round the headland to Repulse Bay for a romantic (and expensive) evening's dinner at the Verandah Restaurant. Bus N° 6 or 61 can whisk you back to Central from here. You'd be hard pushed to pack this entire Shek O to Repulse Bay tour into one day, but any combination of the various sections offers some great hill and coastal journeys as well as some fine end-of-the-road destinations.

The vast New Territories offers considerably more choice for the adventurous traveler. For a survey of the most popular destinations, see the New Territories chapter. But if you're willing to take on a full day's exploration of a more remote spot, I'd suggest **Plover Cove**, north of Tolo Harbour, which has a reservoir, Country Park and plenty of hiking potential. This area gets packed out with cars, picnickers and hikers at weekends so try and choose a weekday to make the most of its rural surroundings. To get here, take the MTR to Kowloon Tong, change to the KCR line and get off at Tai Po Market. The N° 75K bus at the terminal outside takes you directly to Plover Cove, a 30-minute ride which ends at a hamlet called Tai Mei Tuk at the edge of the reservoir.

If you're interested in engineering, the Plover Cove Reservoir is something of a marvel of water conservation. It was once part of the sea. In the early 1970s the inlet was closed off, the entire bay sealed, the seawater pumped out — and the monsoon rains did the rest. Now, it's one of Hong Kong's main guarantees against its old summertime agony, either too much rain, with accompanying land slips

and death and injury, or not enough, with accompanying strict water rationing.

It's also become a popular recreational spot. You can rent bikes and rowing boats here, cook yourself a barbecue at one of dozens of sites (though you'll have to bring your own supplies!) or follow a choice of two short nature trails. The Country Park Visitor's Centre at Tai Mei Tuk (head north from the bus stop for about 400 m (438 yards) and it's just off the main road) has information about these trails as well as displays on the local flora, fauna and geology of the area. But to be sure of getting the detailed trail brochures in English, call in at the Country Parks Office before you go (393 Canton Road, Kowloon) or the Government Publications

Centre. The Countryside Series map for the area is N° 5.

The easiest trail is the one-km Bride's Pool Nature Trail, which passes the 15 m (50 ft) high Bride's Pool waterfall, named after a bride who supposedly plunged to her death here long ago as she was being carried in her sedan chair on the slippery path above the waterfall. To get to the start of the trail, though, you'll have to walk along the main Bride's Pool Road for about an hour or hail a passing taxi (the N° 75K bus goes to Bride's Pool from the Tai Po KCR station, but only on Sundays and public holidays). The trail is well signposted.

I personally prefer the Pat Sin Leng Nature Trail, a four-km hike which starts near the Visitor's Centre and ends at Bride's Pool. It's more demanding but more rewarding, with wonderful views of the reservoir and Pat Sin mountains. You should allow about two hours for the walk, though you can always cut it short and take a side loop just after Stop N° 8 which will bring you back to the start in about half-an-hour. The really energetic can combine both trails in one go.

If you're not into a day's walking, some sights in and around **Tai Po** can also be combined on this tour or made into a separate visit. Tai Po itself, a former pleasant market town north of Shatin is now a fast-changing New Town. For

A bird's eye view of Stanley.

railway enthusiasts, the old Tai Po Market station has been preserved and tarted up and turned into the Hong Kong Railway Museum (2653-3339, featuring an exhibition gallery, old coaches and a mock-up of a modern-day electric-powered coach. It's open daily except Tuesday from 9 AM to 5 PM. Nearby, two Tin Hau temples have also been restored — one is near the Railway Museum on Fu Shin Street and the other across the river on Ting Kok Road.

At Shek Kong, west of Tai Po, you'll find **Kadoorie Experimental Farm** on the northwestern slope of Hong Kong's tallest mountain, Tai Mo Shan. Established in 1951, it was originally set up to teach modern agricultural techniques to refugees from over the border. The farm is beautifully landscaped with steep terraces of pools, crops and trees, and the view from the top of the slope is magnificent. Livestock such as pigs and ducks are specially reared. If you're interested in visiting, please give the farm at least two day's notice. For inquiries call (2488-1317. To reach the farm from Tai Po Market KCR station take bus N° 64K or 65K. Keep your eyes peeled for the farm entrance, on the left side of the road, as it's easy to miss.

To really feel as if you're getting away from urban Hong Kong, however, the best touring option is to take a short ferry ride across the South China Sea, westwards to Lamma, Cheung Chau or Lantau islands. They offer wonderful

Cheung Chau (HK$30) which will point you in the right direction while you're there, although you don't need to go far beyond the waterfront village to get a memorable flavor of the place, with its busy shops and marketplace (the fresh fish display is incredible), its harbor full of fishing boats and junks and its ancient Pak Tai temple, set back a little from the harbor.

Arriving at Mui Wo at 12.50 PM you're just in time for lunch: in addition to a market of cheap fast food restaurants and even a McDonald's — all near the ferry terminal — you can also find a couple of more congenial open-air Chinese restaurants just above the road leading to the beach. My favorite of the two is the Sang Lee (2984-8478, which has some great sizzling dishes and hotpots during the winter months.

Since the last ferry back to Central from Mui Wo is at 11.10 PM, you've got plenty of time to tour the island. Taxis are available at the ferry pier if you prefer that mode of transport, though you'll find buses (also at the ferry pier) can get you practically everywhere. Two of the most popular destinations are the Po Lin Monastery on the high Ngong Ping plateau, and the far western coastal village of Tai O. There are buses to Tai O from the monastery, too, so you can visit both places in a day if you fancy. Take a look at THE OUTLYING ISLANDS chapter and TOP SPOTS, HIKE THE TRAILS OF HIDDEN HONG KONG, page 14 for more ideas on how best to enjoy this huge and varied island. The HKTA's *Explorer's Guide to Lantau* (HK$30) is also worth buying before you set off, though if you're likely to be exploring this and the other islands in some depth, the Countryside Series map N° 3 from the Government Publications Centre is the one to buy. It features Lantau in detail, with smaller box maps on the other islands. An alternative pocket-size map of both Cheung Chau and Lantau is published by Universal Publications and available at major bookstores (HK$18).

country walks, casual open-air dining, Buddhist monasteries and temples or simple strolls by the seaside. Lamma has to be considered as a single day-trip destination since it has no inter-island ferry connections, but it's quite conceivable to visit both **Cheung Chau** and **Lantau** in a long, but rewarding day.

You'd need to start early, taking the 8 AM or 9 AM ferry to Cheung Chau from the ferry pier in Central. This will give you time for a few hours on Cheung Chau before catching the charmingly old-fashioned little ferry at noon to Lantau's main village and ferry terminal of Mui Wo (Silvermine Bay). The Hong Kong Tourist Association has a useful Explorer's Guide walking tour booklet on

ABOVE: Outlying Islands ferry glides through lighters and fishing trawlers off central "bottleneck" of Cheung Chau Island.

If you're seriously into island hopping you could consider taking in yet another island on your way home: **Peng Chau**. This little island lies off Lantau's eastern coast, between Mui Wo and Discovery Bay to the north and is connected by ferry from Mui Wo seven times a day (a convenient one to consider taking on this triple-island visit would be the 3.05 PM or 5.20 PM). Peng Chau is a microcosm of Hong Kong in many ways, with a narrow old street of shops and market stalls representing its ancient, traditional face, while modern housing estates and a scattering of expat-run bars and restaurants reveal the changing times. Apart from a couple of tempting shops selling Chinese furniture and hand-painted ceramics, there's not a lot to see or do here, but the Sea Breeze Club (2983-8785, at 38 Wing Hing Street (on the waterfont a short walk from the ferry terminal) is a very pleasant spot to sit in the sun and snack on pizzas while waiting for your ferry back to Central (you can relax, the last one is at 11.30 PM).

Backpacking

Hong Kong is a challenging place for those who are on a tight budget. For a start, there are few decent rock-bottom budget places to stay. Even **Chungking Mansions** in Tsimshatsui — the long-established backpacker's ghetto which is notorious for its filthy stairwells, its tiny, crowded lifts and its occasional night-time raids by police has had to upgrade facilities and raise prices following a crackdown on fire-safety violations in the mid-1990s.

Nevertheless, this 17-story complex of five blocks at 30 Nathan Road still offers the cheapest accommodation in town — around HK$200 for a single room or HK$300 to $400 for a double (usually with private bath). Most of the guesthouses are on the upper floors of Block A and B. Recommended places in Block A are the popular **Travelers' Hostel** (2368-7710, 16th floor; **Peking Guesthouse** (2723-8320, 12th floor; and

Chungking House (2366-5362. In Block B, you could try **Carlton Guesthouse** (2721-0720 on the 15th floor; **New Washington Guesthouse** (2366-5798, on the 13th floor; or **Hong Kong Guesthouse** (2723-7842, on the 11th floor. The only cheaper options than these are dormitory beds (around HK$80 to HK$100) which you can find both in Chungking Mansions (try the Travelers' Hostel) or nearby, such as **Golden Crown Guesthouse** (2369-1782, at 66-70 Nathan Road.

If you can't bear the closet-size rooms of Chungking Mansions, the interminable queues for the lifts or the 24-hour bazaar bustle in its ground floor shopping arcade, there are plenty of reasonable, if slightly pricier, alternatives nearby. Recommended are **Golden Crown Guesthouse** (single rooms for HK$280) and the **Victoria Hostel** (2376-0621, at 33 Hankow Road, which has both dorm beds (around HK$100 a bed or $180 for a place in a three-person dorm) and doubles for HK$450. Another decent place is the friendly **Man Hing Lung** (2722-0678, at 58 Nathan Road, Flat F2, Mirador Arcade, 14th floor. Singles here are HK$280 with air-con and TV, doubles HK$380. Such budget accommodation is rare anywhere other than Tsimshatsui, but an exception is **Noble Hostel** (2576-6148, at 27 Paterson Street, 17th floor, Flat A3, which is in Causeway Bay on Hong Kong Island. Rooms here (all with shared bathroom) start at around HK$300.

Staying in Hong Kong's seven **youth hostels** isn't very convenient, because nearly all of them are located in remote parts of the New Territories. Only one, Ma Wui Hall (2817-5717, on Hong Kong Island's Mount Davis is fairly central, situated high above Kennedy Town with great views of the harbor and beyond. If you've got heavy luggage, you'd be best to take a taxi; bus N° 5B or 47 from Central come fairly close but you're still faced with a stiff half-hour walk.

Moving up several notches in the price and comfort bracket, you could try the Salvation Army-run **Booth Lodge** (2771-9266 FAX 2385-1140, which is at

11 Wing Sing Lane, Yaumatei. Twin rooms here start at HK$580 but you'd need to book well in advance. Two other reasonable places in Yaumatei are the **Caritas Bianchi Lodge** (2388-1111 FAX 2770-6669, at 4 Cliff Road, where singles are around HK$750, doubles HK$850; and **King's Hotel** (2780-1281 FAX 2782-1833, at 473 Nathan Road, which has singles for around HK$570 and doubles for HK$700.

A very pleasant alternative to staying in the city is to base yourself on one of the **outlying islands** — an especially attractive option if you'd rather go hiking than shopping. Note, however, that although guesthouses here are a bargain midweek, prices rocket at weekends. Cheung Chau does a booming trade in cheap holiday flats for weekenders: you'll see a row of booths on the waterfront advertising rooms as soon as you get off the ferry. Despite the flattering photos you'll be shown, the flats (which have tiny attached bathrooms and a miniscule kitchenette) are very poky and often located in an ugly ghetto of flats. Weekday prices are around HK$300 a night.

On Lamma you could try **Man Lai Wah Hotel** (2982-0220, near the Yung Shue Wan ferry pier, where doubles are HK$400 on weekdays and HK$700 at weekends.

On Lantau, there's everything from campsites and youth hostels (the **S G Davis Youth Hostel** (2985-5610, at Ngong Ping, near the Po Lin Monastery, is a popular choice) to cheap guesthouses and up-market hotels (in Mui Wo). Among guesthouses, the **Lantau Tea Gardens** (2985-5161 on Ngong Ping, has basic rooms for HK$200, while the **Mui Wo Inn** (2984-8597 on Tung Wan Road, Mui Wo, has attractive seaside rooms from HK$320 (HK$600 at weekends). Billed as "the smallest hotel in Hong Kong", the charming three-room **Babylon Villa** (2980-3145 FAX 2980-3024, has a remote, romantic setting right on Cheung Sha beach. Rooms here cost from HK$440 ($590 at weekends).

Once you've got your accommodation sorted out, you'll find you can survive in Hong Kong quite cheaply if you're careful. Transport is reasonable (to cut costs, stick to trams and the Star Ferry, and buses instead of the MTR). Eating out needn't be expensive as long as you avoid expensive yuppy ghettos such as Lan Kwai Fong in Central. In Tsimshatsui, Chungking Mansions is the best place to track down cheap meals — it has some great Indian and Pakistani restaurants — though you can find similarly budget-price Indian eateries elsewhere, too. **Woodlands** (2369-3718, at 61 Mody Road has superb vegetarian Indian fare. For homely Cantonese noodle and rice dishes, you can't beat the prices at **Happy Garden Noodles & Congee Kitchen** (2377-2604, at 76 Canton Road, or **The Sweet Dynasty** (2375-9119 at 88 Canton Road.

Wanchai is another good hunting ground for drinkers and diners on a budget. You'll find everything here from *dai pai dongs* (typical Chinese street stalls) and bars with extraordinarily long happy hours (see TOP SPOTS page 16 for some ideas) to places like **Brett's Seafood Restaurant & Takeaway** (2866-6608, at 72 Lockhart Road, which is famous for its fish 'n' chips; and **Hawker Noodle** (2528-6219 at 146 Queen's Road East, which can serve up cheap and filling noodle dishes of your choice.

If you hanker for some fresh seafood (you haven't lived in Hong Kong until you've eaten this popular fare) you better head for the outlying islands of Lamma or Cheung Chau where prices will be lower than in town. Expect to pay around HK$100 a person here for a simple seafood meal, less without the seafood. Wherever you eat in a Chinese restaurant, you'll find it works out cheaper if you can get a group together.

As for late night entertainment, you better stick to places like the Temple Street night market if you're trying to save your dollars and cents: bar prices and discos aren't cheap in Hong Kong, though there are generous happy hours (typically from 5 PM to 8 PM although often much longer). Pick up a copy of the free weekly *HK Magazine* or monthly *bc Magazine* (both available at many bars, bookshops and cultural centers) for listings and price ratings of bars, clubs and restaurants.

Living It Up

THE FINEST HOTELS

You'll have no trouble at all living it up in Hong Kong: some of the world's most luxurious accommodation can be found here, in hotels which host some of Asia's most expensive and extravagant restaurants and nightclubs. Famous for decades and still topping the list in hotel rankings worldwide — are the **Mandarin Oriental (** 2522-0111 FAX 2810-6190 in Central and **The Peninsula (** 2366-6251 in Tsimshatsui. Business executives choose the Mandarin for its superbly convenient location at the heart of Hong Kong's financial center, although VIPs of any distinction love it for its discreet and utterly efficient service. The harbor-facing Peninsula is ideal for forays into Tsimshatsui's shopping malls and famous for its gold-glittering lobby and spectacular restaurants. At both hotels you can expect luxury down to the finest detail and room rates soaring around US$450 a night.

Newer boys on the block include the trio of excellent hotels in Central's Pacific Place — the **Conrad (** 2521-3838 FAX 2521-3888, the **Island Shangri-La (** 2877-3838 FAX 2521-8742 and **J.W. Marriott (** 2810-8366 FAX 2845-0737. Located between Central and Wanchai and above one of Hong Kong's classiest shopping malls (Pacific Place), they're also a short walk away from the relaxing Hong Kong Park. Other deluxe choices in the Central neighborhood include the **Ritz-Carlton (** 2877-6666 FAX 2877-6778, an exclusively small hotel with just 114 rooms and 29 suites, and its older neighbor, the **Furama (** 2525-5111 FAX 2845-9339, which has a health center, conference facilities and discounts for families. If you're attending a conference at the Convention & Exhibition Centre in

Wanchai, or prefer to be closer to the Wanchai nightclub scene, the best choices of up-market accommodation are the **Grand Hyatt (** 2588-1234 FAX 2802-0677, which boasts an outdoor swimming pool and a slick disco among its facilities, and the larger though less ostentatious **New World Harbour View (** 2802-8888 FAX 2802-8833, which has a full range of facilities including a pool. Both these hotels also have specially equipped rooms for disabled guests. Despite warnings of an over-supply of rooms when these newer hotels first appeared in the early 1990s, they've survived very well indeed — as their US$400 a night room rates testify.

Over in Tsimshatsui you have even more choice of luxurious accommodation. The superbly-situated **Regent Hotel (** 2721-1211 FAX 2739-4546, bags the best view of the harbor from this side of Hong Kong (its glass-fronted lobby is unbeatable), while its neighbors, the **New World (** 2369-4111 FAX 2369-9387 and **Sheraton (** 2369-1111 FAX 2739-8707, both offer outdoor pools and health centers, and extensive shopping malls.

In the nearby shopping enclave of Tsimshatsui East there are a clutch of very popular newer places, notably the 692-room **Kowloon Shangri-La (** 2721-2111 FAX 2723-8686, as sumptuous as its Hong Kong Island counterpart; the small but well-equipped **Royal Garden (** 2721-5215 FAX 2369-9976 (which is one of the few hotels in town with both an indoor and outdoor pool); and the 444-room **Hotel Nikko (** 2739-1111 FAX 2311-3122, which offers discounts to honeymooners. See listing under the ACCOMMODATION on page 207 for these hotels' full addresses.

THE FINEST RESTAURANTS

Not surprisingly, the best hotels also boast some of the territory's finest restaurants. The French cuisine of the Mandarin's **Pierrot Restaurant (** 2522-0111, the Peninsula's **Gaddi's (** 2366-6251, the Island Shangri-La's **Petrus (** 2877-3838, and the Conrad International's **Brasserie on the Eighth**

The lavish creativity of Hong Kong's nighlife — string duo and piano perform amid the huge atrium of Royal Garden Hotel in Tsimshatsui East.

(2521-3838, is as memorable as their very elegant settings, while the dramatic decor alone of the Peninsula's **Felix** has to be seen to be believed! For Chinese cuisine, don't miss the Grand Hyatt's **One Harbour Road** Cantonese restaurant (2588-1234, or the Island Shangri-La's **Summer Palace** (2877-3838, both very classy acts indeed, while lobster and seafood aficionados will find lobsters at their most succulent at the Island Shangri-La's **Lobster Bar** (2877-3838.

Beyond the hotels' lush environments, you'll find no lack of deluxe dining all over the territory, though most places are concentrated on Hong Kong Island. The long-established **Landau's** (2827-7901 in Wanchai, is a comfortable old favorite for Continental cuisine, **Grappa's** (2868-0086 in Pacific Place, famous for its huge Italian menu, and the **Camargue** (2525-7997 always a delightful dining experience (despite its Central office block location). One restaurant that has carved a special place for itself in the upper echelons of Hong Kong's restaurants is **M at the Fringe** (2877-4000 by the Fringe Club in Central. Run by the talented Michelle, this operation is unique in every way — decor, cuisine (a range of Middle Eastern and Continental), and most of all, an atmosphere and service that makes you feel special as soon as you arrive.

For epicureans of French cuisine, there's the unbeatable trio of Central's **Papillon** (2526-5965, **Pavilion** (2973-0642, or **Le Tire Bouchon** (2523-5459. Italian pasta in a stylish setting? You can't go wrong at **Toscana** (2877-6666 or **Tutta Luna** (2869-0099 (both in Central), **Sabatinis** (2721-5215 in Tsimshatsui's Royal Garden Hotel, or the trendy new candlelit nook of **Club Casa Nova** (2869-1218 in the Mid-Level's up-and-coming "SoHo area (South of Hollywood Road).

Some places are definitely worth going out of your way for: The Peak's **Café Deco Bar & Grill** (2849-5111 fits into this category (top marks for its heady views

and art deco fittings), as does the Continental restaurant of **Tables 88** (2813-6262 in Stanley, on the south side of Hong Kong Island, and **The Verandah** (2812-2722, in nearby Repulse Bay whose colonial-style setting right by the sea makes it the ultra-romantic deluxe dining spot for Sunday brunch (book well ahead for this one), afternoon tea or dinner.

Outside of the hotels, elegant Chinese restaurants are thinner on the ground than the Continental ones. But **Fook Lam Moon Restaurant** (2866-0663, in Wanchai has a mind-bogglingly extravagant menu (stick to the shark's fin and abalone if you really want to impress your guest) while **Lei Garden** (2892-0333 (also in Wanchai) manages to be almost as classy without burning such a big hole in your pocket. For a more unusual Asian dining experience, try the **Indochine** (2869-7399, a Vietnamese restaurant in Lan Kwai Fong, Central which recreates the French-influenced romance and aura of 1920s Vietnam with superb style.

NIGHTLIFE

Hong Kong's nightlife operates at the same tempo as the business of the day fast, furious and in a constant boom. It follows the same pattern as the business world too every few years it bursts beyond its own conventions and attempts the impossible, or at least the decidedly improbable. And within no time at all another improbable dream is just another convention.

The latest nightlife triumph is to after-dark entertainment what the Jumbo 747 was to the airline industry when the monster airliner first nosed its way out of Boeing's assembly plant in Seattle. Youll find it in Tsimshatsui East — three huge hostess clubs called the **Club Bboss** (2369-2883, LG/F New Mandarin Plaza, 14 Science Museum Road, **Club Metropolitan** (2311-1111, LG/F Chinachem Golden Plaza, 77 Mody Road, **China City Night Club** (2723-3278, 4/F Peninsula Centre, 67 Mody Road the biggest and most astonishing entertainment centers anywhere in the world.

A Rolls Royce replica and hostesses await customers at Club Bboss.

When you stroll into the Club Bboss, for example, you enter a vast 6,510 sq m (70,000 sq ft) luxuriously appointed dance-lounge and are driven to your plush, discreetly positioned personal "relaxation zone" in a full-sized battery-powered replica of an antique Rolls-Royce — gliding down a long glass-smooth boardwalk which glitters and twinkles with overhead lighting and, as it streaks into the distance before you, looks like the main runway of an international airport at night, turned upside down.

Both Bboss and China City have huge laser-lashed dance floors, non-stop big-band entertainment and teams of Cantonese and Filipino rock and soul singers, romantically lighted hospitality lounges and nooks as far as the eye can see, and absolute regiments of hostesses and service staff. Bboss boasts no fewer than 1,000 hostesses on its books, up to 400 of whom will be on duty any night of the week. Specially selected for their looks, poise and their conversational skills and costumed in elegant thigh-split traditional silk *cheong-sams* theyre supervised by a legion of *mama-sans* who carry walkie-talkie radios to keep in touch with customer requests.

Different sector managers carry special pager beepers which show a digital code that corresponds with a particular request or area of the huge nightspot. The waitresses, selected again for their looks and poise, wear black bow ties and tails,

kneel at your table to serve drinks and snacks and are so well tuned in to customer service that theyll have a cigarette lighter poised before you while the cigarette is still on its way to your lips.

In both Bboss and China City entertainment palaces, digital clocks over the seating areas begin operating the moment a tall, slim, raven-haired hostess is led like a vestal virgin to your divan by a radio-equipped *mama-san*. There is a minimum HK$500 charge for a drink and snacks. If your desire goes beyond that, companionship, conversation and reasonably restrained flirtation will cost an extra HK$65, strictly for 15 minutes. For a full night outside on the town the fee is a flat HK$2,400 — reasonable by

any standards for the beauty and intellect of the girls, and certainly a much more attractive proposition than the high-priced hustle of the hostess bars of Wanchai and Tsimshatsui.

Both complexes have special segregated areas for Japanese visitors — quiet, private and almost Zen-like in mood. While the Club Bboss has the most imaginative decor, the style and tone of a kind of high-class Star Wars bordello, the China City offers a lush and romantic patio garden with an aviary full of lovebirds. Club Metropole is an elaborately decorated hostess club with an XO tunnel of cognac and whisky bottles.

Laser-lashed dance floor of Club Bboss, one of the biggest and most astonishing entertainment centers in the world.

These huge nightspots have to be seen simply to be believed (and such is the level of discretion on which they operate that you don't necessarily have to contract a hostess to visit one). They are a forward glimpse of the twenty-first century, a promise of the extravagant style of entertainment to come in the great Asiatic cities of the future. As one manager described it: "Compared with us, every other nightclub in Hong Kong is just a small store. We're the supermarkets of the nightlife business."

There are lots more cheaper and less palatial hostess clubs around. Most of them have big-band entertainment and non-stop Filipino and Cantonese singers, legions of pretty, well-groomed hostesses and, like Bboss, Metropole and China City, all sorts of extravagant and bizarre gimmicks to make the visitor feel pampered.

The giant **New Tonnochy Night Club** (2511-1383, 1-5 Tonnochy Road, Wanchai, for example, greets its visitors with a turbaned honor guard, and violins play guests to their seats. While the bands

crash from one swing number to the next, 200 hostesses chat and dance with their clients. There's no minimum charge but drinks are pricey. Tonnochy's main rival is **Mandarin Palace Night Club** (2575-6551 at 24-28 Marsh Road, a nightclub (with nonstop dance-floor entertainment) where big spenders will feel right at home.

For the gentleman with no jacket, Hong Kong abounds with hostess and girlie bars, most of them aimed specifically at the lonesome wolf and nearly all devoted to vacuuming your wallet as fast as it can be done. Top of the bill is **Bottom's Up** (2721-4509, 14-16 Hankow Road, Tsimshatsui, which has been around since the early heady 1970s and was Hong Kong's first topless bar. Nowadays it has become as much a cultural landmark as a den of titillation and welcomes wives and girlfriend. It even has HKTA's stamp of approval.

Tsimshatsui has a much wider range of nightclub options to choose from than Hong Kong Island, but you'd be well-advised to check in detail first about the prices of drinks, companionship and cover charge before you enter. The management won't mind being questioned; they prefer to discourage Western customers

---

ABOVE: Bottoms Up bar. OPPOSITE: The neon sign announcing yet another bar–restaurant.

rather than end up with dissatisfied and possibly troublesome guests. For the best and most reputable, try two establishments in the **New World Centre** on Salisbury Road — **Club Cabaret** (2369-8432 and **Club Deluxe** (2721-0277.

Not all nightlife in Hong Kong is as awesome and futuristic, and as male-oriented, as Club Bboss, China City and Metropole. Like eating out, stepping out on the town is to face a myriad of different nightspots and an almost impossible variety of choices of entertainment. If you simply want a drink and some music, you'll find that most bars offer Happy Hour (two drinks for the price of one) from around 5 PM to 9 PM. At the bigger venues which offer music and dancing, you'll probably have to pay a cover charge which, depending on where you are, can vary from HK$50 to $200. During the week, nightlife usually ends around 2:30 AM but at weekends you can party till 5 AM or 6 AM.

On Hong Kong Island's Central District, the fashionable **Lan Kwai Fong** bars and restaurants are often so busy at weekends that finding even elbowroom may not be easy, especially after 10:00 PM.

For starters you can try the three affiliated venues of **Nineteen 97** (2810-9333, 8-11 Lan Kwai Fong drinks upstairs at **Post 97,** dinner downstairs in **La Dolce Vita 97** and then dance the night away in **Club 1997**. Across the road, at California Entertainment Building, 2/F, the **Jazz Club** (2845-8477, frequently features top international performers, along with their regular, first-rate house band.

Around the corner, **California** (2521-1345 restaurant turns into a thumping disco in the late evening, **Yelts Inn** (2524-7790 at 42 D'Aguilar Street has loud music and plenty of soul. Across the road at **Hardy's Folk Club** (2522-4448, you can listen to folk music or even get up on stage yourself and sing. Just around the corner from there, up Wing Wah Lane, the popular **Club 64** (2523-2801, offers alfresco drinking on hard stools and the occasional rat scampering by. The friendly **Le Jardin** (2526-2717 is at the top of the steps. Elsewhere there are plenty of other places to choose from — just wander around and go with the flow.

From there you can head to Wanchai which used to be the notorious **Suzy Wong** bar, brothel and nightclub district of Hong Kong but has now become a respectable business and restaurant area with a surviving core of fairly tame topless bars and nightclubs along with karaoke lounges, discos and bars. For live rock and roll, Suzy Wong and old Hong Kong memorabilia, try **The Wanch** (2861-1621 at 54 Jaffe Road. **Joe Bananas** (2529-1811, which is also a restaurant, at 23 Luard Road, has a resident DJ, extra loud disco music and dance floor but if you're wearing fur, shorts or a shirt without a collar, you won't be allowed in, company policy. During the weekends the place is packed, so get there early. Nearby, the dark and drab, but friendly and informal discos, **Neptune Disco II** (2865-1883, Basement, 98-108 Jaffe Road (with another branch at 54 Lockhart Road), and **New Pussycat** (2527-6767, 17 Fenwick Street, are a home away from home for Filipina housemaids working in Hong Kong, and can be a lot of fun. On the edge of Wanchai, one of the hottest nightspots in town is **JJ's** (2588-1234, in the Grand Hyatt Hotel, which features live rhythm and blues, disco dancing, videos and excellent bar food. In Causeway Bay, the **Jump Bar & Restaurant** (2832-9007, 7/F Causeway Bay Plaza, Phase II, 463 Lockhart Road,

has the latest in pop music and a disco from 11:00 PM. Wednesday is Ladies Night and Sundays you get two drinks for one. Check out its homepage on http://www.thejump.com. **Strawberry Café & Disco** (2866-1031, Basement, 48 Hennessy Road, is another lively spot, with a special promotion every night and an extra long happy hour, lasting from 3 PM until 10 PM. If you want to rock the day or night away, head for **Carnegie's** (2866-6289, G/F, 53-55 Lockhart Road, which bops with jazz and rock 'n' roll practically nonstop.

Over in Tsimshatsui, try the **Bar City** nightlife complex (2369-8571, live Latin music in the **Latino Bar** and a country and western theme in the **Crazy Horse Saloon.** Also in the center, the chic **Cat-walk** (2369-4111, on the 18th floor of the New World Hotel has a resident six-piece salsa band, disco floor, video wall, karaoke lounge area and private karaoke rooms. For just disco, the long-standing **Rick's Café** (2367-2939 at

4 Hart Avenue. If it's reggae beats you want, head for Tsimshatsui's mini-version of Lan Kwai Fong Knutsford Terrace where you'll find **Bahama Mama's Coconut Bar** (2368-2121.

For those who yearn for the relaxed conviviality of the British, Irish or Australian pub, the trail begins in Central at **Mad Dogs Central**, 1-13 D'Aguilar Street. From there wander along to Hutchison House on Harcourt Road to the Tudor-style English Free House **Bull & Bear** (2525-7436, then over to the long-established **The Godown** (2524-2088 or (2527-9174 at 104 Lockhart Road and the nearby **Horse & Groom** (2507-2517, (2894-8888. Also in Causeway Bay, at 66-72 Paterson Street, is the **Brewery Tap Pub & Restaurant** (2576-2075, which has all the familiar British pub trappings of billiard-felt green walls, a brass rail bar and lots of varnished wood.

For real Irish ale (including, of course, Guinness on tap) and some exclusive all-natural ales from Hong Kong's very own micro brewery (The South China Brewing Company), popular **Delaney's** (2804-2880, at 2/F One Capital Place, 18 Luard Road, is the place to go to. It has live Irish music on Tuesdays, Fridays and Saturdays. Another Irish haunt

ABOVE: Trio belt out disco beat in Rick's Café in Kowloon. OPPOSITE: Draught beer and pint glasses at a Kowloon pub — a legacy of the British administration and commercial presence in Hong Kong.

not far away is **O'Brien's** (2890-8830 at Basement 2, Lee Theatre Plaza, 99 Percival Street, Causeway Bay.

From here the trail switches to the other side and slips simultaneously Down Under — the **Kangaroo Pub** (2376-0083, 1/F, 35 Hai Phong Road, and the long-standing doyen of them all, **Ned Kelly's Last Stand** (2376-0562 at 11A Ashley Road, with a decor celebrating the modern-day folk hero of the bush-ranging era who challenged the Victorian state constabulary in a bullet-proof iron mask and breast-plate, and got shot in the legs. The roof of the place is blasted off in the evenings by a traditional Dixieland jazz band.

For more sedate English and Irish drinking, with food to go with it, seek out the Tsimshatsui branch of **Mad Dogs** (2301-2222, on 32 Nathan Road and **Delaney's** (2301-3980, at 3 Pratt Avenue. And if you want to extend your pub-crawl you can sally as far as Stanley and find among others the rustic **Smuggler's Inn** (2813-8852, 90A Stanley Main Street.

In the background to the disco blast, Hong Kong's nightlife trail is dotted with more traditional cocktail joints and supper clubs, mostly at the hotels, which offer live music, and sometimes dancing, to go with the menu.

In Central District you can try **Mandarin Oriental's** (2522-0111 somewhat renowned mezzanine Clipper Lounge in which the seating is plush, the clientele drip with Rolexes and 22-carat gold and there's unobtrusive live music each afternoon and early evening, or the revolving **La Ronda Restaurant and Lounge** (2525-5111, at the Furama Hotel. Over in nearby Pacific Place, The Island Shangri-La Hotel's posh **Cyrano Lounge** (2820-8591 is billed as Hong Kong's highest, with a sky-high panorama of the harbor, while the **Conrad Lobby Lounge** (2521-3838 of the Conrad International Hotel is an equally respectable venue. Also in Pacific Place, on Level 3, is a branch of **Pomeroy's** (2523-4772, a popular place for after-work drinks or business rendezvous.

In Wanchai, there's the sophisticated **Oasis Lounge** (2802-8888 at the New World Harbour View Hotel, and the very elegant **Champagne Bar** (2588-1234, at the Grand Hyatt Hotel. In Causeway Bay, **Tott's Asian Grill & Bar** (2837-6786, on the roof-top 34/F of the Excelsior Hotel, has a sushi bar and cognac bar; the Park Lane Hotel has the **George & Co bar** (2890-3355.

In Tsimshatsui, the most relaxing and sophisticated bars are also in the main hotels: especially recommended are the Peninsula Hotel's **The Bar** (2366-6251; the Regent Hotel's **Club Shanghai** (2721-1211; the Hyatt Regency's cosy **Chin Chin Bar** (2311-1234; and the Hongkong Hotel's **Gripps** (2736-0088.

Family Fun

Hong Kong can be hard going for visiting children, especially if they're not into the amount of shopping or sightseeing their mums and dads probably want to do. But take heart, kids, there's a place which will please all of you: **Ocean Park,** Southeast Asia's largest oceanarium and fun park, is just half-an-hour away from Hong Kong Island's Central district (take bus N° 70 from Central and get off immediately after Aberdeen Tunnel or take the special Ocean Park Citybus service from Admiralty MTR station which goes directly to the entrance).

Ocean Park was established on the southern slopes of Hong Kong Island in 1977 and has expanded over the years to incorporate some of Asia's greatest thrills: it's got Asia's first and largest water playpark, called Water World (try the 20-m- (65-ft)-high Super Slides for a six-second adrenaline splash); the world's largest reef aquarium, the Atoll Reef (6,000 fish on three levels); and, the biggest thrill of all, one of the world's longest and fastest roller coasters, a heart-stopping loop-the-loop appropriately called The Dragon. This monster ride takes you soaring up to the sky and back again in a furious two-and-a-half-minute ride which reaches speeds of 48 kph (29 mph) and has you suspended upside down, on the edge of a cliff. Conquer that one and you're obviously brave enough to tackle some of the other thrill rides here like the Flying Swing, which will lift you in a seasickening wave-like motion up to seven meters (23 ft) high; the gravity-defying Eagle

Ride; and the new Film Fantasia-Simulator Ride whose hydraulically-actuated seats take you through an "illusionary" window while life-like images are projected on a 15-m- (50-ft)-high screen. There are plenty of less taxing attractions at Ocean Park: after the Atoll Reef my own favorite is the Ocean Theatre where you can watch a bunch of very talented dolphins, sea lions and a killer whale called Hoi Wai put on a show of incredible aquatic tricks. There's the park's latest attraction, Discovery of the Ancient World, a 300-m (985-ft) trail winding through tropical forest and enlivened by animated reptiles; and the already popular Dinosaur Trail. And then there are the Aviaries, whose spectacular space-age design offers free-flying room for over 2,000 birds including swans, ducks, cockatoos and hornbills (don't miss the flamingoes, either). There's even a special section in the park, Kids' World, for the younger members of the family, offering carousel and model train rides, a theater with animated shows and even a Dolphin University where you can watch the dolphins' training. And near the Tai Shue Wan (upper level) entrance, the Middle Kingdom recreates 5,000 years of Chinese history through crafts demonstrations, theater, opera and dance. As you can imagine, you'll need a full day to see just a fraction of Ocean Park's attractions.

If you manage to get mum and dad hooked on this kind of alternative entertainment while you're in Hong Kong, lead them further astray by visiting a couple of museums which are great for youngsters (and pretty enthralling for us oldies, too): the **Space Museum** and Science Museum, both in Kowloon. The Space Museum, dominating the Tsimshatsui waterfront with its huge planetarium (featuring Omnimax screenings and Sky shows several times daily) has some brilliant displays about astronomy and space technology, while the **Science Museum** in Tsimshatsui East is very much a "hands-on" experience and has displays for practically every age range, including robotics, transportation, computers and virtual reality. The 20-m- (65 ft)-high

OPPOSITE: Fun, amusement and excitement for all the family at Ocean Park.

Energy Machine is worth the visit alone. One word of warning: don't come on a Wednesday (free admission day) or you'll be engulfed by crowds of excited local school kids. That might be just enough to push mum and dad out to those shopping malls again.

Two malls, however, which may have some attraction for youngsters are the Cityplaza Shopping Centre in Tai Koo Shing (take the MTR to Tai Koo station) and the Whampoa Gardens in Kowloon's Hung Hom (easiest to reach by ferry from Central). Both have **ice-skating rinks** (see the SPORTING SPREE page 34 for details) and the Whampoa's concrete model of a ship (which is the mall itself, in fact) also has a playground on the top floor.

But perhaps the best and easiest family outings are those which involve a trip on a tram, train or ferry. The **Peak Tram** is an obvious must (see TOP SPOTS page 18) and its recently-opened Peak Tower could keep the kids on high for hours, thanks to its trio of attractions: the Rise of the Dragon train ride, taking you through the history of Hong Kong; The Peak Explorer motion ride with its individually moveable seats; and a branch of Ripley's Believe it or Not! Museum with 500 oddities from around the world. When you come down from The Peak, pop into **Hong Kong Park** (near the tram terminal) to see its fabulous walk-through aviary and three-level children's playground.

Train buffs can make the journey by MTR and KCR to Tai Po Market to visit the **Train Museum** (a good outing for adults and kids), while the **trams** trundling from Kennedy Town in the west of Hong Kong Island to Shau Kei Wan in the east are the simplest, cheapest ride of all and a lot of fun for everyone, especially if you can grab the front upper-deck seats. For the best roller-coaster bus ride in Hong Kong, don't miss the N° 6 from Central to **Stanley**, on the south side of Hong Kong Island. One of Hong Kong's best beaches is also near here, at **Repulse Bay** — a pleasant place to hang out after

Repulse Bay and its high cost condominiums which overlook Hong Kong's most popular beach.

Stanley's crowded market. Other **beaches** which will suit the kids can be found on Lantau (Cheung Sha is the best), Cheung Chau (you can windsurf here, too) and in the New Territories areas of Sai Kung and Clearwater Bay.

Recommended jaunts by ferry range from the hop across the harbor by the famous **Star Ferry** (dare I mention that there's a Toys "R Us store in Ocean Centre near the Tsimshatsui Star Ferry terminal?) to the hour-long ferry rides to the Outlying Islands of Cheung Chau, Lamma or Lantau — great destinations in themselves for family outings (see THE OPEN ROAD page 38).

Lastly, for something with an environmentally educational edge to it, you could consider taking a day-long **Dolphinwatch cruise** to try and spot the last of Hong Kong's Chinese white dolphins (see THE GREAT OUTDOORS page 28).

Cultural Kicks

TRADITIONAL CHINESE TEMPLES
Major cultural events in Hong Kong revolve around its temples, of which there are no less than 600, an amazing number for so small a place. About half of them are Buddhist, 200 Taoist, and the rest a mixture of both. They pay homage to animist beliefs and spiritual codes that sprang out of the early mists of Chinese history as a formula for that most crucial of all Chinese creeds — man's harmony with nature and the entire universe. Where ancient animism endowed all of the physical world with various guardian or malignant spirits, Taoism produced dozens of different gods and deities, all of them entrusted with the care and protection of some aspect of moral life. When Buddhism invaded China from India along the Silk Road in the fourth century, Taoism flexed and bent like bamboo in its path, and thus survived the challenge. Rather than battle for supremacy, the two religions adapted to each other, virtually borrowing each other's gods, and have since stood alongside Confucianism as

the paramount Three Teachings of the Chinese culture.

The most common gods and goddesses represented in Hong Kong's temples are Tin Hau (Goddess of the Sea), Pak Tai (Emperor of the North), Kwun Yum (Goddess of Mercy), and Kwan Kung (God of War). Architecturally, the temples are often fantastically ornate and colorful affairs, with curving roofs (to deter evil spirits), ceramic or carved wooden friezes depicting deities, and a series of alcoves or chambers holding altars to the different gods and goddesses.

Hong Kong's oldest and most famous temple is the **Man Mo Temple** on Hollywood Road, below the island's Mid-Levels, built within a few years of

the colonial land-grab of 1841. In typical
Taoist style it's dedicated to the God
of Literature and civil servants, known
as Man, and the God of War, Mo and
is an ornately decorated old building,
its interior blackened by years of joss
smoke. Even the newer temples —
notably, Kowloon's huge Wong Tai Sin
temple which was opened in 1973 —
follow traditional architectural lines.
At Chinese New Year, the Wong Tai Sin
complex is packed with hundreds of
thousands of worshippers praying for
a prosperous and happy new year —
an indication of how important the
traditional cultural beliefs still are among
Hong Kong people, despite modern
Western influences.

YOUR CHOICE

ARCHITECTURE

Colonial architecture has fared poorly
in the face of development: there are
few vestiges left of Hong Kong's early
years. The old Legislative Council
building in Statue Square, the clock
tower in Tsimshatsui, the Edwardian
Helena May Club on Garden Road,
St John's Cathedral, the restored
Western Market and the Main Building
of the University of Hong Kong are
among the few buildings left which

ABOVE: The Star Ferry, Cultural Centre and the
preserved clock tower of the old railway terminus.
OVERLEAF: The Convention & Exhibition Centre —
where the hand-over ceremony of Hong Kong to
China took place — seen here from the Tsimshatsui
East promenade across the Victoria Habour.

date from the turn of the century or early 1920s.

Architectural buffs should perhaps look instead at Hong Kong's soaring modern replacements — notably the Sir Norman Foster-designed Hongkong Bank headquarters in Central, and its neighbor, the triangular-shaped China Bank Building, designed by I.M. Pei. For modern architectural feats on an engineering level, the new Chek Lap Kok Airport terminal (also designed by Foster) is also well worth seeing as are the world's longest suspension bridge, Tsing Ma (linking the airport to Kowloon) and the soaring new extension to the Convention & Exhibition Centre in Wanchai.

ARTS FESTIVALS

Hong Kong has certainly graduated from its old reputation as a cultural desert — theater, films, ballet, Chinese opera and orchestral concerts and performances by the highly regarded Hong Kong Philharmonic Orchestra are now held on a regular basis.

In January and February each year Hong Kong puts its growing cultural reputation bravely on the line with the Hong Kong Arts Festival and Fringe Festival, drawing top-class orchestras, soloists, dance troupes, theater companies, movies and fringe events from all over Asia and the West.

In alternate years, in October and November (the last one was held in 1996), there's also the Asian Arts Festival every August (held around the Central Lan Kwai Fong area), which is a banquet of food promotions, street entertainment, open-air music performances and other special events.

As part of its five-year "Spotlight Hong Kong towards the millennium" program, the HKTA is also initiating or promoting a series of world-class events and cultural extravaganzas to appear in Hong Kong in the next few years, including the Stars of the Bolshoi Ballet (December 1997), Nutcracker on Ice, Jesus Christ Superstar and the Kirov Ballet.

PERFORMING ARTS VENUES

The main venues are, in Wanchai, the Hong Kong Arts Centre (2877-1000, 2 Harbour Road and, next door, the Hong Kong Academy for Performing Arts (2584-1500. In Central, City Hall (2922-1284 and (2521-7251, on 2 Lower Albert Road, which stages more offbeat theater and music shows. The open-air Hong Kong Stadium (2895-7895 in Eastern Hospital Road, Causeway Bay, stages some of Hong Kong's biggest pop and music shows, as does the indoor Queen Elizabeth Stadium (2591-1347 at 18 Oi Kwan Road, Wanchai.

In Tsimshatsui, the Hong Kong Cultural Centre (2734-2010 next to Star Ferry, offers a gigantic 2,100-seat Concert Hall with a 93-stop pipe organ, a Grand Theatre with a revolving stage and seating for 1,750, a studio theater for smaller performances and six exhibition galleries, along with restaurants and bars. Recent performers have included such international stars as soprano Dame Kiri Te Kanawa.

In Hung Hom, the 12,500-seat Hong Kong Coliseum (2355-7233, 9 Cheong Wan Road, regularly stages massive spectator events — sports meets, ice shows, ballet and pop and rock concerts. Also in Hung Hom, the 2,600-seat amphitheater at the Ko Shan Theatre (2740-9222, on Ko Shan Road, is the main venue for pop concerts by local underground, and sometimes international, bands. Cantonese opera performances are held at least once a month. For more pop shows and opera, as well as foreign and Chinese films, you can also try the Academic Community Hall (2339-5182, at the Baptist College, near the Kowloon Tong MTR station. Major classical concerts and Chinese opera performances are often held at the Tsuen Wan Town Hall (2414-0144 at 72 Tai Ho Road, Tsuen Wan.

For other venues along with a weekly rundown of events, consult HKTA's Hong Kong Diary and Hong Kong This Week, the South China Morning Post newspaper or the free weekly HK Magazine. The Urban Council also publishes a City News digest of events, available free at the City Hall,

Cultural Centre or HKTA Information Centres. Or you can check the HKTA website, http://www.hkta.org or another entertainment guide website, http://www.webhk.com.

Tickets for events organized by the Urban Council or at Urban Council venues can be booked at URBTIX box office outlets (at nearly all the theaters mentioned above) or by calling the URBTIX number (2734-9009 (daily 10 AM to 9 PM). Tickets can be reserved with an ID card or passport or paid for by credit card.

CINEMAS

Hong Kongers love going to the movies — even though they probably have the latest VCRs and laser-disc players at home. There are over 30 cinemas in Hong Kong, the most popular in multi-screen complexes such as UA Queensway (Admiralty), UA Times Square (Causeway Bay), Silvercord (Tsimshatsui), and Golden Gateway (Tsimshatsui). Theaters showing more unusual, offbeat films include Columbia Classics in Wanchai (2827-8291, and the Arts Centre's basement Lim Por Yen Film Theatre (2582-0232.

Cinema tickets cost around HK$60 (half price on Tuesdays) and can be booked three days in advance. Phone bookings are often for weekday shows only but with a system called Cityline you can book tickets at most major theaters by calling (2317-6666, paying with a credit card and collecting your tickets from a vending machine outside the theater. There's an additional HK$7.50 charge per ticket for this service.

The home-produced Chinese-language films (usually with English subtitles) tend to be violent martial-art movies or slapstick comedies; watch out for films by mainland directors which are often richly photographed historical dramas. The annual International Film Festival (see above) is also a chance to see some excellent mainland movies. Major English-language movies arrive here soon after release but you may well have to queue to get a seat for the popular

blockbusters — or choose a weekday matinee show.

The *South China Morning Post* carries weekend film reviews and a daily listing of current films; even more comprehensive is the free *HK Magazine* (available at many bars, restaurants and bookshops) which unlike the *SCMP* also lists all the cinemas' Chinese names: an essential aid to getting to the theater of your choice by taxi since few drivers know the theaters' English names.

MUSEUMS

Hong Kong has some 17 museums illustrating everything from traditional teaware to 2000-year-old tombs, from horse-racing to trains. The HKTA has a Museums leaflet (available at their Information Centres) giving full details; they can also provide you with a special visitor's pass which gives you unlimited admission to four Urban Council museums — Hong Kong Museum of Art, Science Museum, Space Museum and Museum of History — for only HK$50. The pass is valid for one month and includes a 10 percent discount at museum gift shops.

If you've got children in tow, the Science Museum and Space Museum are probably the most appealing (see FAMILY FUN page 52) but a trio of charming folk museums are also ideal for family visits: the **Law Uk Folk Museum** (2896-7006 is a converted 200-year-old Hakka village house in the midst of urban development in Chai Wan which reveals what traditional life was once like for these rural Hong Kong settlers. The **Sheung Yiu Folk Museum** (2792-6365, way out in the Sai Kung Country Park, makes a very pleasant goal for a day's outing. Once a fortified Hakka village, the museum expands on the Law Uk idea, with displays of typical belongings and furnishings. The **Sam Tung Uk Museum** (2411-2001, in Tsuen Wan, is also a restored 200-year-old rural walled village, now surrounded by the new town of Tsuen Wan.

Hong Kong's most important art collection is housed in the **Hong Kong**

Museum of Art (2734-2167, in the Cultural Centre complex in Tsimshatsui. There are seven exhibition galleries, of which four concentrate on Chinese antiquities, fine arts and historical pictures — one of the most comprehensive Chinese art displays in Southeast Asia. Other specialist Chinese art museums include the **University Museum & Art Gallery** (2859-2114 (with the world's largest collection of Yuan Dynasty bronzeware); and the **Tsui Museum of Art** (2868-2688 (with a notable collection of Chinese ceramics).

The museum which houses the earliest historical monument in Hong Kong — an early Han Dynasty tomb dating back some 2,000 years — is the **Lei Cheng Uk Museum**, a branch of the Museum of History, at Sham Sui Po (2386-2863. Don't get your hopes up — the tomb isn't actually very exciting and only worth a visit if you're in the area. My own favorite museum — and a favorite for many visitors — is the **Flagstaff House Museum of Teaware** (2869-0690, conveniently located in a strikingly handsome nineteenth-century house (once the home of the Commander-in-Chief of the British forces) in Hong Kong Park.

CONCERTS

The **Hong Kong Philharmonic Orchestra** performs a season of classical concerts from September to July at the City Hall Concert Hall, Hong Kong Cultural Centre and Tsuen Wan Town Hall. You'll find details of their program at these major venues (or check the *South China Morning Post*).

For a new slant on traditional Chinese music, it's worth inquiring about the **Hong Kong Chinese Orchestra**, the largest of its kind in the world. It combines Chinese instruments and Western orchestrations and gives regular performances at the major venues as well as at district arts festivals. If this unconventional style of Chinese music isn't to your taste, try and track down a performance of traditional **Chinese opera**. This usually takes place to celebrate Chinese festivals (especially major festivals such as the Tin Hau Festival or locally important festivals in honor of a temple god) or as part of the Asian Arts Festival or Hong Kong Arts Festival. The style you're most likely to witness is Cantonese, though the big troupes may well come from the mainland and perform the Peking style. Be prepared for a good deal of untuneful (to Western ears) noise and clamor, and for some fabulous costumes and face makeup. The free monthly *bc Magazine* (available at bars, restaurants and Hong Kong Book Centre outlets) keeps tabs on where you can hear a performance.

More familiar music can be heard at the **lunchtime concerts** in St John's Cathedral in Central every Wednesday. Call (2523-4157 for details or turn up at the door before 1:20 PM.

Shop Till You Drop

Whether a bargain-packed Emporium of the East or a latter-day showplace of the latest fashions and consumer electronics, Hong Kong has always been an exciting but hard-nosed shopping center — the great Oriental emporium that the early China traders envisioned it as being, and something that must be making the ghost of Lord Palmerston chew on his top hat.

And Hong Kong is a place where you won't find toilet paper advertised on TV, or mouth-wash, or any other of the mass-marketed household essentials that crowd the commercials channels of the West. Hong Kong's English-language ATV World and TVB Pearl programming pushes Swiss watches, French perfumes, high-class jewelry, up-market Japanese electronic consumer products, the target and tone of its commercials reflecting the same tone of its mainstream shopping — Gucci, not anything as crass as the morning gargle.

Hong Kong's commercial extravaganza — the vast atrium of New Town Plaza shopping mall in Shtain.

This up-market trend makes shopping a covetous experience, and the Hong Kong version of a window-browsing far more than just a stroll in the streets. Since the beginning of the eighties, huge self-contained, climate-controlled, luxury-packed shopping malls have sprung up all over the place to revolutionize the retail industry, many of them featuring multi-story atriums, decorative fountains and regular cultural exhibitions and performances — anything from police brass bands to string quartets or Chinese acrobats — to attract the crowds. Just as the ultra-modern infrastructure of Hong Kong has made the place something of a capitalist funland, these great retail palaces have made shopping an adventure playground.

Like some kind of living, growing organism, they've also gradually linked up in certain districts, providing environments in which you can browse in airconditioned comfort for hours, crossing from mall to mall, without actually exposing yourself to the outside air; a blessed relief in the sweltering and humid high-summer months.

Though you can virtually shop everywhere in Hong Kong, the main concentration of shops and shopping centers are in Central District along Des Voeux Road Central to Wanchai, Causeway Bay, and Taikoo Shing, across the harbor they are in Tsimshatsui East, Tsimshatsui along Nathan Road down to Yaumatei, and the recently developed New Town centers in Shatin and New Territories all have their big shopping complex.

In **Central District**, for example, you can stroll from Star Ferry to the converted pedestrian overpass between Jardine House and Exchange Square that gives you the choice of either continuing along the waterfront towards the **Shun Tak Centre** shopping arcades and going across another overpass to the **Wing On** and **Sincere** department stores, giving blissful shelter from rain and the fierce

The riot of colored neon that competes for attraction along Nathan Road, Kowloon.

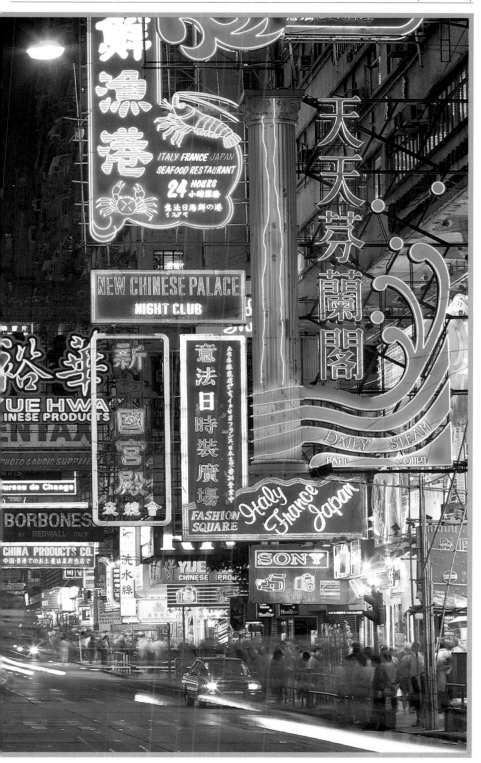

summer heat, not to mention the traffic. Or you can go straight ahead into the bargain outlets of World-Wide Plaza on your right or to the high-class boutiques in **Swire House** on your left, with access to more shopping floors in St George's Building and the **Mandarin Hotel** and, via other pedestrian crossovers, **Prince's Building, The Landmark** and the posh **Galleria.**

This is the start of the Gucci Trail — alongside Gucci you'll find Chanel, Christian Dior, Lanvin, Hermès, Giorgio Armani, Nina Ricci, Issey Miyake and Salvatore Ferragamo. You'll find Rolex, Seiko, Girard Peregaux and Cartier watches. You'll drool over heavy 22-carat gold necklaces, bracelets and other high-fashion jewelry, Italian pig-skin shoes and silk ties, French perfumes, fine porcelain, the latest in American and Japanese sports equipment and fashions, Burmese jade, crystal glassware and antique fine arts — and you'll feel strangely avid and perhaps a little embarrassed at the long-suppressed instinct for the luxuries of life that is rising out of your soul.

From here, the trail extends past a new branch of **Marks & Spencer**, on the corner of Wyndham Street, to **Lane Crawford** on Queen's Road Central, the traditional home of Harrods-style upper-drawer British shopping. All along Queen's Road Central are high class boutiques, watch and gold-jewelry shops. Heading eastwards from the Landmark, take the pedestrian overpass into the walk-through of Queensway shopping plaza that runs between the Far East Finance Centre and Admiralty Towers, above the Admiralty MTR station, from where another pedestrian bridge takes you into the glistening shopping mall of Pacific Place.

This vast complex houses a wide range of up-market boutiques, a **Marks and Spencer, Seibu** (a Japanese department store with a range of trendy merchandise and prices that have to be seen to be believed), specialty shops, restaurants, cinemas and the **Marriott, Conrad** and **Island Shangri-La** hotels.

From there it runs down into Wanchai and Causeway Bay, where the accent changes from Western to Japanese high fashion and luxury accessories in the giant Tokyo-style department stores, **Mitsukoshi, Daimaru, Matsuzakaya** and **Sogo**. Just around the corner from Mitsukoshi, between Russell and Sharp streets, you'll find the spectacular **Times Square** with its inside scenic elevators, up-market boutiques, huge music store, restaurants and cinemas. There's also another branch of **Lane Crawford** in this district, and a range of boutiques and shops selling everything from silk scarves to cameras and electronics to Chinese antiques in the **Excelsior Hotel Shopping Arcade**.

Beyond Causeway Bay in the Taikoo Shing housing development at Quarry Bay, you'll find another enormous emporium, **Cityplaza,** which has four towers for up-market and bargain shopping and a variety of eating places. And if you feel like a little exercise in between window-browsing there's an ice-skating rink in one of the atriums. Cityplaza is easily accessible by MTR — just take the train to Taikoo station and one of the exits takes you right into Tower I.

The giants of the shopping world are clustered over the harbor in Tsimshatsui and Tsimshatsui East. From the moment you get off the Star Ferry, in fact, you're drawn into the luxury vortex of shopping plazas, all interlinked **Star House, Harbour City (Ocean Terminal, Ocean Centre** and **Ocean Galleries)** and **China Hong Kong City,** containing no less than five hotels and hundreds of shops. It's such a mammoth place that an information desk in the Ocean Terminal, staffed by English-speaking guides, will provide you with maps and even a computer print-out of suitable shops to help you find your way through the retail maze.

Some other malls in Tsimshatsui include **Park Lane Shopper's Boulevarde** on the Nathan Road side of Kowloon Park and opposite, Park Lane Square. Also, the **New World Centre,** across Salisbury Road on the southern fringe of the Tsimshatsui reclamation. For the discerning buyer there are smaller shopping arcades in the Peninsula, Hyatt Regency, Sheraton, Holiday Inn Golden Mile and Regent hotels.

From there you can wend your way into the heart of Tsimshatsui East and take your pick of a half-dozen shopping plazas around the Royal Garden, Regal Kowloon, and Grand Stanford Harbour View hotels.

Finally, for jewelry-lovers Hong Kong offers high-quality diamonds and other gems, all of which are exempt from tax and duty charges, at reasonable prices. Gold and platinum are also competitively priced. As with other shopping, where to go for the best buys is always a problem and before rushing into the first shop you see, please consult HKTA's *Official Shopping Guide*, which tells you what you need to look for in a stone, and lists reputable retailers. (For more on jade, see the BARGAIN TRAIL, page 71)

TAILORMADE CLOTHING

Gone are the days when you could walk into any tailor shop in Hong Kong and have a man's or woman's suit or dress shirt made in 24 hours at ridiculously cheap prices. A lot of the 24-hour tailors are no longer around, and the conventional ones, which require at least 72 hours, are now charging prices comparable with designer-label fashion off the hook. However, one tailor who's still keeping the tradition alive is the famous and long-established **Sam's Tailor** ℂ 2721-8375, Burlington Arcade, K, 92-94 Nathan Road, Tsimshatsui, whose prices, depending on the material, range from around HK$1,800 to HK$6,000.

THE SPACE-AGE BAZAAR

For the latest in high-tech consumer products, Hong Kong has them all, in the thousands of shops and plazas that make up this city. With the help of the territory's free-port status, as fast as they come off the space-age assembly lines in Japan, South Korea, Taiwan and China they're

usually available here months before they appear in most other countries. And at competitive prices.

But with a combination of spiraling shop rents, increasingly slim profit margins, the deteriorating caliber of retail employees and sheer greed, shopping for these goods can be an unpleasant experience. Particular consumer complaints in recent years have been over bait-and-switch tactics, where what you get is not what you were shown. Also, components or accessories are often removed from the product boxes and, when the deal is done, the shop assistant claims that these are optional extras — which you must have or the product itself won't work properly, and which he'll sell you at a 50 percent discount because you're such a nice customer. Don't rush into a deal — prices can vary from shop to shop, sometimes considerably. For example, in one store I was quoted HK$1,800 for a portable compact disc player which was selling for HK$1,300 in another.

Tailor-made clothes ABOVE are still possible in Hong Kong.

The Tsimshatsui district is famous for its bargains (and unscrupulous deals) in cameras and consumer electronics, especially in the honeycomb of brightly lit, fixed ghetto blasters that are the cutthroat stores on Nathan Road and back-streets either side. Like most of the smaller stores in Hong Kong, these places operate on the principle of high turnover, which means that some of them have profit margins on their most popular lines shaved down to as little as HK$40 to HK$80. On Hong Kong Island, you can try the row of shops running along Queen Victoria and Stanley streets in Central. In Wanchai, Johnston and Hennessy roads and in Causeway Bay, Cannon Street (which leads to the Excelsior Hotel) and along **Yee Wo Street**.

But if you're concerned about getting ripped off, or just don't want to deal with the frequently rude assistants, the following are some reputable dealers recommended by HKTA.

Hong Kong Island
The Sony Service Centre's **Chung Yuen Electrical Co** stores at Shop 104-105 Prince's Building (2524-8066, Chater Road in Central and 2/F In Square, Windsor House, 311 Gloucester Road (2890-2998 Road in Causeway Bay; **Crown Photo Supplies** (2524-5039, Shop 103 Prince's Building, Central; **Fortress** (2544-1665, 107-111 Des Voeux Road, Central; and **Universal Audio & Video Centre** (2801-6422 in Shop 135 at The Mall in Pacific Place. For cameras only, go to the **Photo Scientific Appliances** (2522-1903, 6 Stanley Street, Central.

Tsimshatsui
Crown Photo Supplies (2376-1836, 27 Hankow Road; **Fortress** (2735-8628, Shop 281, Ocean Terminal; and **Wood's Photo Supplies** (2736-8128, Room 1004, 10/F Silvercord, Tower 2, 30 Canton Road. For cameras only, the **Camera Shop** (2730-9227 in Shop 121, Ocean Terminal.

For computer buffs, I recommend the following two shopping complexes in Tsimshatsui: **Silvercord**, 30 Canton Road, and **Star Computer City**, 2/F Star House, 3 Salisbury Road. Also, **Plug & Play Systems** (2581-9113, G/F, 113 Des Voeux Road, Central.

Lastly, and not mentioned in any of HKTA shopping guides, you'll find a multi-level computer bazaar in Shamshuipo called the **Golden Shopping Arcade** where you can get hardware, software, accessories and spare parts for just about any brand you can name. You can also get software (and the possibility of viruses) that you'd swear could not be offered at the prices you're being quoted, if you know what I mean. It's a freelance establishment in the truest sense of the word and you'll find that matters like warranties and guarantees have to be treated with something of a wink and a nod so be careful, and if you feel unsettled about the equipment or the price, take the prudent route and don't buy. If you know all about computers, and know exactly what you want, you should come out satisfied.

THE ANTIQUE/ARTS & CRAFTS TRAIL

For Chinese and Asian antiques there's really only one place to go, the area in Central starting from the upper end of Wyndham Street, continuing all the way along Hollywood Road until you reach "Cat Street", just by the Man Mo Temple.

Here you'll find a wide range of high-priced boutique-style stores offering everything from Chinese and Thai carved buddhas to Indonesian masks and batiks, Persian and Indian carpets, rosewood furniture, Thai and Himalayan artwork and a fascinating array of snuff bottles, porcelain, silver jewelry, Korean and Japanese wooden chests and traditional Chinese silk paintings and scrolls.

If the prices frighten you off, there's an irresistible junk shop on the corner of Hollywood Road and Lyndhurst Terrace laden with an incredible assortment of second-hand Western and Chinese collectibles Mao paraphernalia, watches, cameras, Chinese coins, black and white photos of old Hong Kong and China and books and magazines. For much the same thing, but on a larger scale, hawkers at "Cat Street" display their "antiques" along the pavements of two narrow streets.

Another interesting place for Asian arts and crafts is the **Amazing Grace Elephant Company** in Ocean Centre, and a smaller branch at the Excelsior Hotel Shopping Arcade.

THE BARGAIN TRAIL

Outside the big plazas, there are literally thousands of department stores and smaller shops to choose from, offering just about anything your heart desires. Their prices are cheaper because their rents are lower, the competition between them is

fierce, and, as already mentioned, they operate on the basis of a swift turnover. Many of them also cater more for the domestic Chinese buyer, which in some cases means better prices and, in the case of clothing, means some very good deals if you can fit into the generally smaller Chinese sizes.

Starting in the western area of Central District, the **Shun Tak Centre** in the Macau Ferry Terminal offers several levels of shops selling the latest in fashion and informal gear. Nearby, the **Wing On** and **Sincere** department stores not only offer high fashion but reasonable bargains in clothing, luggage, shoes and body-care products, particularly when there's a sale on.

For watches and jewelry, there are dozens of stores running virtually parallel with each other on Des Voeux and Queen's roads. For really good value,

Cameras and electrical goods OPPOSITE TOP are among the top items of the tourist' shopping list in Hong Kong. Jewelry shops OPPOSITE BOTTOM abound on and off the Golden Mile on Nathan Road — the main tourist shopping mecca of Kowloon. ABOVE: Beautifully painted antique screen.

the City Chain watch shops — there are around 70 branches scattered throughout Hong Kong — have permanent 30 to 50 percent discounts.

A relatively cheap place for quality men's shirts, suits and casual ensembles is **Crocodile**, which has a number of outlets in Central, Pacific Place, Causeway Bay and Kowloon. Even more popular is the **Giordano** chain of shops (offering casual clothes for both men and women) which initiated the unfamiliar concept in Hong Kong of service with a smile. On-the-spot hem-alterations will also be done here and goods exchanged without question. Elsewhere in Central, you'll find haberdashery items on the steps on Pottinger Street, and across Queen's Road in The Lanes, or Li Yuen Streets East and West, which run down to Des Voeux Road, cheap clothing, underwear, shoes, silkwear, make-up, fashion jewelry and Gucci look-alike handbags. Nearby on Des Voeux Road, **World-Wide Plaza** has

lots of small shops selling much of what's to be found in the lanes.

For mainly Chinese products, the five floors of the **Chinese Merchandise Emporium** at 92-104 Queen's Road, just past Pottinger Street. The prices are good and style and quality are steadily improving as the society modernizes. It's also a treasure house of interesting souvenirs — herbal medicines, Chinese teas, mahjong sets, jewelry, down garments and duvets, carpets and antiques, silk embroidery, fine linenware, carved marble and soapstone figures, jade and nephrite jewelry and sculptures, intricate cloisonné and bamboo ware, traditional kites in the form of hawks and ducks, mouth organs, ping-pong sets, calligraphy and painting sets, ornate old-fashioned treadle-style sewing machines, *kung fu* swords and tom-toms, dragon masks and even the sturdy Phoenix and Swallow bicycles of China, modeled on the old British workhorse, The Raleigh Roadster.

In Wanchai around the Wanchai Road and Spring Garden Lane area there are stalls and shops selling designer jeans, children's clothes and casual wear for both men and women. Further along in Causeway Bay, the bargain shopping is more concentrated, largely in the area between Hysan Avenue and the Excelsior Hotel. Again, there's just about everything you'd want to know on sale in the myriad stores and boutiques that absolutely throng with shoppers. The area is particularly rich in women's clothing and shoes and a popular place you can try is **Jardine's Bazaar**, which is similar to the lanes in Central. Also in the vicinity is another huge Chinese emporium, **China Products.**

No shopping visit to Hong Kong is really complete without a browse through the open market and bargain boutiques at Stanley. To get to Stanley, take the bus N° 6 or the airconditioned bus N° 260 from the Exchange Square terminal in Central. Famous for years for its cut-price clothing and arts and crafts, the market has become a mainstream tourist attraction these days, with tour

ABOVE Chinese calligraphy set — one of the many traditional Chinese items available from the Chinese Merchandise Emporium. You can also select some calligraphy or a hand-painted sourvenir from an open-air studio OPPOSITE.

coaches thundering out there every day. At weekends the place is packed, and if you want my advice, go there during the week. Stanley isn't as cheap as it used to be and bargaining doesn't seem to be the thing to do anymore. But you won't be disappointed, it's still a good place to shop, and a lot of fun.

In Tsimshatsui, the most interesting place for browsing and buying both day and night is along the Golden Mile of Nathan Road, checking out the side streets if you have the time. One area off Nathan Road that shouldn't be missed is Granville Road, which is noted for its cheap clothes. Most of the shops are outlets selling factory seconds and production overruns and if you've got the patience to sort through the endless racks and piles of clothes you'll find some amazing bargains.

Other locations for more overruns of designer brand clothes as well as electronics, carpets, lamps and porcelain, etc are the factories themselves. Personally, the last place I'd want to shop in Hong Kong is at the factory, but if the discounts appeal to you I suggest you obtain *The Complete Guide to Hong Kong Factory Bargains* a handy pocket-sized book found in most book shops for tips and the best and most reliable places to go. Also available is the HKTA's *Factory Outlets/Locally Made Fashion Outlets* brochure, which lists all HKTA members dealing in the manufacturing and retailing of ready-to-wear.

For Chinese products, **Chinese Arts & Crafts** in Star House, by Star Ferry, sells happy coats, silk dressing gowns, embroidered linen, inexpensive to very pricey jewelry and jade items, porcelain and antiques, along with rosewood furniture and beautiful Chinese carpets. Good for souvenirs and gifts and like its competitor in Central, prices are very reasonable.

For more browsing and buying, **Temple Street** is Hong Kong's most popular night market and can be reached by MTR, alighting at Jordan station. From the Jordan Road entrance

you make your way through block after block of stalls and shops selling fake Rolex, Dunhill and Cartier watches and designer clothes, more cheap watches, sunglasses, silk ties, trousers, shirts, sweaters, jackets, suits, men's underpants at HK$20 for three pairs and T-shirts for HK$15 to $20. You can pick-up electronic keyrings that beep, solar calculators the size of credit cards (which also double as FM radios), or FM radios the size of cigarette lighters, or cigarette lighters that double as FM radios. You'll find Nepalese hawkers sitting on the sidewalk selling Nepalese jewelry, masks and colorful bags. You'll see street dentists, Chinese opera, and for HK$50 to $80 you can have some of your fortune told — the full story will cost more.

Where Temple Street caters mainly to men, Tung Choi Street in Mongkok is the Ladies' Market selling bright sweaters, scarves, jeans, underwear and makeup.

Back in Yaumatei, another of Hong Kong's traditional open-air bargain centers, the **Jade Market**, under the flyover near Kansu Street, offers a range of jade, and prices. But be careful, if you

have the time, they're definitely worth visiting.

THE SAFETY TRAIL

Being the frenetic open market that Hong Kong is, the trading rules and practices naturally get a little twisted and bent here and there, and there are certain precautions that should be taken before buying anything of technical or financial value. The first rule is this: don't go shopping until you've obtained a copy of the HKTA's *Official Shopping Guide.* This handy little booklet is packed with information on where to go and who to trust on your shopping spree, and it offers the added guarantee of its own membership system — every retail outlet in the book has the HKTA stamp of approval. If you have any complaints or queries about a member, you can contact the **HKTA Hotline** (2807-6177.

When you're shopping outside the major retail plazas, take cash and not plastic. Such is the low-profit turnover in most shops, especially the clothing, camera and electronics places, that the retailers put a five percent "handling" charge on the cost to discourage credit cards. If this happens to you, suggest you report the shop to your credit card company.

Always shop around and compare prices before making any decision, and even then make sure that the best bargain price you get includes not only the camera or stereo unit you want to buy but the standard accessories and manufacturers' garantee that go with it. For complaints or advice call the **Consumer Council** (2929-2222.

Again, outside the major plazas, the question of a warranty on cameras and electrical goods is a constant problem. The best way to tackle it is to shop only where you see the HKTA sign, meaning the establishment has been vetted for good customer service and honesty, and insist that a warranty be provided and stamped with the dealer's chop before you hand over the money.

Don't be timid. Bargain where you feel you can. Go for whatever discount you

know nothing about the stone, don't spend a lot of money unless you have an expert with you.

East of Tsimshatsui East in **Hung Hom,Whampoa Garden** is another place for value for money. When you arrive, if you think you see a large ship in the middle of the shopping area you're not mistaken. The Whampoa hasn't run aground and was, in fact, especially built as a shopping mall — inside, a Japanese department store, Chinese restaurant and a coffee shop. Nearby, the **Hong Kong Place** arcade stages a Musical Fountain Show. To get there from Kowloon, take a taxi and if you're coming from Hong Kong Island, Star Ferries will take you directly there.

Not forgetting the children, these days about the only place specializing in toys, apart from the department stores, is the massive **Toys R Us** in the basement of Ocean Centre.

Out in the New Territories the shopping plazas in the New Towns at Shatin, Tsuen Wan and Tuen Mun — all conveniently accessible via the MTR/KCR — have added to the bargain market, forced by their locations to undercut the prices in the central tourist districts. If you

can get, it's accepted practice in most "freelance" outlets in Hong Kong. But then again, don't lose your cool if you get cold-shouldered. Try at all times to make shopping a fun experience, not a cultural collision remembering that, with the vast variety of stores throughout Hong Kong, and the fierce competition, if one shop won't give you the price you want you'll get it somewhere else.

Don't let touts physically drag you into their shops. It means you're stepping into a tourist trap. When you're buying ivory or jade, shop only at an establishment recommended by HKTA and go there armed with HKTA advice. There are some very clever bone and plastic imitations of ivory around Hong Kong, and plastic and ordinary stone "jade". Remember also that some countries have now banned the import of ivory, so check on that with your consulate or trade commission before you bother to look around.

If you're buying Chinese or Asian furniture to ship home, make sure you get all receipts from the retailer, the total price, shipping information and check requirement for disinfestation before or after importation to the destination country. The HKTA advises that on

major purchases you take out All Risk Insurance as well to cover the possibility of in-transit damage. Remember also that rattan and certain other Asian woods and materials dry out and become brittle or even crack when they're shipped from constant humidity to centrally heated homes.

Lastly, be careful about the amount of luggage you try to hand-carry on to your plane at the airport. For most airlines, United States carriers excluded, there's a size limit to cabin luggage, and there's a team of female inspectors inside the departure barrier which is so zealous you'd swear it trained with Delta Force or the SAS. Anything beyond a reasonably sized hold-all will not get through, and you'll leave Hong Kong in anger when you should have a contented, perhaps over-stimulated and exhausted smile on your face.

Many shades and shapes of jade are displayed in the jade market ABOVE but care is needed if true jade is the quest. OPPOSITE: Hong Kong's traditional arts — ornately sculptured marble and jade chops in Man Wa Street store, Western District.

Short Breaks

OUTLYING ISLANDS

Most visitors to Hong Kong base themselves in a city center hotel and explore the territory on day-trips. Thanks to the efficient transport system you can easily see Hong Kong's central highlights in a few days and get out even to the furthest corners of the territory and back again within a day.

But if you'd rather be walking over the hills in Hong Kong's Country Parks than through the shopping malls of Tsimshatsui you might like to base yourself in the countryside for a day or so.

The outlying island of Lantau is the ideal choice since it offers excellent hiking trails within easy reach of its main village and ferry terminal, Mui Wo (Silvermine Bay). There's the budget-price Mui Wo Inn here (for details on this and other budget places, see BACKPACKING, page 40) as well as the up-market **Silvermine Beach Hotel** (2984-8295 FAX 2984-1907 where doubles are around US$100 a night on weekdays.

The neighboring island of Cheung Chau is another alternative — not so much for hiking, since the island is too small and developed for that, but for easy-going days and nights (there are no cars on Cheung Chau), fascinating strolls through the village or lazy hours on the main Tung Wan beach. The up-market accommodation choice here is the **Warwick Hotel** (2981-0081 FAX 2981-9174, which overlooks the beach and is similar in price to the Silvermine Beach Hotel.

MACAU AND CHINA

Another enticing option is to extend a visit to **Macau** beyond a quick day-trip into a relaxing two or three-day visit. With this length of time, you can not only get to see most of Macau's cultural sights but also catch its Portuguese flavors most enjoyably by lingering over meals in typical Portuguese style — that means several hours spent over a three-course lunch that naturally includes aperitifs (a dry white port, perhaps?), wine and a vintage port with your coffee. Sightseeing after such lunches is invariably a strain: best to follow the Portuguese way and have a quick siesta back at your hotel. Two days spent like this in Macau pass very quickly and pleasantly, I can assure you. Check MACAU, page 231 for details of its various temptations and for information on how to get there.

A short trip from Hong Kong further into **mainland China** is an even more popular extension to a Hong Kong holiday. You can do this on one- to three-day tours organized by tour operators such as China International Travel Service or Swire Travel, or by going by yourself.

The quickest, easiest hop is to **Shenzhen,** a Special Economic Zone (SEZ) which lies just across the border from Hong Kong's Special Administrative Region. Shenzhen is a modern, high-rise business city — not so very different from Hong Kong, in fact — but it does have a couple of **theme parks** which are very popular with Hong Kong visitors and make a suitable destination for a day-trip, especially if you've got kids in tow: Splendid China (China's major monuments and architectural wonders, all in miniature) and the adjacent China Folk Culture Villages (recreations of minority villages, folk dances and crafts).

From Hong Kong, it's an easy trip to Shenzhen by express bus (call **Citybus** (2735-7764, or **The Motor Transport Company of Guangdong & Hong Kong** (2601-1151 for details), train (regular services from Hung Hom to the border crossing at Lo Wu; call the **Kowloon–Canton Railway** on (2602-7799 for timetables) or hoverferry to Shekou, Shenzhen's port west of town (regular departures from China Hong Kong City on Canton Road or the Macau Ferry Pier). If you'd rather someone else made all the arrangements, there are regular day-trips to Shenzhen's theme parks (about HK$750 adult, HK$670) with tour operators such as Swire Travel (see page 76) .

Another quick trip to China can be made by hopping across the border from Macau to visit the **Zhuhai Special Economic Zone**. This area, too, is developing at lightening speed although it's still slower-paced than Shenzhen and in many ways a more attractive place to visit. It's got a pleasant stretch of beach and several up-market holiday resorts and golf courses (playgrounds for rich visitors from Macau, Hong Kong and even the mainland). The birthplace of Dr Sun Yatsen (China's most famous revolutionary and republican) is in Cuiheng village in **Zhongshan** county, just north of the Zhuhai SEZ border (minibuses go here directly from the Macau border crossing), and is the focus of organized day-trips to Zhuhai.

Going to Zhuhai by yourself couldn't be simpler: just walk across the border from Macau! Alternatively, you can take a jetcat directly from Hong Kong's China Hong Kong City ferry terminal. Alternatively, consider a tour such as the two-day package from CITS (costing around HK$2,000) which starts in Hong Kong and includes a quick visit to Guangzhou, Foshan (famous for its pottery and temples) Zhongshan and

Macau. You could even leave the tour in Macau and linger there a while before returning to Hong Kong.

If you want to push on further into Guangdong county and visit the capital city itself, **Guangzhou,** you can catch a minibus from Shenzhen railway station or a bus from Zhuhai. for further details. Express air-con buses operated by **The Motor Transport Company of Guangdong & Hong Kong Ltd** (2601-1151 also make regular trips to Guangzhou from Hung Hom pier, the Hong Kong Coliseum or Shatin Central. Again, there are plenty of tour options to Guangzhou, ranging from one to three days, if you prefer to do it this way.

Although regulations may change, at the time of writing you still need a **visa** for day-trips to Shenzhen and Zhuhai (and be sure to bring your passport). The tour operator will arrange this if you're joining a tour but if you're going on your own, visas are quite easy to obtain. In theory, on-the-spot visas are available at the Lowu checkpoint for

The electrified Kowloon–Canton Railway ABOVE links new towns with urban centers and provides regular services from Hung Hom Railway Station to the border corssing at Lo Wu.

day-trips to Shenzhen but travel agents usually recommend getting one beforehand, just to be safe. The fastest and cheapest way is to go to the **Visa Office, Ministry of Foreign Affairs of the People's Republic of China** (2827-1881, 5/F, 26 Harbour Road, Wanchai. Take along one photo with your passport — processing takes one working day and the fee is HK$100 for single entry, HK$250 if you need it the same day. (American passport holders have to pay HK$160 more). You can also go to China International Travel Service (CITS), China Travel Service (CTS) or any travel agent for your visa, but expect to pay a little more. If you don't want to join their tour they can just get you by train to Guangzhou, where you can plot and book your itinerary from there. After traveling as an "individual" on the trains through 20 cities myself, handling my own bookings as I went, I can promise you that, apart from the immense people-pressure along the routes, you can travel alone and unaided in China as well as in any other country.

Besides the train and bus there are several other ways of traveling around China. **By air,** the Chinese national airline, **CNAC (CAAC)** (2861-0322 fly directly to most cities in China and cover virtually the entire country from Guangzhou. Their ticketing office is located on ground floor of CNAC Building, 10 Queen's Road Central. In addition, **Hong Kong Dragon Airlines (Dragonair)** flies directly to 24 destinations, such as Beijing, Guilin, Kunming, Shanghai and Xian, along with stopover packages. They're located at 6/F, Wheelock House, 20-Pedder Street, Central, or call reservations (2590-1188, ticketing (2868-6777 and for information on tours (2590-1194.

Journeys **by sea** can be booked through CITS, CTS, a travel agent or from the China Ferry Terminal, China Hong Kong City, 33 Canton Road, Tsimshatsui, where hovercraft and steamers leave daily for Shenzhen, Shekou, Guangzhou and many other cities in southern China. Or you can take a leisurely two-day cruise to Shanghai aboard the cargo liners *Shanghai, Hai Xing* and *Hai Hua* which offer comfortable staterooms, cabins and berths. Amenities include lounge and disco, bar, coffee shop, swimming pool, barber and beauty salon and cinema.

The addresses of CITS, CTS and some major tour operators are as follows: **CITS (Head Office)** (2732-5888 FAX 2367-6785, 6/F, Tower II, South Seas Centre, 75 Mody Road, Tsimshatsui; Central branch (2810-4282 FAX 2868-1657, 1807 Wing On House, 71 Des Voeux Road Central; Connaught Road Central branch (2853-3888 FAX 2877-2033; Kowloon branch (2315-7188 FAX 2721-7757, 1/F Alpha House, 27-33 Nathan Road, Tsimshatsui.

Hong Kong

Concorde Travel (2524-5121 FAX 2845-0485, 7/F (China tours), 8-10 On Lan Street, Central.
Swire Travel (2579-6688 FAX 2590-0099, 18/F Devon House, 979 King's Road, North Point.
Thomas Cook Travel Services (2545-4399 FAX 2545-7477, is conveniently located at 18/F Vicwood Plaza, 199 Des Voeux Road Central.
The Travel Shop (2851-0108 FAX 2851-7441, 17/F Hollywood Tower, 49-51 Hollywood Road.
Wallem Travel (2876-8200 FAX 2876-1220, 46/F Hopewell Centre, 183 Queen's Road East.

Kowloon

Associated Tours (2722-1216 FAX 2369-5687, 811-814 Wing On Plaza, 62 Mody Road, Tsimshatsui East.
Morning Star Travel (2736-8368 FAX 2375-5100, G/F, 5C Star House, 3 Salisbury Road, Tsimshatsui.
Silkway Travel (2736-0338 FAX 2375-0888, 1/F Victoria Heights Building, 192 Nathan Road.

Festive Flings

Hong Kong's spiritual calendar is full of observances, rituals and festivals

A Chinese New Year welcome OPPOSITE at Ocean Park/Middle Kingdom complex.

that govern the Chinese reverence for life, death, good luck, good health, their forebears, their new-born and the various gods that preside over their interpretation of the universe and the firmament. On virtually any day, some ritual expression is being made somewhere in Hong Kong, whether it's the relatively simple slow-motion, highly controlled dance and calisthenics of traditional *tai chi* exercises (usually seen in parks such as Hong Kong Park in Central or along the harbor frontage of Victoria Park in Causeway Bay), or a full day's explosion of feasting, praying, joss-stick burning and gift-giving that marks a major spiritual event.

For exact dates and details of festivals and events, call and check with the **HKTA** (2807-6177 or you can visit their website: http://www.hkta.org. Another website devoted to local events and things to see and do can be found on http://www.webhk.com.

Major Festivals

Chinese New Year

The most important observance of the Chinese, their New Year, comes well after the Western event, marked by the first new moon after the sun enters the constellation Aquarius and falling somewhere between January 21 and February 19. It is a time of celebration and of reckoning, and it involves a full week of feasting, observances and rituals during which most business in Hong Kong grinds to a crawl or stops altogether.

As the magic hour approaches, families, merchants and factory chiefs clean out their homes and offices and settle all outstanding debts. Apartments and homes are decorated with peach blossom trees, kumquat trees, jonquils (Water Fairies) and chrysanthemums.

It is at this time that the Kitchen God is believed to visit households to report on the families' conduct during the year, so pictures of the god are

Chinese New Year festivities — protective door gods and banners ABOVE proclaiming prosperities and red inscribed envelopes or *laisee* packets OPPOSITE BOTTOM with "lucky money" enclosure are handed out to relatives, friends and colleagues and Lion dance OPPOSITE TOP adds color to the festive celebrations.

worshipped and smeared with sugar or honey so that the reports will be sweet and not sour.

For the visitor, the atmosphere of Chinese New Year can best be captured by meandering around the enormous flower markets, erected specially for the occasion, in the **Victoria Park** in Causeway Bay on Hong Kong Island and **Fa Hui** in Boundary Street, Kowloon. It is a carnival of jostling, jovial couples and families ambling around in search of flowering symbols fit to decorate their homes for the auspicious occasion. The most patient can be seen near dawn scurrying away almost hidden behind their bargains of enormous potted flowering trees which anxious sellers must clear at any price before the market closes.

On New Year's Day, the Cantonese dress in their finest new clothes — the children swaddled in brightly colored Chinese padded jackets — and go visiting close relatives, exchanging red envelopes, or *laisee* packets, containing "lucky money". On the second day it's time to visit and exchange laisee with close friends. It's also the time to reflect upon any late lunches, long sojourns around the water cooler or office misdemeanors during the previous year. This has traditionally been the day when employers could inform any superfluous or unsatisfactory staff that their services are no longer required — either presenting them with a symbolic piece of chicken or greeting them with the words "Thank you for your assistance in the past year", which in the Cantonese tradition is equivalent to an American vice-president gently telling one of his executives, "You've done a great job. What you need now is a rest".

Although mainly a time of rest, reflection and family obligation, Chinese New Year has its pageantry and color too. In China itself, the period features huge Spring Festival parades in most major cities and towns. In Hong Kong, especially in the more "Chinese" villages and centers like Stanley,

Aberdeen, Shaukeiwan and Cheung Chau Island, people celebrate with lion dances to the frenzied thunder and clash of tom-toms and cymbals and, here and there, the crackle and splutter of fireworks — banned for all except official occasions in Hong Kong since the Red Guard troubles of the late sixties.

There are many other festivals throughout the year that have less feasting and formality and far more fun and color.

Ching Ming Festival

In April, an even more astonishing ritual takes place. On this occasion, known as the Ching Ming Festival, thousands upon thousands of people flock to the graves of their forebears to pay homage by sweeping, cleaning and repairing the tombs and sites, making offerings of food and, in some cases, actually taking out the skulls and bones and polishing them. Bizarre as it sounds, it's actually a rather tender event — it's a family communion and transaction with the dead in which their wishes and needs are anticipated and their blessings sought for the future course of the living.

A similar ceremony to this is held in October during the Chung Yeung Festival.

Tin Hau Festival

The most revered of all Hong Kong's deities is Tin Hau, the Goddess of the Sea and protector of fisherfolk, and the annual Tin Hau Festival, which falls in April or May is by far the most colorful and dramatic of all the territory's spiritual events.

There are Tin Hau Temples all over Hong Kong, but the most popular mecca of the festival takes place at **Ta Miu (Green Temple)** in Joss House Bay. Huge armadas of colorfully decorated junks, launches, cargo lighters, ferries and even harbor tugs flood across the harbor waters to crowd the foreshores below the temple, tom-toms beating, gongs clanging and maybe firecrackers exploding over the decks and bows.

Lions and dragons prance, leap and twist across gangplanks to the shore, and behind them come spectacular, lavishly decorated paper altars loaded with offerings of food, wine, tea, "lucky" money and even toys. And then come the worshippers themselves, carrying giant wrist-thick joss sticks and more offerings of fruit, pastries and even whole roasted piglets. One after another, the cavalcades stream ashore and up through the temple doorways, cramming

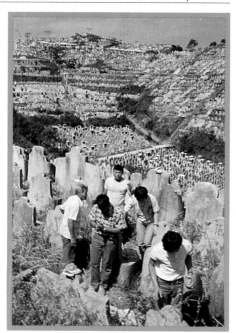

into the prayer halls and chambers in a murky bedlam of billowing joss smoke, in the thick mists of which hundreds of figures kneel, kowtow and pray to the looming, impassive images, others haul the garish paper altars up the walls to hang on display in the temple rafters, others shake canisters of bamboo tapers, inscribed with numbers, taking the sticks that slide out of the tight clusters to nearby soothsayers to have their fortunes read for the coming year. And over it all, the drums boom and the gongs clash and whine, and engines grumble and roar as wave after wave of fishing junks and harbor craft pull into the crowded bay.

OPPOSITE: Tin Hau Festival — worshippers offer food, joss and prayers at Wong Tai Sin Temple. The major event takes place at Ta Miu where the worshippers pray to the Goddess of the Sea. Filial piety ABOVE at graveyards at Wo Hop Shek Cemetery. Ching Ming and Chung Yeung Festivals are the occasions to pay respect to one's ancestors in Hong Kong.

The Bun Festival

There's one other major festival in Hong Kong that began as an observance but has now become more of an extravagant seven-day Mardi Gras. The Bun Festival on the island of **Cheung Chau,** held in April or May on dates that are not announced until about three weeks beforehand, was originally held to placate the spirits, so the story goes, of people murdered by a ruthless pirate who used the island as a base before the colonial British appeared on the scene.

Now, it's a huge fiesta that features religious ceremonies, Chinese opera performances and various other cultural displays and, on the third day, a tumultuous parade of lions and dragons, traditional drum, pipe and gong bands, ornately decorated floats with tableaux depicting moral themes — and, riding majestically above the whole procession, children dressed in theatrical and historical costumes and suspended on the tips of poles with hidden harnesses and metal rods so that they appear to

be levitating amidst the banners and flags.

Throughout the week-long celebration, mammoth images of three deities — the Gods of the Earth, Good Luck and Hell — preside over the festivities. But all the feasting and fun is really focused on the central symbol of the festival, three big bamboo towers literally covered with bread buns. These small round loaves are there as offerings to the dead, but at the climax of the festival they are taken down and distributed to the revelers — the idea being to grab as many as possible for good luck in the coming year. Until a few years ago, it was the tradition at each Bun Festival to make a massed scramble up the towers for the buns, but the free-for-all was abandoned when it got out of hand and one of the towers collapsed, injuring several revelers..

The Birthday of Lord Buddha

This inherent exuberance and excitement of the Cantonese somehow complements, rather than shatters, the more placid, reflective character of Buddhism in Hong Kong. Its major Buddhist monastery and temple, **Po Lin (Precious Lotus)** on Lantau Island, offers retreat, meditation and escape from the urban clamor for most of the year, but during the most important observance, the Birthday of Lord Buddha, held in May, peace and tranquillity give way to pandemonium as thousands of worshipers flock across to the island to fill the sanctified air once again with clouds of joss, the blood-stirring thunder of drums and the massed murmur and chorus of prayer. Similar spiritual explosions take place at the Buddhist **Castle Peak Monastery, Miu Fat Monastery** and the celebrated **Ten Thousand Buddhas Monastery** in the New Territories, while at the **Tam Kung Temple** in Shaukeiwan, Taoism and Buddhism put on one of their spiritual "double features" in which homage is paid to

Beautifully dressed doll-like young girl LEFT and costumed child OPPOSITE "floats" on a pole over crowd secured by hidden braces, at Cheung Chau Bun Festival.

YOUR CHOICE

Tam Kung, the latter-day second patron saint of Hong Kong boat people, and honor is given to the other Great Teaching with a spectacular Washing the Buddha ceremony at the harbor foreshores — with more drums and gongs, more extravagant altars and offerings, and dancing, writhing lions and dragons.

The Dragon Boat Festival

Usually held in June, the Dragon Boat Festival is an ancient Chinese commemorative event that Hong Kong has turned into a combined sporting extravaganza and beer fest with the added underlying attraction of rivalry between Chinese and *gweilo* (Cantonese for "foreign devil" and the name by which

Caucasians are often known) teams. The event has traditionally paid homage to the memory of an imperial adviser, Chu Yuan, of the Warring States Period (403–221 BC), who committed suicide by throwing himself into the Mi-Lo River in what is now Hunan Province in a desperate act of protest against official intrigue and corruption.

It is said that Chu was so popular and respected that the villagers, hearing of his death, rushed in their boats to the spot where he'd disappeared and beat the water with paddles, banged drums and gongs and threw rice to keep the fish away from his body. It's been a custom since to make offerings of colored packets of rice on the day of the festival,

If there's an essential spirit to the competition it's making as much noise as possible. While hundreds of spectators on the surrounding vessels beat gongs to frighten evil spirits away, hundreds of others yell and scream encouragement from the shores as the boats leap and lurch through great explosions and cascades of water thrown up by each massed strike of the paddles, the tom-toms pounding out a kind of primitive blood-curdling tattoo above all the hullabaloo and excitement. Some heats end with boats foundering and sinking with their crews, amid more waves of hysteria.

The races are held at a variety of locations in the New Territories, Kowloon and on Hong Kong Island.

The Hong Kong Tourist Association will give advice on the current year's program and venues, and these are also published in the daily and tourist newspapers. A week or so later, it's all done again, with crews from all parts of southeast Asia and even the West taking part in the strictly competitive International Dragon Boat Races, held on the Tsimshatsui East waterfront.

The Festival of Hungry Ghosts
There are ritual occasions in Hong Kong when the full ceremony of ancestor-worship can be seen. The Festival of Hungry Ghosts, for instance, held on the 15th day of the seventh moon (August), is the day on which vast symbolic fortunes in gifts and provisions are consigned by ritual fire to the awaiting dead. Hungry ghosts mean underworld spirits who are financially down on their luck, whose homes have leaking roofs, whose TV set has blown a fuse, who need a car, bicycle or maybe even a horse and carriage to get around, and hungry or discontented spirits can mean trouble for the living. So, on this festive day all over Hong Kong, the urban pavements, temple forecourts, ancestral halls and grave sites blaze with paper offerings.

and the symbolic beating of the waters survives in the very nature of the dragon boat races.

Today's dragon boats are anything up to 40 m (131 ft) long, have huge ornately carved and decorated dragon's heads on their prows and look very much like a hybrid of an ancient Chinese war canoe and a modern racing shell. They're manned by as many as 80 oarsmen who lash at the water with their paddles to the heavy rhythmic beat of big drums carried in the middle of the vessels. There are many heats, culminating in a grand championship of the three fastest boats, and the races are held over courses that are packed with pleasure junks, launches, ferries and other small craft.

Dragon Boats prepare for international heats near Tsimshatsui East Promenade.

Causeway Bay — the entire grounds festooned with thousands of lighted lanterns ranging from the traditional pot-bellied candle-lit paper designs to ornate laser-operated versions that revolve and play music. But, from my own experience, the location that offers the most romantic combination of lanterns and moon worship is **Stanley Beach.** There, in the full flat glow of the rising moon, the sands are packed with picnickers and moon-gazers; and there are not only lanterns of all shapes and designs to behold — everything from butterflies and fish to tanks and warships — but the children carve castles and ornate patterns in the sands and place hundreds of small candles in them, creating astonishingly sophisticated fairylands of flickering pools and caverns of light.

Moon Festival

In contrast, there are other traditional events and observances in Hong Kong that are noted more for their reverence and beauty than their decibel level. And none is more beautiful than the Moon Festival, held in mid-autumn on the 15th day of the eighth moon. Also known as the Mid-Autumn (Chung Chiu) Festival, it combines a Chinese version of the Western harvest celebration with a lantern festival and a fourteenth century tradition of preparing and eating moon cakes, a sweet confection filled with sesame seeds, duck eggs and ground lotus seeds. But it is also a moment of simple nature worship in which thousands of people make their way to beaches and the peaks of Hong Kong's many hills to picnic through the night and gaze upon the full moon.

For the Lantern Festival, there's no better venue than **Victoria Park** near

The Galloping Gourmets

Eating out in Hong Kong is not just a culinary experience, it's a taste of high adventure. With over 19,000 restaurants offering different cuisines, noodle shops, snack and fast-food outlets throughout the territory (more for the population than probably anywhere else in the world), simple choice is the big biggest challenge — the culinary landscape crowded with thousands of neon signs, all beckoning the taste buds and promising ecstasy.

The choice is vast and complicated enough even for the Hong Kong resident with all the time in the world for leisurely exploration. For the average visitor, with not more than three or four days in which to find the best that there is on offer, the variety is so overwhelming that it can paralyze the decision-making processes, turning a once-in-a-lifetime culinary challenge into a retreat into the safe sanctuary of hotel restaurants. With a little courage and a reliable route-map, what lies before you is not so much a bewildering neon-lit maze but one of the world's biggest and most celebrated food bazaars.

Moon Festival: ABOVE Ornate lanterns await buyers in Happy Valley store. OPPOSITE: String duo and piano complement the gourmet food and lavish atmosphere.

Running right through the peaks, pinnacles and myriad path ways of the gastronomic jungle is one paramount and immediately recognizable route — the broad sweep of Chinese cuisine. Every other cuisine and national taste, and there are dozens of them in Hong Kong ranging from French, German, Swiss and Italian to Indian, Malaysian, Indonesian, Japanese, Korean, Thai, Mexican and many more, are wayside stopovers, chosen for their particular excellence and the reputation of their restaurants but purely complementary to Chinese fare.

It is Chinese food that reigns above all others in this teeming high-tech "Chinatown". It packs the restaurants, *dim sum* dining halls and food stalls each lunch time and it awaits the immense, scurrying flood of growling bellies that pours out of the airconditioned discipline of the office blocks each evening, into the muggy heat and exhaust and clamor of the packed streets, into the dying fires of the sun and the soaring neon-decorated shadows and silhouettes of the urban jungle, where most of the glowing trail-markers point to one thing: food.

With such a enormous selection of restaurants in Hong Kong, the only reliable guide or route-map is one that breaks it down into the four main tourist districts — Central and Wanchai–Causeway Bay on the island, and the central and eastern sections of Tsimshatsui in Kowloon. Of course, there are other top-class restaurants and seafood spots further afield, in Aberdeen and Stanley, in the New Territories and on the islands of Lamma and Cheung Chau, and the best of these are mentioned later in this section of the guide.

In all the restaurants highlighted in this book, the standard of cuisine is high. Most of them are also recommended by the Hong Kong Tourist Association, which has a department staffed by some 30 people keeping a constant check on restaurants and nightclubs and promoting only those that show

a consistent determination to please. Most places have a menu printed in English, and restaurants recommended in this guide certainly do unless otherwise stated. Pick up a copy of the HKTA's *Official Dining and Entertainment Guide* for a complete listing of their recommended restaurants, bars and nightclubs.

CENTRAL DISTRICT

This, the crowded business and banking center of Hong Kong, spins like a human treadmill during the day and then winds down into a quiet, almost serene backwater with a few ripples of activity at night — the towering office blocks lighted up but empty and the nightlife scattered around the neighborhood. But nightlife there certainly is. The main action is in a wedge of neon signs and strolling crowds bounded by **Lan Kwai Fong** and **Wellington** and **D'Aguilar Streets.** Lan Kwai Fong itself is a cluster of streets that has become a distinct neighborhood of bistro-style eating places, bars and discos, particularly popular with the *gweilo* community, especially the trendy young from The Peak, the Mid-Levels and middle-class apartment and tract housing developments like Discovery Bay on Lantau Island.

Grabbing some of Lan Kwai Fong's limelight recently is the up-and-coming area around Staunton and Elgin streets, easily accessible by the Mid-Levels escalator. Known as SoHo ("South of Hollywood Road") this is one of the most exciting areas in Hong Kong for eclectic culinary adventures, with cuisines on offer that range from French to Nepalese, Scandinavian to Spanish.

Chinese Cuisine
CANTONESE
The imperial courts of the Chinese Cuisine in this district are the **Yung Kee Restaurant** (2522-1624, a multi-story gaudily decorated Cantonese eating place in Wellington Street, and the famous **Luk Yu Tea House** (2523-5464, in nearby Stanley Street, which is such a popular *dim sum* establishment and restaurant that you virtually need to camp outside overnight to get a table. The Yung Kee is noted for its Cantonese roast duck and pork and its wide selection of Cantonese and Shanghainese specialties, while the Luk Yu is worth a visit not only for its food but also its fairly faithful re-creation of the bustling tea-house atmosphere of bygone years.

For an absolutely superb *dim sum* and a memorable experience of the pandemonium of tea-house life, you can go no better than the **Diamond Restaurant** (2544-4708, at 267 Des Voeux Road Central — but again, you need to be quick off the mark and determined to beat the hordes of office workers that pour into it at lunch-time. You'll also have to make an advance booking or move pretty swiftly on your feet to get a table at the **City Hall Chinese Restaurant** (2521-1303, in the City Hall on the waterfront side of Connaught Road near the Star Ferry, which combines the best traditions of the tea-house with splendid harbor views.

For some other good-value eating places for both lunchtime *dim sum* and

evening meals there's the award-winning **Tai Woo Seafood Restaurant** (2524-5618, 15-19 Wellington Street, for seafood hotpots, steamed garoupa, garlic prawns, sautéed scallops, beef in taro's nest and mango pudding. Tai Woo has other branches on Hong Kong Island as well as a number of outlets in Kowloon and the New Territories. Or you can try the **Jade Garden** restaurants: Basement, Jardine House (2524-5098, 1 Connaught Place and 1/F Swire House (2526-3031, 11 Chater Road — where specialties include double-boiled duck with parsley and pan-fried stuffed beancurd.

Well worth a visit is **Tsui Hang Village** (2524-2012, New World Tower, 16-18 Queen's Road Central. The restaurant is purportedly a place of homage to the home village of Dr. Sun Yatsen, founder of the Republic of China, and is well known for both classic and modern Cantonese dishes such as succulent pigeon and chicken, tasty thick soups and fried milk fritters.

One of a trio of charmingly cosy cafés which evoke the feel of a traditional *dai pai dong* street-side restaurant is the **Dai Pai Dong** (2851-6389 at 128 Queen's Road Central. Like its other branches in Causeway Bay, it is decorated with nostalgic old-style posters and bric-a-brac. You can get light snacks, noodle dishes, omelettes and sweet soups here but the real attraction is the various coffees, teas and *yuan yang* (a unique blend of both) prepared and served in a manner that has all but disappeared from the Hong Kong dining scene.

At the hotels you can expect to pay more. Highly recommended are the **Island Restaurant** (2848-7305 at the Furama Hotel, and the elegant **Man Wah** (2522-0111 at the Mandarin Oriental, with its spectacular views of the harbor. In Pacific Place, restaurants noted for the quality of their cuisine are the **Golden Leaf** (2521-3838 at the Conrad International Hotel; **Man Ho** (2810-8366, J.W. Marriott Hotel; and

---

OPPOSITE: A *dai pai dong* (street-side restaurant).

the **Summer Palace** (2820-8552 at Island Shangri-La.

CHIU CHOW

This cuisine comes from the coastal region around the Swatow district of eastern Guangdong and is similar to Cantonese food, but a little heavier and spicier. It features its own variations of duck, goose and pigeon dishes, along with oysters fried in egg batter and clams in a biting chili and black bean sauce. Chiu Chow restaurants are also noted for their shark's fin and bird's nest soups — the disgorged linings of sea swallow nests reputed to do wonders for rejuvenation — and a particularly sturdy tea called Iron Maiden, drunk from tiny thimble-sized cups before and after the meal. The best place to go is the **Chiu Chow Garden Restaurant** (2525-8246, Basement, Jardine House, 1 Connaught

ABOVE: The skill required to make Chinese noodles is featured in a fascinating demonstration presented during the evening at the Peking Garden Restaurant. OPPOSITE: Many Chinese restaurants in Hong Kong offer not only food but fun too — foursome ponders mahjong game.

Place, or to their branch near Admiralty MTR (2845-1323, G/F Lippo Centre, Queensway.

HUNAN

Another restaurant which will put fire in your belly with lots of chilies and garlic is **Hunan Garden** (2868-2880, 3/F The Forum, Exchange Square, where many dishes are served in the traditional way, in bamboo stems or earthen pots. Levels of hotness are clearly, mercifully, and thankfully indicated on the menu.

SICHUAN

The **Sichuan Garden** (2521-4433, 3/F Gloucester Tower (in the Landmark shopping complex) and at Shop 4, The Mall, Pacific Place, specializes in smoked duck with camphor, ducks' tongues, beancurd with minced beef in a pungent sauce and scallops with hot garlic sauce.

SHANGHAINESE & PEKING

The **Shanghai Garden Restaurant** (2524-8181, Hutchison House, at 10 Harcourt Road, is a popular venue for dishes such as "drunken" chicken, fried Shanghai noodles and sweet black sesame dumplings. A good place to try for Peking food — Peking duck, beggar's chicken clay-breaking ceremonies and nightly noodle-making shows — is **Peking Garden** (2526-6456, Basement, Alexandra House, 6 Ice House Street, or it's branches at the Excelsior Hotel in Causeway Bay, Cityplaza in Taikoo Shing and in the Mall at Pacific Place.

International Fare

INDIAN & SRI LANKAN

An establishment that has earned a reputation for good food and friendliness over the years is the **Ashoka** (2524-9623 at 57 Wyndham Street. You won't be disappointed. Also, **Tandoor** (2845-2299, (2524-0107, 1/F Carfield Commercial Building, 75-77-Wyndham Street, and **Koh-I-Noor** (2877-9706, 34 D'Aguilar Street, Lan Kwai Fong, where Halal food is always available.

For Sri Lankan, the homey **Club Sri Lanka** (2526-6559, Basement, 17 Hollywood Road, offers very reasonably priced buffet dining.

JAPANESE

Japanese food is very popular in Hong Kong and, as with Western cuisine, the prices vary radically. In Lan Kwai Fong, the **Yorohachi** (2524-1251, 5-6 Lan Kwai Fong, and the **Hanagushi** (2521-0868, 7–22 Lan Kwai Fong, offer set dinner courses, tempura and beef sukiyaki, soya noodles and other traditional fare at reasonable prices. If you don't mind paying more, there's **The Benkay** (2521-3344,First Basement, Gloucester Tower (in The Landmark), and the **Nadaman** (2820-8570, 7/F Island Shangri-La Hotel, Pacific Place.

THAI

For such favorites as spicy *tom yum* soups and red and green curries, king prawns and Thai beer, the very popular **Supatra's Thai Gourmet** (2522-5073, 50 D'Aguilar Street, Lan Kwai Fong, and the trendy **Phukets Seafood Grill** (2868-9672 at 30 Robinson Road in the Mid-Levels above Lan Kwai Fong — the new escalator will take you nearly there — are two of many excellent Thai restaurants to open in Hong Kong in recent years.

VEGETARIAN

A casual spot for a vegetarian lunch buffet is the **Fringe Club**; ring ahead at (2521-7251 for reservation. Another no-frills place is **Vegi-Table** (2877-0901 at G/F, 1 Tun Wo Lane (next to Petticoat Lane). Its extensive menu includes both Chinese and Western fare, such as congee, Hawaiian beancurd, pumpkin and chickpeas and lots of garden-fresh vegetables, all at bargain prices (and without that bane of Cantonese cooking, MSG — monosodium glutamate). For vegetarian sandwiches, herbal teas and lunch buffet, try **The Original Health Foundation** (2815-0398, 27/F Wing Shan Tower, 173 Des Voeux Road. The most up-market vegetarian place around is **Joyce Café** (2810-1335, at 9 Queen's

Road Central, where all the beautiful people come to eat healthy goodies such as sautéed wild mushrooms, Mexican green rice and carrot juice combos. There are some deliciously sinful desserts, too, such as rose petal strawberry profiteroles.

VIETNAMESE

Since the advent of the "boat people" and their desperate refugee voyages across the South China Sea, Vietnamese cuisine has taken root and flourished in Hong Kong. In ingredients, preparation and style it's probably closest to the Cantonese school of cooking, with the addition of crisp lettuce and fresh mint and an assortment of condiments based on fiery red and green peppers. It features a particularly savory spring roll, eaten in jackets of lettuce and mint, a delicious barbecued prawn with sugar cane, an interesting variety of beef dishes and a range of fragrant meat and noodle-based soups. In Central, you can find superb Vietnamese cuisine, in a setting oozing with French colonial nostalgia, at the very up-market **Indochine** (2869-7399, 2/F California Tower, 30-32 Lan Kwai Fong.

WESTERN

Central District offers some of the best Western restaurants around, probably because it is also the territory's business and banking citadel. The menus range from hamburgers and fried chicken to French and Italian haute cuisine, and the decor from trendy high-tech to homespun. Fast-food and take-away restaurants such as **Hardie's, Kentucky Fried Chicken, Wendy's, McDonald's, Domino's, Marco Polo Pizza, Pizza Hut, Spaghetti House** and **Oliver's Super Sandwiches** abound not only in Central but throughout Hong Kong.

From the beginning of the day, there are several reputable breakfast spots in Central, headed by **The Landmark's** mezzanine **La Terrazza** (2526-4200, and the ground-floor **Fountainside Restaurant** (2526-4018. Both feature fairly hearty American and Continental breakfasts and good coffee. For value,

Jim's Eurodiner would be hard to beat: fruit, two eggs, and a choice of sausage, ham or bacon will cost you as little as US$5. You'll find **Jim's** (2868-6886 in the Basement, Tak House, 5-11 Stanley Street. Or you can try the **DeliFrance** fast-food restaurants in Queensway Plaza, 20-22 Queen's Road Central, in World-Wide Plaza on the corner of Des Voeux Road Central and Pedder Street, and several other well-marked locations. More genuinely French (and slightly more expensive) is **Fauchon** (2537-2938 in The Forum, Exchange Square 3, which has snacks, pastries and punchy real coffee. For a good hearty English breakfast, try the **Bull & Bear** (2525-7436, G/F Hutchison House.

Going up-market, head for the **Mandarin Oriental's Coffee Shop** (2522-0111, or **Brown's** (2523-7003, in the bowels of Exchange Square, where young stockbrokers tend to gather. In Central's mad lunch-time scramble, it's not so much where to eat but where you can grab a table.

In the Lan Kwai Fong neighborhood, the **California** (2521-1345, G/F California Tower, 24-26 Lan Kwai Fong, serves a satisfying array of hamburgers, open

sandwiches and chili dishes, but the food is pricey. At night, the chrome and sunset and the in-house video monitors wink and flash on supper club diners, and at weekends the dance floor is thrown open to writhing disco dancers and blazing lasers. Among some of the other Lan Kwai Fong and nearby establishments that offer good value for lunch and dinner, or to just simply sit back with a drink and watch the Lan Kwai Fong scene, take your pick from the following:

The three popular adjacent venues for dining and nightlife are **Club 1997**, **Post 97** and **La Dolce Vita 97** (2810-9333, 8-11 Lan Kwai Fong. Open 24-hours over the weekend, Club 1997 is a disco and bar, Post 97 a café-restaurant and La Dolce Vita a sleek, open-to-the-street Italian restaurant.

For a modern-day setting and French cuisine **Papillon** (2526-5965, 1/F, 8-13 Wo On Lane, and the open-plan **Café des Artistes** (2526-3880, UG/F California Tower, 30-32 D'Aguilar Street. For those

The Lan Kwai Fong neighborhood above Central District features French bistros and American hamburger restaurants.

hankering after sauerkraut and draft pils, the **Schnurrbart** (2523-4700, at Winners Building, D'Aguilar Street, offers a relaxed and informal bar-restaurant setting, with a menu that's more on the snack side than a full meal.

For good Italian food, try the **Ristorante Il Mercato** (2868-3068, Basement, 34-36 D'Aguilar Street, and **Va Bene stile veneziano** (2845-5577, 58-62 D'Aguilar Street. Around the corner at 24-30 Ice House Street, **La Taverna** (2523-8624, is packed with the usual Chianti bottles and features a good menu with a particularly well-prepared range of *antipasta*. In Pacific Place, **Grappa's Ristorante** (2868-0086, at Shop 132, Level 1, is popular with business and media trendies.

If you're lusting for backhome American food, **Trios** (2877-9773, 9B Wo On Lane, specializes in Maine lobster and US steaks, and **Al's Diner** (2869-1869, 27-39 D'Aguilar Street, US prime sirloin, root beer floats and golden oldies juke-box music. For a cheap hamburger, fries and apple pie, there's a small **McDonald's** across the road. Down on Chater Road, at N° 11, there's the Hong Kong Island branch of the popular **Hard Rock Café** (2377-8168 (in Kowloon it's at 100 Canton Road), where you can get great burgers and shakes and non-stop music. In Pacific Place, the very American **Dan Ryan's Chicago Grill** (2845-4600, is the place for extra large portions of dishes such as Maryland crab, barbecued ribs, charcoal-grilled Swordfish and salads. The **La Café** (2526-6863, G/F Lippo Centre (opposite Pacific Place), has American "nouvelle cuisine", and in the Sports Bar you can watch American and international football, baseball and basketball on a giant one-meter (40-inch) screen.

A short walk from Lan Kwai Fong you'll find the cozy **Mozart Stub'n** (2522-1763 at 8 Glenealy (at the top of steps), which has great Wiener schnitzel, veal goulash, bread dumplings and Austrian soufflés. At the bottom of Glenealy, in the old colonial building — you can't possibly miss it— **M at the**

Fringe (2877-4000, 1/F South Block, 2 Lower Albert Road, has an impressive Mediterranean menu. Along the top end of Wyndham Street, at N° 31, **La Bodega** (2877-5472 offers paella and a tasty selection of *tapas*. Nearby, **Le Tire Bouchon** (2523-5459, 9 Old Bailey Street, is noted for its excellent French provincial cooking, wines and cheese board at reasonable prices. For bistro-style dining and a very fine selection of wines, try **Pomeroy's Wine Bar and Brasserie** (2810-1162, G/F On Hing Building, On Hing Terrace (off Wyndham Street), and at **Pacific Place** (2523-4772, Shop 349, Level 3.

In Prince's Building, next to Statue Square, you'll find Creole and Cajun fare at **Prince's Tavern** (2523-9352, on the mezzanine floor and excellent, but not cheap, seafood at **Bentley's Seafood Restaurant and Oyster Bar** (2868-0881, in the basement.

But for those who can't really enjoy themselves without a bit of "Hurry on now, gents" nostalgia you can try two traditional British pub-style haunts: **Mad Dogs Central**, Century Square, 1-13 D'Aguilar Street, with its ale, Trivial Pursuit nights, Scottish football, live music and no-nonsense culinary fare, and the **Bull & Bear** (2525-7436, at G/F Hutchison House, 10 Harcourt Road.

In the up-and-coming SoHo (South of Hollywood Road) area — an old-fashioned residential neighborhood quickly becoming a funky alternative to Lan Kwai Fong — you'll find an extraordinary range of restaurants and cuisines. The first of the restaurants to open here in 1994, **Casa Lisboa** (2869-9631, 21 Elgin Street, is still one of the best, a romantic little haunt serving huge portions of Portuguese dishes. Other European ventures are **Club Casa Nova** (2869-1218, 47B Elgin Street, for mellow Mediterranean atmosphere, Italian fare and late-night dancing; **Le Fauchon** (2526-2136 at 6 Staunton Street, for minimalist decor and haute cuisine; and three less-expensive places — **La Piazzetta** (2522-9505, 5 Tsun Wing Lane (just below Staunton Street); **Rico's** (2840-0937, at 44 Robinson Road, a bustling Spanish restaurant; and **O'Wien** (2525-8810, at 5 Staunton Street, for freshly-prepared Austrian, Greek and Finnish (yes, even Finnish fare has come to Hong Kong!) food. Also recommended in this area is a great Nepalese restaurant, **Nepal** (2869-6212, 14 Staunton Street; and **Desert Sky** (2810-7318, 36 Elgin Street, for unusual Middle Eastern dishes.

Back down in Central, there are several distinguished restaurants that have built abiding reputations from their lunch and supper menus. On the lower end of Wyndham Street in the basement of the South China Building, the family-owned **Jimmy's Kitchen** (2526-5293, has been operating for more than 60 years and is one of the most popular and most reputable of all Hong Kong restaurants. Its menu is varied — Western, Cantonese and Indian — and unless you're on a tight budget, affordable. At the Mandarin Oriental Hotel, **The Pierrot** offers superb French cuisine, and for perhaps the most sumptuous and meticulously prepared Western food in Hong Kong, the **Mandarin Grill** is in a class of its own. For reservations for both restaurants (2522-0111. The other hotels, Ritz-Carlton, Furama, Conrad, Island Shangri-La and Marriott also have fine restaurants that certainly will not prove disappointing.

At night, the most romantic spot to my mind, offering a bird's-eye view of Central and across the harbor to Kowloon, is **La Ronda** (2525-5111 in the revolving restaurant of the Furama Hotel.

Other than the major restaurants there are various tourist attractions and services that present movable feasts on night- time harbor cruises (see TAKING A TOUR page 110 for details) or the adventure of eating out alfresco style from the thousands of open-air food stalls that are found throughout Hong Kong.

The **Pearl of Hong Kong** (2561-5033, a converted vehicular ferry, and the **Pearl of the Orient** (2516-6022 have evening harbor cruises along with Chinese and Western cuisine, dancing and a cabaret.

WANCHAI AND CAUSEWAY BAY

While Central District breathes a kind of weary sigh of relief in the evening, a financial powerhouse at rest, Wanchai and Causeway Bay come into their own as teeming neon-lit centers of food, shopping and entertainment. In Wanchai, the blazing, beckoning signs of its old Suzy Wong scene, the "girlie" bars and big hostess clubs, now seem slightly tacky and against the district's rising reputation as one of Hong Kong's best dining out domains. In Causeway Bay, the lure of bargain clothing boutiques, even better bargains on the hawker stalls that line the sidewalks, and the huge Japanese department stores — Daimaru, Matsuzakaya and Sogo — that have chosen the district as their own, have turned the area into a restaurant and nightlife center so packed with people that it's often difficult to find space to stroll on some streets.

Causeway Bay, its main attractions centered on Times Square with its impressive food floor, the Excelsior Hotel and the Japanese emporiums, is to my mind a glimpse of the East Asian urban giants of the future. If you can recall the futuristic Harrison Ford movie, *Bladerunner,* and add the stunning visual effect of virtual wall-to-wall neon, you

ABOVE: Sampans, divers and a floating kitchen vie for space in the Causeway Bay Typhoon Shelter.

YOUR CHOICE

have the color, drama and excitement of Causeway Bay.

Chinese Cuisine

The two most outstanding restaurants are undoubtedly the **Tao Yuan** (2827-8080 and **Forum** (2892-0248 both in the Wanchai area. The Tao Yuan, which you'll find in the Great Eagle Centre 3/F in Wanchai North, near the Hong Kong Exhibition and Convention Centre, is an up-market new-style Cantonese establishment with harbor views and a pleasant peach decor, and a menu which features the novel "nouvelle cuisine", drunk prawns. Already well noted for its seafood dishes, it also offers succulent baby lobster, stuffed scallops, baked crab, baked oysters in port wine and satay sauce, sautéed sea whelks, and a range of more exotic recipes that include braised civet cat fillet, sautéed tender tortoise, snake soup and stuffed bamboo fungus with vegetables.

As for the **Forum** (2891-2516, at 485 Lockhart Road, one dish reigns above all the others — braised abalone. The rubbery ear-shaped mollusk is braised for a full 15 hours in a stock of ham, chicken and beef, and the result (and the price) is truly sensational.

Elsewhere, for the most popular Cantonese restaurants take your pick, in Wanchai: **Canton Room** (2866-2166, in the Luk Kwok Hotel, 72 Gloucester Road; **East Ocean Seafood Restaurant** (2827-8887, 3/F Harbour Centre, 25 Harbour Road; and the **Lei Garden Restaurant** (2892-0333, at 1/F CNT Tower, Hennessy Road.

For panoramic views of Victoria Harbour (but be prepared to pay for it), you can try **One Harbour Road** (2588-1234, in the Grand Hyatt Hotel, and for even more spectacular views at more reasonable prices, the **Round Dragon Chinese Restaurant** (2861-1668, 60/F Hopewell Centre, 183 Queen's Road East.

For those not counting every penny or cent, **Fook Lam Moon** (2866-0663, 35-45 Johnston Road, serves such delicacies as shark's fin and bird's nest soups, bird's nest in bamboo pith and abalone. Also, you might take a look at **Sun Tung Lok Shark's Fin Restaurant** (2882-2899, G/F Sunning Plaza, 1-5 Sunning Road, Causeway Bay, where waiters will explain the shark's fin grading and price differences before you order.

Elsewhere in Causeway Bay: the **Tin Tin Seafood Harbour** restaurant at 4/F Elizabeth House, 250 Gloucester Road, offers such dishes as sautéed oysters with port wine, prawns fried with chili and pungent preserved beancurd sauce and Thai-style curry-fried crab. The value-for-money **Farm House Restaurant** (2881-1881, 1/F AIA Plaza, 18 Hysan Avenue, has healthy dishes free of MSG (monosodium glutamate), such as scallops and shrimp hotpot and braised pigeon with garlic. For other home-style dishes, health-enhancing casseroles and "male" and "female" soups, try the renowned **Ah Yee Leng Tong,** which has eight outlets in Kowloon, three in the New Territories and three in Wanchai and Causeway Bay at 13 Fleming Road (2573-0402; 503-505 Lockhart Road (2834-3480; and Basement, Hang Lung Centre, 2-20 Paterson Street (2576-8385.

Lastly, to experience something completely different, how about some snake soup? The **King of Snake 2** (2831-0163, at 24 Percival Street (it has another branch on Russell Street) is the place to come to sample this popular winter soup, which isn't nearly as disgusting as you may think but rich, tasty and warming. The restaurant serves other dishes, too, in case you chicken out.

CHIU CHOW/SHANGHAI

In Causeway Bay, check out the following for good Chiu Chow cuisine: the **Chiuchow Garden Restaurant** (2577-3391, Hennessy Centre, 500 Hennessy Road, the **Carriana** (2511-1282, 151 Gloucester Road, the **Harbour City Chiu Chow Restaurant** (2833-6678, 2/F Elizabeth House,

---

OPPOSITE TOP: Typical *dim sum* restaurant in Central District. BOTTOM: Chinese food is a religion worshipped in the vast majority of some 19,000 restaurants and other food outlets in Hong Kong.

254 Gloucester Road, and the **Regal Chiuchow Restaurant** (2837-1787, 2/F Paliburg Plaza, 68 Yee Wo Street. For Shanghainese, the **Wu Kong Shanghai Restaurant** (2506-1018, 1201 Food Forum, Times Square, 1 Matheson Street and the deluxe **Lao Ching Hing Restaurant** (2598-6080, Century Hong Kong Hotel, 238 Jaffe Road, Wanchai.

PEKING

The most popular venue is the **Hong Kong Chung Chuk Lau** (2577-4914, 30 Leighton Road, Causeway Bay, which specializes in Mongolian hotpots, very popular do-it-yourself dishes during the winter months. For more northern Chinese fare in Causeway Bay, **Imperial Kitchen** (2577-2018, 3/F Caroline Centre, 28 Yun Ping Road, and **King Heung Restaurant** (2577-1035, G/F Riviera Mansion, 59-65 Paterson Street.

SICHUAN

The top choices are located in Causeway Bay and include the family-run **Red Pepper** (2577-3811, 7 Lan Fong Road, for strange taste spiced shredded chicken and sizzling prawns. At **Sze Chuen Lau** (2891-9027, 466 Lockhart Road, house favorites include spiced perfumed chicken, kumquat beef and chili and camphor-flavored tea-smoked duck.

VEGETARIAN

For some traditional Buddhist culinary artistry in which mushroom and beancurd recipes have the shape, texture and even the taste of chicken, pork or beef, try the **Vegi Food Kitchen** (2890-6603, 8 Cleveland Street, and **Kung Tak Lam** (2890-3127, 31 Yee Wo Street, which specializes in chili-flavored Shanghainese dishes. Both are located in Causeway Bay.

International Fare

JAPANESE

Because of the big multi-story Japanese department stores in Causeway Bay, the area abounds with Japanese restaurants. At the top of the range you'll find the **Kanetanaka** (2833-6018, 22/F East Point Centre, 545-563 Hennessy Road, **Sui Sha**

Ya (2591-1511, 1/F Lockhart House, 440 Jaffe Road, **Isshin** (2506-2220, 13/F Times Square, and **Tomokazu** (2893-0682 at 491-499 Lockhart Road. But for something a little different, and certainly more exciting, try the department stores themselves. The giant **Sogo,** for example, has a vast basement food stall which is divided into various Japanese and Cantonese kitchens and informal eating areas where you can enjoy full à la carte meals or just pick snacks from various stalls and counters.

KOREAN

For pungent peppery *kim chi,* or assorted vegetables pickled and spiced and then fermented (they're buried in the ground for several months), tabletop barbecues and hotpots, try **Arirang** (2506-3298, 11/F Food Forum, Times Square, and **Koreana** (2577-5145 at 55 Paterson Street, Causeway Bay.

INDIAN & BURMESE

The **Viceroy Restaurant & Bar** (2827-7777 at 2/F Sun Hung Kai Centre, 30 Harbour Road, Wanchai, has built up an enviable reputation for its curries. It's also noted for its marvelous harbor views, fountain-decked outdoor terrace and its Saturday night entertainment — come 10:30 PM the tables disappear, a live band or DJ sets up and the trendies pour in to dance and drink the night away. Otherwise, the tiny and enjoyable **Café Malaya** (2577-3277, 1/F Dragon Rise Building, 9-11 Pennington Street. For milder Burmese food, the **Rangoon** (2893-1182, 265 Gloucester Road in Causeway Bay.

INDONESIAN

The **Shinta** (2527-8780, 2/F Kar Yau Building, 36-44 Queen's Road East (not far from Pacific Place), offers excellent Indonesian fare such as spicy beef *rendang,* satay (charcoal-grilled meat with spicy peanut sauce), *gado gado* (vegetable salad) and curries, and on Saturday nights a sumptuous buffet. For a mixture of Indonesian and Filipino, the **Cinta** (2527-1199, Basement, Hotel New Harbour, 6 Fenwick Street, Wanchai, and

for Indo-Malaysian, **Banana Leaf**
☎ 2573-8187, 440 Jaffe Road, Causeway
Bay. This restaurant is always very busy
so it would be best to reserve a table to
avoid waiting around.

THAI

In Wanchai, the cheap and cheerful **Thai
Delicacy** ☎ 2527-2598 at 44 Hennessy Road
or the popular **Chili Club** ☎ 2527-2872,
1/F, 88 Lockhart Road. In Causeway Bay,
Thai Kitchen ☎ 2577-0018, 6/F Goldmark,
1 Jardine's Bazaar, is highly recommended.

Western
Landau's ☎ 2827 7901, 2/F Sun Hung Kai
Centre, Wanchai, has dominated the
traditional scene for some years, offering a
range of hors d'oeuvres, pickled herrings,
snails and tasty whatnots like goose
terrine to go with it. The **Excelsior Hotel
Coffee Shop** ☎ 2894-8888 in Causeway
Bay, is also highly recommended, for its
harbor views as well as its food, and the
Amigo ☎ 2577-2202 at 79A Wongneichong
Road in Happy Valley, is the place if you
want good French cuisine in a romantic
Spanish-style setting. For more romance,
the **Revolving 66** ☎ 2862-6166, 62/F
Hopewell Centre, 183 Queen's Road East,

offers à la carte candle-lit dinners, seafood
and steaks, afternoon tea and magnificent
views of Hong Kong.

For Mexican specialties, US steaks
and seafood, margaritas and nightly
entertainment with Ben Abellaneosa
and Los Mexicanos, try **Casa Mexicana**
☎ 2566-5560, G/F Victoria Centre,
15 Watson Road, North Point. However,
be warned that half-way through the
evening the waiters shove wide-brimmed
hats on your head and everybody goes
completely wild: it is definitely not a place
for a pleasant, peaceful evening out. On
the same premises, **Texas Rib House &
Lounge** dishes up the finest spare ribs this
side of the Panhandle.

Another place for some high jinks is
Bacchus ☎ 2529-9032, Basement, Hop Hing
Centre, 8-12 Hennessy Road, Wanchai.
This Greek restaurant is romantic and
mellow every night except Tuesday,
Greek Party Night, when it erupts with
plate-smashing and dancing.

Also in Wanchai, some Italian
restaurants of note include the "friendliest
Italian restaurant in town", **La Bella**

Dai pai dong (street-side restaurants) ABOVE are a
convenient and cheap way to dine out.

Donna (2802-9907, at 1/F Shui On Centre, 8 Harbour Road, the **Rigoletto** (2527-7144, U-G/F East Town Building, 16 Fenwick Street, and the up-market **Grissini** (2588-1234 in the Grand Hyatt Hotel, which has an extensive all-Italian wine list. In Causeway Bay, on the first floor of the Excelsior Hotel, **Cammino** (2837-6780.

Also in Wanchai, **Harry Ramsden's** (2832-9626, at 213 Queen's Road East, next to the Hopewell Centre, has brought real English fish and chips to Hong Kong. **Brett's Seafood Restaurant** (2866-6609, 72-86B Lockhart Road, has an excellent selection of seafood, flown in from Australia, along with your basic fish and chips. The restaurant is open practically round the clock, from 7:30 AM to 3:00 AM.

TSIMSHATSUI

Tsimshatsui and the Kowloon peninsula were once known as the other side of Hong Kong, linked only by the Star Ferry with the island and providing a huge urban dormitory for the territory's Cantonese industrial work force. But the district was also the conduit for arrivals at Kai Tak Airport and, being at the very southern tip of China and the strategic Kowloon–Canton Railway, it had a tourist district centered on the Peninsula Hotel and Nathan Road, the main thoroughfare into the Kowloon hinterland down which, it was often half-jokingly predicted, Mao Zedong's occupation forces would one day march.

In the past two decades, the tourist development in Tsimshatsui has been phenomenal, with major new hotels soaring up around the Peninsula and along Nathan Road's so-called Golden Mile, and, more recently, a whole new district, Tsimshatsui East, springing up on largely reclaimed land to add a series of gigantic new hotels, shopping plazas, restaurants and nightclubs to the Hong Kong extravaganza.

In many respects, the district offers Hong Kong's best variety of restaurants, largely because its tourist facilities and amenities have been concentrated into the Tsimshatsui East area and the Golden Mile. Certainly, for Chinese cuisine, you can take your pick of dozens of establishments, and many regional tastes, which have a high, proven reputation.

Chinese Cuisine

You can choose the opulence and glitter of several palatial restaurant/nightclubs. Among them, **Ocean City** (2369-9688, Level 3, New World Centre, 18 Salisbury Road, is one of Hong Kong's largest dinner-dance venues with entertainment by some of Hong Kong's more well-known cabaret performers. **Ocean Palace** (2730-7111, 4/F Ocean Centre, Harbour City, Canton Road, has a Chinese classical dance performance every evening, followed by cabaret shows and dancing.

If you prefer a cozy atmosphere, there are hundreds of smaller restaurants in the area — take your pick:

For "drunken" prawns, Peking duck, game dishes and roast pigeon, the **Flower Lounge** restaurant (2730-2200 at 11 Canton Road. For gourmet favorites such as shark's fin soup with crab and fish roe and roasted pigeon with cheese sauce, **Heichinrou** (2375-7123, 2/F Lippo Sun Plaza, 28 Canton Road.

The following outstanding groups also have branches on the Hong Kong Island:

Ah Yee Leng Tong (2317-6082, Shop A, 1/F Hanley House, 68-80 Canton Road (and four other Kowloon locations) is very popular with the local community for health-enhancing casseroles and "male" and "female" soups. **Tai Woo Seafood Restaurant**, at 14-16 Hillwood Road (2369-9773, and 20 Granville Road (2739-8813, offers reasonably priced seafood dishes such as hotpots, steamed garoupa, sautéed scallops and garlic prawns. For home-style cooking, "drunken" prawns and seasonal specialties, **Tao Yuan** (2736-1688, at 1/F, Departure Level, China Hong Kong City, 33 Canton Road, is highly recommended.

For those not watching their budgets, two excellent restaurants to try for shark's fin soup, seafood specialties and game dishes are **Sun Tung Lok Shark's Fin Restaurant** (2730-0288, G/F Harbour City, 17-19 Canton Road, and **Fook Lam**

Moon (2366-0286, 1/F, 53-59 Kimberley Road.

Almost all the hotels in Kowloon have excellent Chinese restaurants and the following are just a few of the more well-known ones, in the lower price range:

Dynasty (2369-4111 at the New World Hotel; **Celestial Court** (2732-6991, 2/F Sheraton Hotel & Towers; **Loong Yuen** (2369-3111, 1st Basement, Holiday Inn Golden Mile. At the higher end: the **Chinese Restaurant** (2311-1234, 2/F Hyatt Regency; **Golden Unicorn** (2730-6565, 6/F The Hongkong Hotel; the waterfront **Lai Ching Heen** (2721-1211, Regent Hotel, which has splendid views of the harbor and Hong Kong Island; **Spring Moon Chinese Restaurant** (236-6251, The Peninsula; and **T'ang Court** (2375-1133, Hong Kong Renaissance Hotel.

CHIU CHOW

City Chiu Chow Restaurant (2732-6226, 1/F East Ocean Centre, 98 Granville Road, Tsimshatsui East, and **Golden Island Bird's Nest Chiu Chau Restaurant** (2736-6288, 2/F, East Half, Star House, 3 Salisbury Road or at 3/F BCC Building, 25-31 Carnarvon Road (2369-5211.

SHANGHAI & PEKING

Try **Tien Heung Lau** (2368-9660, G/F, 18C Austin Avenue — this restaurant is small so reservations are necessary — and the art deco **Wu Kong Shanghai Restaurant** (2366-7244, Basement, Alpha House, 27 Nathan Road. For Peking food, the **Peking Garden** restaurants at two locations: 3/F Star House (2735-8211, 3 Salisbury Road and at 1/F Empire Centre (2721-8868, 68 Mody Road, Tsimshatsui East. You can also try the long-established, modestly priced **Spring Deer** (2723-3673, 1/F, 42 Mody Road, and another value-for-money oldie, the **Great Shanghai Restaurant** (2366-8158, 26 Prat Avenue.

SICHUAN

Fung Lum's (2367-8686, 1/F Polly Commercial Bldg, 21-23 Prat Avenue, specialties include tea-flavored smoked duck, boneless chicken and prawns with chili and garlic sauce. Also worth a try is the **House of Tang** (2761-1711, at The Metropole Hotel, 75 Waterloo Road.

Hong Kong's Cantonese teahouse-restaurants ABOVE are packed at mealtimes — some of them so crowded that people wait alongside diners for a place to sit and eat.

VEGETARIAN

One of my favorite vegetarian restaurants is **Bodhi** (2366-8283, 1/F, 32-34 Lock Road, which has a wonderful selection of beancurd, fungi and bamboo shoot dishes. Other recommended places are **Kung Tak Lam Shanghai Vegetarian Cuisine** (2367-7881, 1/F Wang Seng Building, 45 Carnarvon Road, **Winner Vegetarian Restaurant** (2723-6331, Shop Nᵒs 41-53, China Hong Kong City, 33 Canton Road, Tsimshatsui, **Woodlands** (2369-3718, G/F Mirror Tower, 61 Mody Road, Tsimshatsui East, and **Light Vegetarian Restaurant** (2384-2833, G/F New Lucky House, 13 Jordan Road, Yaumatei.

International Fare

INDIAN

Curry lovers are well taken care of at the famed **Gaylord Indian Restaurant** (2376-1001, 1/F Ashley Centre, 23 Ashley Road, where tandooris are a specialty and where you can watch breads and kebabs being prepared for clay-oven baking. Also worth trying are the **Koh-I-Noor** (2368-3065, at 1/F, 3-4 Peninsula Apartments, 16C Mody Road (with another branch on Hong Kong Island), and **Swagat** (2722-5350, 103 Chungking Mansions (the only fully licensed Indian restaurant in the Mansions).

INDONESIAN

Java Rijsttafel (2367-1230, 38 Hankow Road, and, like its counterpart on Hong Kong Island, the busy, fast-food style **Banana Leaf** (2382-8189, 3/F, 438 Prince Edward Road and 3/F Golden Crown Court, 68 Nathan Road (2721-4821, for Indo-Malaysian food.

ITALIAN

Branto Pizzeria and Snack Bar (2366-8171, 1/F, 9 Lock Road.

JAPANESE

One novel establishment to try is **Ah-So** (2730-3392, 159 Craigie Court, World Finance Centre, South Tower, Harbour City, Canton Road, which calls itself "Hong Kong's Only Floating Sushi Bar" — the food being served from floating "boats". If you'd prefer a place with its feet a little more firmly on dry land, there's **Kotobuki** (2368-2711, Flat A & B, 1/F Good Result Building, 176 Nathan Road, or **Sui Sha Ya** (2722-5001, G/F, 9 Chatham Road. **Nadaman** (2721-2111 in the Kowloon Shangri-La Hotel, is one of the most popular Japanese restaurants in town, with bargain lunch prices and wonderfully authentic Japanese decor and cuisine.

KOREAN AND VIETNAMESE

For Korean, **Arirang** (2956-3288, 2/F The Gateway, Canton Road, and **Sorabol Korean Restaurant** (2375-2882, 4/F Miramar Tower, 1 Kimberley Road. For Vietnamese, two branches of the **Golden Bull** (2730-4866, at 101 Ocean Centre, Harbour City, 5 Canton Road, and (2369-4617 at L1, 17 New World Centre, 18 Salisbury Road.

THAI

Two good ones are the **Chaophraya Thai Restaurant** (2382-6618, 2/F, 440 Prince Edward Road, Kowloon City, and the **Thai Restaurant** (2735-9181, Bangkok Royal Hotel, 2-12 Pilkem Street, Yaumatei.

Western

When it comes to Western food, Tsimshatsui outshines Hong Kong and once again it's difficult to know where to start.

For years the **Au Trou Normand** (2366-8754, 6 Carnarvon Road has been rated the finest French restaurant in town, and its classic recipes, its variety of wines and decor are still five-star. Its main competition traditionally coming from the mainland branch of **Jimmy's Kitchen** (2376-0327, excellent European restaurants **Gaddi's**, the Swiss-style **Chesa**, the **Verandah Grill** and the extraordinary new East-meets-West **Felix**. But new competition is now rising among the many hotels that have sprung up in the last decade or so, and at most you'll usually find a classy French, Italian or Continental restaurant. A selection are:

For French cuisine, **Le Restaurant de France** (2722-1818, 3/F Regal Kowloon Hotel, **Les Celebrités** (2739-1111, Hotel Nikko, and **Margaux** (2721-2111, at M/F Kowloon Shangri-La. For Continental cooking, **Hugo's** (2311-1234, 2/F Hyatt Regency, **Plume** (2721-1211, Regent Hotel, **Tai Pan Grill** (2113-0088, 6/F The Hongkong Hotel,

and the **Delicatessen Corner** (2369-3111, Holiday Inn Golden Mile. And for Italian, **Sabatini's** (2721-5215 at the Royal Garden Hotel and **Capriccio** (2375-1133 at the Ramada Renaissance. The **Mistral** (2721-5161 at Holiday Inn Crowne Plaza Harbour View is a venerable old-timer for Italian fare, while the **Bostonian** (2375-1133, in the Hong Kong Renaissance Hotel, is a delightfully quirky place which provides a wax sheet and crayons on each table in case you fancy doodling between courses.

Moving out of the hotels, the Kowloon branch of **Grappa's** (2317-0288, Shop 105, 1/F Ocean Centre in Harbour City offers home-style Italian pastas, sausages, breads and desserts at reasonable prices. Other recommended Italian restaurants are the hip and trendy **Tutto Bene** (2316-2116, 7 Knutsford Terrace and **Wild Poppies** (2368-8642, 65A Kimberley Road.

Discos OPPOSITE and bars ABOVE offers a wide range of venues for a convivial night out.

For Australian tucker and a cold Foster's, **Kangaroo Pub** (2376-0083, 1/F, 25 Haiphong Road, and for large helpings of British and Irish pub food, along with a good selection of vegetarian dishes, **Mad Dogs Kowloon** (2301-2222, Basement, 32 Nathan Road, and **Delaney's Kowloon** (2301-3980, at 3A Prat Avenue.

There's an endless number of American restaurants in this area at the moment and you can take your pick of a few of the more popular ones: **Dan Ryan's Chicago Grill** (2735-6111, Shop 200, Ocean Terminal, Harbour City, Canton Road; and the **San Francisco Steak House** (2735-7576, at 7 Ashley Road, for US beef and seafood, salad bar and burgers. Also, **Planet Hollywood** (2377-7888, 3 Canton Road, owned by movie stars Arnold Schwarzenegger, Bruce Willis and Sylvester Stallone, features Californian cuisine and trendy Hollywood decor, while **Hard Rock Café Kowloon** (2377-8118, 100 Canton Road, has its rock 'n' roll memorabilia and Top 40 soundtracks.

Another venue worth mentioning, though not especially for its food, is **Someplace Else** (2369-1111 in the basement of the Sheraton Hotel on Nathan Road. It's a crowded watering hole for young executive types, especially on Friday and Saturday nights, with American-style Victorian bric-a-brac decor, Mexican food, exotic cocktails and live entertainment.

For Ocean Terminal shoppers, **Ruby Tuesday** (2376-3122, Shop 283, Deck 2, Ocean Terminal, is a welcome break for lunch and snacks.

OTHER CULINARY TRAILS
Eating out in Hong Kong needn't be confined to Central District, Wanchai–Causeway Bay and Tsimshatsui area, especially if you have a weekend, or even if it's only a day or night, to spare. Hong Kong is a very compact city, with an efficient transportation service, and reaching the areas outside the normal tourist beat is not as difficult as you might think.

Hong Kong Island
Anyone who saw *Love is a Many Splendored Thing* is familiar with the much-publicized gastronomic symbols of Hong Kong, the palatial floating restaurants in Aberdeen, and they can be visited directly or by organized tour, or by way of harbor cruises from Central District or Tsimshatsui. The most well known is the **Jumbo** (2553-9111, which is moored beside its sister ships the **Jumbo Floating Palace** (2554-0513 and **Tai Pak** (2552-5953. All are excellent for *dim sum*, seafood (you can select your own from tanks) and the usual Cantonese fare. At The Peak, the very classy **Café Deco Bar and Grill** (2849-5111, in the Peak Galleria, features a mixture of Asian and Western cuisine and about HK$8 million worth of original deco items such as a restored 1939 Wurlitzer juke box, a 1930s bronze canopy from a hotel in Miami, toilet basins from the 1920s, an old porcelain and nickel ice box from a New York City church kitchen, a 1920 oyster bar with zinc top, 1925 wall sconces and old brass doors. And this, of course, is another location from where you'll get absolutely fantastic views of Hong Kong and Victoria Harbour. Opposite, the old **Peak Café** (2849-7868, serves a mixture of Asian and American cuisine. During the weekends barbecue dinners are served in the pleasant garden area.

Repulse Bay may have lost its graceful time-honored landmark, the Repulse Bay Hotel, but a replica of the romantic **Verandah** (2812-2722 has been built into the high-rise luxury apartment block that now occupies the site. The restaurant serves excellent Continental cuisine, or you can just go for afternoon tea. Also in this complex, choose from the Euro-Japanese **Kagiya** (2812-2120 at Shop 202, **Hei Fung Terrace Chinese Restaurant** (2812-2622, on the first floor and for a variety of Asian dishes, **Spices** (2812-2711 on the ground floor.

Down on the beach in the Lido complex near the huge Tin Hau and Kwun Yum statues, you'll find a

McDonald's (2812-1544, **Kentucky Fried Chicken (** 2812-0230 and some other fast-food restaurants. At Stanley you can spend the day browsing through the cut-price boutiques and stalls of the open market and lunch or dine in one of the many restaurants or pubs scattered about the town. These include **Beaches (** 2813-7313, at 92B Stanley Street, an open-fronted café-disco serving mainly Western food, and on Stanley Main Street, **Lord Stanley's Bistro & Bar (** 2813-1876, and **Ristorante Firenze (** 2813-9090.

Also in Stanley Main Street, the elegant **Stanley's French Restaurant (** 2813-8873, was the first Western establishment to open there, and more than a decade later is still one of the best restaurants in the southern island area. Located in an old village house, Stanley's French features two glassed-in verandas which offer fine views of the bay, and at night you can enjoy rooftop dining. In much the same vein is **Stanley's Oriental (** 2813-9988, whose menu is a mixture of Asian and Western dishes, served either inside the restaurant or on the veranda. During the day and at weekends both restaurants are quite casual but in the evenings, when the candles come out, more formal attire is expected.

Outlying Islands

Lamma and Cheung Chau are both famous for their seafront Cantonese seafood restaurants, so many that they stand virtually check by jowl. In Yung Shue Wan, Lamma's main village, recommended restaurants include **Lung Wah Sea Food (** 2982-0281 at 20 Main Street, which also serves Western-style fish and chips, the **Man Fung Seafood (Lamma Seaview) (** 2982-1112 on 5 Main Street and the funky, very popular **Deli Lamma (** 2982-1583 at 36 Main Street. Other places to look out for are the **Waterfront Bar & Restaurant, Toochkas (** 2982-0159 at 44 Main Street, for Indian fare and pub grub, and the **Sampan Seafood Restaurant (** 2982-2388 and **(** 2982-0680 at 16 Hung Shing Yeh Road, is one of my favorite spots on the

island. To reach it: just before you arrive at the beach, walk up the steps on your left and near the top on the left you'll see a large terrace with tables and umbrellas. It's a bit of a climb but worth the effort for the baked pigeon, minced quail with lettuce, fried pepper prawns, cold beer and seaviews.

On the other side of the island the small fishing village of So Kwu Wan, or Picnic Bay, is a popular destination for expatriates, who flock there in junkloads during the weekends and evenings to drink and gorge on peppered prawns, chili crab and baked lobster in the many open-air, waterfront restaurants. Recommended are the **Lamma Mandarin (** 2982-8128 no relation of the Mandarin Oriental), **Peach Garden (** 2982-8581, and the **Rainbow Seafood Restaurant (** 2982-8100.

On Cheung Chau, the **Warwick Hotel (** 2981-0081 on the east side of the island serves Western and Chinese food. But if you'd rather not be in an airconditioned environment there are plenty of open-air Chinese restaurants along the waterfront promenade including **Baccarat Restaurant (** 2981-0606 (run by English-speaking "Fat Larry"), at 9A Pak She Praya Street. You can also try the **Garden Café** at 84 Tung Wan Road, the popular pub, **Morocco's (** 2986-9767 at 117 Praya Road (near the market complex) for Indian and imaginative Western dishes; and the **Lotus Thai Restaurant (** 2981-2432, 1 San Kai Shi Lane (opposite Morocco's).

If you really want to get away from the crowds, take a sampan from Cheung Chau to Tai Long Wan on Lantau island to the **Frog and Toad (** 2989-2300. The restaurant is about a half-mile walk from the beach along a concrete path that takes you through farms (and patches of cow dung). Open from 1:00 to 9:00 PM, it's best visited for lunch but let them know you're coming if it's a weekday. The food is nothing to write home about but the setting is great. At weekends the place gets packed out with junk parties

FOLLOWING PAGES: The ornate floating seafood restaurants at Aberdeen.

of expats. There's no regular sampan service back to Cheung Chau: at weekends they go to and fro fairly frequently but on weekdays you may have to ask the restaurant to arrange one for you.

For those touring around Lantau, **Charlie's Restaurant and Bar** (2984-8329, 13-14 Law Uk Village, Pui O, is a welcome stopoff point for lunch. The Australian-operated alfresco restaurant offers Cantonese, Indian and Western cuisine, as well as afternoon tea, and has an extensive wine list. Visa, Master Card and American Express credit cards are accepted. It's closed for Tuesday lunch and all day Wednesday unless you make a prior booking. A little further along the coast is **The Gallery** (2984-7645 at Tong Fuk which serves a popular open-air barbecue on weekends and public holidays (bookings on Sundays essential).

If you've ventured as far Tai O fishing village, **Ho King Restaurant** (2985-5115, 15 Wing On Street, is another good place for lunch.

For those with less time to spare, Lantau's largest residential area, Discovery Bay (or Disco Bay as it's locally referred to) is only about 30 minutes by high-speed ferry from Star Ferry in Central and can be a pleasant interlude either during the day or at night. The restaurants, all located in the shopping complex by the ferry terminal, are casual and reasonably priced: **Chili 'n' Spice** (2987-9191, **Jo Jo Indian Restaurant** (2987-0122, and the **Seoul Garden Korean Restaurant** (2987-0073. But if you'd rather just sit on the beach, takeaways include **McDonald's** and **Cajun Chicken**.

Lei Yue Mun and the New Territories
For adventurous seafood lovers, the village of Lei Yue Mun, on Kowloon's eastern tip of the harbor, shouldn't be missed. Here you select your own seafood from rows and rows of tanks that line the alleyways and if you can decide whether it's to be scallops, prawns and snapper or abalone, crabs and lobster or all six, you take your catch to a nearby restaurant which will gladly cook the

food for you. Great views of the harbor from a different perspective, along with close-ups of jets flying in and out of Kai Tak — an experience in itself. To get there, take the MTR to Kwun Tong and from there either a Kowloon Motor Bus (KMB) N° 14C or minibus to the Sam Ka Tsuen terminus.

Out in the New Territories, Shatin offers some reputable restaurants. Firmly docked on the Shing Mun River Channel, the three-decked marbled concrete **Treasure Floating Restaurant** (2637-7222 offers *dim sum* and seafood. At the night the restaurant is a blaze of lights and quite an amazing sight. A good place to eat after a day at the races. It's land address is 55 Tai Chung Kiu Road. On the same road you can try the **Regal Riverside Hotel** (2649-7878, which has Thai, Western and seafood restaurants along with a disco and karaoke rooms. Another good spot is the 50-year-old **Lung Wah Hotel Restaurant** (2691-1594, 22 Ha Wo Che, which is famous for its pigeon and beancurd dishes.

If you've taken time out to explore Sai Kung Country Park, its beaches and surrounding islands, the picturesque fishing port of Sai Kung is a convenient stopoff point for lunch and dinner, or even breakfast. The town has a number of streetside cafés, nothing fancy, as well as excellent Cantonese seafood restaurants such as **San Shui** (2792-1828, G/F, 7 Siu Yat Building, Lot 941, New Town, which has some interesting dishes on its menu — barbecued fish in bamboo stems, fried clams with black beans and chilies and stuffed cuttlefish. On Fook Man Road, the **Duke of York Pub** (2792-8435 offers pub fare and plenty of cold beer, and friendly Susanna's (2792-2139, at 7 Man Nin Street, Mediterranean dishes. For Italian fare, **Pepperoni's** (2792-2083, at 1592 Po Tung Road; and for African and other exotic dishes, the endearingly casual **Black Sheep** (2792-6662, Sha Tsui Path.

For a more serene setting, the **Sampan Thai Seafood Restaurant** (2719-3238 at Hebe Haven — a boating center southwest of Sai Kung — offers delicious food and, in the summer months, outdoor dining. Or hire a sampan from Sai Kung to get to the popular **Sha Kiu Seafood Restaurant** (2792-4733 on nearby Leung Sheun Wan (High Island). Owner Loi Lam (who was brought up in England and still speaks with a strong North England accent) can organize a junk from Sai Kung, too, if there's a group of you.

Special Interests

COOKERY CLASSES
Gourmets love Hong Kong because of its huge choice of cuisines and restaurants, particularly its excellent Chinese cuisine. If you yearn to be able to cook some of those dishes yourself you could take advantage of a cookery class while you're here. During the HKTA-organized Hong Kong Food Festival, held every March, there's a chance to learn a few secrets from master chefs and well-known cooking personalities such as William Mark, Chan Tung and Doreen Leung during the "Hong Kong at Home" program of cooking classes, jointly organized by the HKTA and the YMCA Domestic Centre. Eight classes are offered during the festival, costing HK$380 each. As there's a maximum of only 12 people per class it's advisable to book at least a week in advance.

Another Food Festival program, Cooking with Great Chefs, features executive chefs from some of Hong Kong's finest restaurants and hotels who demonstrate two or three recipes and then help course participants to recreate the dishes. While the "Hong Kong at Home" course concentrates on mainly Cantonese family dishes, this program features everything from Mexican to Mediterranean fare, Japanese to East-meets-West. Again, each class costs HK$380 and there's a maximum of 15 people per course. To participate, contact the HKTA in advance.

Outside of Food Festival times, you could try contacting any of the following places, all of which organize cookery classes: **Chopsticks Cooking Centre**

(2336-8433, G/F, 108 Boundary Street, Kowloon; **Oriental Culinary Institute** (2881-5528 FAX 2822-3333, 12/F, 22 Yee Woo Street, Causeway Bay; **Hong Kong Electric Company (Home Management Centre)** (2510-2828, 10/F Electric Centre, 28 City Garden Road, North Point; **Towngas Centre** (2576-1535, Basement, Leighton Centre, 77 Leighton Road, Causeway Bay. Demonstrations of Chinese and Western cuisine are also available at some of these centers.

EDUCATIONAL AND HISTORICAL TOURS
The HKTA organizes several excellent tours which aim to provide a deeper insight into Hong Kong's social, cultural and religious life. **The Heritage Tour** of the New Territories takes visitors to some of the finest classical Chinese sites in Hong Kong, including the beautifully restored 18th century walled village of Sam Tung Uk, the 18th century Man Shek Tong ancestral hall (a tribute to ancestral worship) and the opulent stately home of Tai Fu Tai, a 19th century scholar of the gentry class. The tour leaves four times a week and costs HK$310 per person.

You'll get a very different look at modern Hong Kong life with **The Family Insight Tour** which takes you inside a large public housing estate and gives you the chance to visit one of the estate's social services organizations such as a day-care center, nursery, kindergarten or hostel for the elderly. About half of Hong Kong's population (some three million people) live in public housing of various types (a little known fact about Hong Kong is that it's the free world's largest public landlord). On this tour, you'll get to see one of the huge estates that have been built since the 1950s when tens of thousands of refugees lived in dangerous squatter huts on Hong Kong's hillsides. Also included in the tour is a visit to Wong Tai Sin temple one of Hong Kong's most popular temples, built in 1973 smack in the middle of a crowded urban area. The tour runs every Thursday and costs HK$260 per person.

Taking a Tour

TOURS TO HONG KONG AND ASIA

Taking a package tour to Hong Kong makes great sense economically, especially in the low to shoulder season periods of January to June. Not surprisingly, considering the long historical, business and tourism links between Britain and Hong Kong, some of the best choices of package tours come from Britain's big operators such as **Kuoni** ((01306) 740500 FAX (01306) 744222, Kuoni House, Dorking, Surrey RH5 4AZ; **Hayes and Jarvis** ((0181) 222-7822 FAX (0181) 741-0299, Hayes House, 152 King Street, London W6 OQU; **Thomas Cook Holidays** ((01733) 332255 FAX (01733) 505784, PO Box 5, 12 Coningsby Road, Peterborough PE3 8XP; **British Airways Holidays** ((01293) 723171 FAX (01293) 722624, Astral Towers, Betts Way, London Road, Crawley, West Sussex RH10 2XA and **Trailfinders** ((0171) 938-3366 FAX (0171) 937-9294, 42-50 Earls Court Road, London W8 6FT.

Most of the tour operators offer a five-night flight and accommodation-only package to Hong Kong from around £700 in the low season. Of course, it depends on the hotel you choose — the cost can rise to over £1,000 if you pick a hotel such as the Mandarin or the Peninsula, or dip to as low as £600 for a less centrally located hotel such as the Metropole in Kowloon's Ho Man Tin district or less luxurious hotel such as The Wesley in Wanchai. Other hotels featured in these packages — such as the New World, J.W. Marriott, Island Shangri-La or Excelsior — all offer high-standard comforts and facilities.

The accommodation-only restriction actually works to your advantage: Hong Kong has such a huge range of choice, so many restaurants to offer and so many varied cuisines the last thing you'd want is to be restricted to your hotel. And incidentally, honeymooners often get complementary extras with these packages — fruit, flowers or champagne or even a room upgrade to a deluxe or harbor-view room.

Since Hong Kong is a major transport hub for the rest of Asia, many European, American and Canadian visitors take the opportunity of combining a Hong Kong visit with a trip to other parts of Asia. Again, a package tour offers excellent deals: for example, Kuoni's Hong Kong and Bangkok package (four nights in each) starts at around £770 and its Hong Kong, Bali and Singapore package (four nights in Hong Kong, seven in Bali and three in Singapore) at around £1,200 (both low season prices). As with several other operators, you also get the offer of several days' free extra accommodation if you stay a certain number of nights within a certain (usually low season) period.

Similar enticing combinations at reasonable prices are offered by British Airways Holidays: their "Multi Centre Options" include a seven-night Hong Kong and Singapore package from £940 and a 12-night Hong Kong and Phuket deal from just under £1,000. Thomas Cook's similar "Multi-centers" feature Phuket, Singapore and Bali, as well as Sabah (in Malaysia): for just over £1,000 you could have two nights in Hong Kong and five in Sabah's seaside resort of Kota Kinabalu. Or how about an even more exotic combination of Hong Kong, Singapore and the Seychelles? An 11-night deal has a low-season tag of around £1,500.

TOURS WITHIN HONG KONG

There's a dozen or so different tours you can chose within Hong Kong, taking you to some of the most popular or difficult-to-reach sights by bus, boat, tram or train and offering everything from dinner cruises in the harbor to open-top tram tours.

The HKTA, for instance, organizes a daily Land Between Tour to the New Territories — the hinterland dividing Hong Kong from the rest of mainland China. Costing HK$365 per person (HK$315 for children under 16), the tour includes visits to monasteries and rural markets, a Country Park and a bird sanctuary, finishing with a stop at the Shatin Racecourse and a Chinese lunch. If the horseracing takes your fancy, you can join the HKTA's special Come Horseracing Tour (provided your period of stay in Hong Kong falls in the June to September racing season): for HK$530 you get to enjoy lunch or dinner in the Visitors' Box within the Members' Enclosure of the Hong Kong Jockey Club's racecourse.

Golf fans, on the other hand, might prefer the **Sports and Recreation Tour** which whisks you off to the exclusive Clearwater Bay Golf and Country Club in Sai Kung for HK$400. See also the SPECIAL INTERESTS section on page 109 for details about the HKTA's special Heritage Tour and Family Insight Tour. For booking any of these tours, contact the Information and Tours Department on (2807-6390 ((2807-6177 on Sundays and public holidays) FAX 2807-6582.

Several private tour operators offer a variety of other tours: MP Tours Limited (2118-6235 or 2845-2324, organizes one-hour **open top tram tours** which trundle from Central to Causeway Bay and back five times a day every day (including a Night Tour starting at 7:45 PM daily except Friday and Saturday). They also offer one-hour **daily harbor cruises** from Tsimshatsui seven times a day (including an Afternoon Chinese Tea Cruise at 3 PM, Sundown Cruise at 7 PM, Evening Cruise at 8 PM and Harbour Lights Cruise at 9 PM. Each tour costs HK$180 per person (HK$140 child fare). You can book the tours at your hotel or at the Star Ferry piers.

Gray Line Limited (2368-7111 FAX 2721-9651, has a variety of land tours and harbor cruises including a popular morning or afternoon **Hong Kong Island** tour (HK$290 adult, HK$190 child under 11) which includes a visit to Victoria Peak, Aberdeen, Repulse Bay, and Stanley Market. Their **Kowloon & New Territories** tour (HK$290 adult, HK$190 child) features a visit to the (sadly over-visited and now commercialized) Kam Tin walled

village, the Wong Tai Sin temple and the new Kowloon Walled City park. Be warned that both tours also feature a visit to a jewelry factory (that's where your tour guide gets his or her commission!).

Gray Line's **dinner cruises** offer some unadulterated romance, however: for HK$630 per person you can cruise the harbor on a modernized Chinese pleasure junk and then enjoy dinner at the Revolving 66 Restaurant, on the 62nd floor of Wanchai's Hopewell Centre. Or for HK$480 take the **Pearl by Night** buffet dinner cruise on board the Pearl of the Orient restaurant cruiser. Gray Line also organizes trips further afield, to Macau Zhongshan and Shenzhen's two theme parks. **Splendid Tours and Travel Limited** (2316-2151 FAX 2721-7014, have similar tours on offer as well as a **Splendid Aberdeen Night Cruise** for HK$680 which includes a Chinese seafood dinner on board the famous floating restaurant in Aberdeen.

ABOVE: One of the relaxing ways to see Hong Kong is on a tourist boat.

Open-top bus tours at night of
Tsimshatsui and Kowloon followed by a
buffet dinner on board the Hong Kong
Bauhinia cruising restaurant is another
attraction option, offered by Tourist
Enterprises (2367-4143. The nightly
five-hour tour costs HK$630 adult
(HK$490 child).

Watertours of Hong Kong Limited
(2739-3302 FAX 2735-1035, offer some of
the most popular tours in Hong Kong —
a trip on a Chinese style motorized junk
to the outlying islands of Lamma, Lantau
or Cheung Chau or the seafood haven of
Lei Yue Mun. Their **Cheung Chau and
Islands Hopping Tour**, for example,
runs daily except Sunday and costs
HK$240 adult (HK$160 child).

Do-it-yourself **walking tours** are
increasingly popular in Hong Kong.
The HKTA publishes five excellent little
booklets (complete with basic maps) to
help you find your way around Central
and Western District, Yaumatei, Cheung
Chau, Lantau or Sai Kung. They're on sale
at the Information and Gift Centres for
HK$30 each.

Visitors explore the spectacular neon-lit streets on
the open-top bus tour before joining a fabulous
dinner cruise.

Images of
Hong
Kong

THE NEW DAWN

On July 1, 1997, one of the most extraordinary events in modern history took place as 156 years of colonial rule in Hong Kong came to an end. Following the Sino-British Joint Declaration on the future of Hong Kong, signed in 1984 and lodged with the United Nations, the sovereignty of Hong Kong — one of the most successful capitalist countries in the world — reverted to communist China. Under a unique arrangement referred to as "One Country, Two Systems," Hong Kong became a Special Administrative Region (HKSAR) of China enjoying a high degree of autonomy, free to continue its capitalist lifestyle for 50 years after 1997.

Seconds before midnight on June 30th, the Union Jack and Hong Kong flags were lowered, the new SAR Bauhinia-flower flag was raised, and British Governor Chris Patten handed over control to the SAR's new Chief Executive, shipping magnate Tung Chee Hwa, who had been chosen by a select 400-member body, handpicked by China, in December 1996.

The handover was celebrated in Hong Kong with celebrity concerts and cultural festivals, processions and parades of floats, a gigantic, 3.3-km- (nearly two-mile)-long dragon lighting display along Nathan Road, and one of the world's biggest and most extravagant firework and laser shows over Victoria Harbour. An event long feared by some and desired by others had finally come to pass, and Hong Kong entered yet another new era in its life, more prosperous and dynamic than ever, with a massive HK$330 billion in the government coffers, and business booming.

RIGHT: The new Hong Kong SAR Bauhinia-flower flag and the national flap of China replace the Union Jack and Hong Kong colonial flags over the Legislative Building in Central Hong Kong. OVERLEAF: Amid celebrative neon signs proclaiming the return of Hong Kong to China stands the contemporary Hong Kong Convention and Exhibition Centre — built especially for the Handover ceremony.

THE RESOUNDING BOOM

Every day on the stroke of noon, a cannon is fired on the waterfront of Causeway Bay on Hong Kong Island, marking the passing of another 24 hours of high-paced business and pleasure in this, the world's most incredible and exotic center of capitalism.

The Noon-Day Gun doesn't just mark the time, it announces achievement and change — for at the frenetic pace at which business goes on in the tropical heat and

business as it does about the business itself. It's believed the cannon was first fired a century ago in a ceremonial welcome to one of Jardine & Matheson's cargo clippers, loaded with opium, as it sailed into the harbor. It was this nefarious trade in "foreign mud" with China that gave birth to Hong Kong, that nurtured its founding business and trading houses in its infancy, that set the swashbuckling and quite disreputable tradition and tone of its business world and the sort of people who inhabited it. And, while that world is infinitely more

humidity and urban clamor of Hong Kong, that past 24-hour period may have seen a new multi-story hotel or a new restaurant open its doors in a celebration of gongs and tom-toms and prancing dragons and lions, a new consortium formed to drive a new tunnel under the harbor, break the ground on a new multi-million dollar high-rise commercial and residential development, or build a new futuristic banking headquarters. And while the cannon signals the end of that day's business race, it's also the starter's gun that triggers the Hong Kong business world out of its blocks for the next mad 24-hour dash for profits. The origin of this noon-day ritual says as much about the philosophy of Hong Kong's approach to

respectable, image-conscious and even virtuous today, it still has a faint ring and clash of cutlass blades, a whiff of musket powder and a slight swagger of the self-made buccaneer in its boardrooms. It is still a place where each noon-day boom on the Causeway Bay harborfront triggers the pursuit of one thing: the fast buck.

FIRECRACKER ISLAND

There have been so many booms in Hong Kong's 150-year flicker of history, that to study its development is like watching a fizzing firecracker, waiting for the next bang. Every five years or so this tiny island

and small wedge of mainland territory, this little ant-hill of probably fewer than seven million people, bursts its seams with ambitious and even impossible business dreams, and five years later it's not only achieved every one of them but is about to do it again.

In 1841 when the island itself was annexed by the British as part of their imperial booty from the first Opium War with China, it was dismissed as an insignificant "barren rock" with hardly a hope in the world of becoming much more than that.

happy cheap labor force harnessed by the colony's second major attribute, its nineteenth century British and European adventure capitalists — dour ledger-worshipping successors to the "merchant princes" whose cannon-bristling East Indiamen had first forced China to open up to trade Hong Kong — couldn't help but make money.

Its magnificent sheltered harbor and its position as an offshore haven, distanced from the collapse, chaos and civil conflict into which China was sliding, gave it some

But almost from that first historic crack of the Noon-Day Gun it astounded everyone by burgeoning into a major trading center and "Emporium of the East", taking advantage of a number of crucial factors that the jaundiced mandarins of Whitehall had obviously failed to anticipate and which have underpinned its various development booms since.

First, from the moment the British flag was hoisted on January 26, 1841 the island was flooded with Chinese from Canton (Guangzhou) and the southern provinces fleeing famine and the harsh rule of the Manchu Qing dynasty, most of them with nothing to lose and thus, with thrift and hard toil, everything to gain. With this grab-

advantage over the mainland treaty ports, where there was always the threat, and often the fact, of "native" unrest. As British maritime power grew, as steam replaced sail, and as the first transoceanic flying boats began linking the capitals of the Far Eastern and Pacific empire, Hong Kong's strategic position made it one of the busiest crossroads of the world.

From the turn of this century until World War II, only one treaty port outshone it, and that was Shanghai with its vastly

Hong Kong then and now — OPPOSITE Pedder Street and old clock tower in late 1860s, and ABOVE modern-day eventide view of Manhattan-style skyline of Central District.

bigger, even cheaper labor market, its huge textile industry and its direct access via the Yangtze River to the resources and trade goods of central China. But even then Hong Kong was virtually twinned through business links and joint investment with the "wickedest city on earth" — through the Hongkong and Shanghai Banking Corporation and the wealthy, powerful Kadoorie and Sassoon hotel families, for example; and when Shanghai collapsed, first in the horrific Japanese bombing and wartime occupation, then in the communist revolution of 1949, Hong Kong was there to pick up the pieces.

It became an offshore refuge and new business base for Shanghai textile barons and their money, fleeing the communist revolutionaries. With the many millions of dollars and even manufacturing equipment that they brought with them, the colony re-tooled, fattened and diversified — no longer just a huge island emporium and port of free trade, but an emerging manufacturing center too, churning out textiles and toys. By the 1960s it had not only gone through a new development boom but was in a near-permanent state of change. Again, Southeast Asia was in the grip of a violent convulsion, and again Hong Kong was in the right place and ready at the right time to take advantage of it.

That convulsion was the Vietnam war, a conflict to which the United States committed more than half a million military personnel and an immense amount of arms and supplies. By 1966, Hong Kong was not only the main Southeast Asian transshipment point for Vietnam war materials — its harbor packed with freighters — but it was also one of the most popular R&R (Rest and Recreation) venues for the American troops, and for the next decade it was playing host to something like 3,000 free-spending GIs a month.

WINDOW ON THE WORLD

But by then the colony had also been taking advantage of a far greater and even more lucrative conflict, and one that underscored not only its innate, imperishable

instinct for survival but also its fundamental survival policy — business above all else — and its unique ability to turn even the most unlikely situations to its own favor. While, in the 17 years since the Chinese revolution, it had become an offshore life-preserver for almost two million mainland refugees, it had also quite incredibly become the communist government's main international trading base, communications center and source of something like US$5 billion a year in desperately needed foreign exchange.

The American embargo on "Red Chinese" exports had fallen like a ripe plum into Hong Kong's lap. It became a "laundry" for Chinese products, vast amounts of which went in one end of its port and emerged the other end as Hong Kong products with new certification to prove it. With China's own transport and trading infrastructure still struggling to repair itself after the many years of civil war, Hong Kong was also the key transshipment point for "legitimate" exports to other countries. On top of that, Hong Kong provided a base, or enclave, for Beijing's trade and diplomatic negotiations and capitalistic endeavors that lay conveniently outside the walls of the revolutionary socialist society.

If the prospect of a communist society practicing capitalism in Hong Kong was surprising enough, Hong Kong's own wheeling and dealing was simply amazing — it was playing international high stakes poker with almost every card in the pack marked. It was a sovereign British colony on the surface, but quite prepared to accept instruction from Beijing on key issues behind the scenes. It was anti-communist and a haven for many anti-revolutionary Chinese, yet it was acting as banker, business agent and sales rep for the communist

and a burst of hedonism after the post-war and post-revolutionary austerity. Its late-fifties' image of the World of Suzy Wong had slipped into a micro-skirt, false eye-lashes and Mary Quant eye-shadow, put a Beatles record on and headed for what was then called the *discotheque*. With its unique blend of Chinese character and familiar red London buses, Hong Kong was "Carnaby Street East".

The island's Wanchai bar district fronted directly on to lapping harbor waters, sampans and American warships, and at night

government. It was supporting the American Vietnam war effort on the one hand as a funnel for war supplies, and on the other it was helping circumvent the United States embargo on mainland Chinese products. And it was making a fortune out of it all.

CARNABY STREET EAST

This was Hong Kong of 1966, the year that I first arrived there, fell in love with the place and began an intimate affair which continues with considerable passion to this day. In 1966 it was at the height of its first resounding boom, and the face of the society reflected it. It was a time of wealth, youth

it was teeming and jumping with hordes of United States servicemen and their military police, tourists, local expatriates and young Chinese office workers. Its bars and discotheques were packed with bar-girls, hostesses and seething masses of dancers. The most popular, crowded, exciting "in" place, and the one with the loudest pop music, was the Cave. Its main rival was The Den at the former Hong Kong Hilton, where you could leap about to the beat of the Stones or the Beach Boys or sway gently in the late hours to Paul McCartney's *Michelle* or Frank Sinatra's *Strangers in the Night*.

Girlie bars still await the U.S. fleet.

Images of Hong Kong

The Hilton was the most popular business and recreation hotel for tourists, American military officers and executives and Vietnam correspondents, and one of three hotels at that time that dominated the Hong Kong scene. On the island's Central District waterfront, massively impressive in that era of comparative low-rise development, the Mandarin (today it's called the Mandarin Oriental) was for British businessmen and visiting Foreign Office bureaucrats who liked a bit of brass and leather with their roast beef and gin. And on the Tsimshatsui waterfront on the other side of the harbor, almost monumental in size, architecture and reputation, famed throughout the whole world for its guardian lions, its fountain, its unending streams of Rolls-Royces and its cavernous gathering place of the international jet-set its lobby coffee lounge stood the Peninsula Hotel.

Amid tall columns, crisp linen tablecloths, potted plants and bustling teams of waiters and uniformed bellboys, you could sit in the lobby of The Peninsula, on the very southern tip of "forbidden" China and the main overland routes of the entire Eurasian landmass, and watch the "in" people of Hong Kong and the rest of the world go by — wealthy ex-Shanghai industrialists, Shaw Bros movie starlets, the great stars of Hollywood, United States congressmen, Commonwealth prime ministers, United Nations officials, British aristocracy, Indian princes, Asian and Western tycoons and the new giants of the British business world, the pop idols. Marlon Brando was there, so was Danny Kaye, and so too were Steve McQueen, Doug McClure and Richard Crenna, filming *The Sand Pebbles*. And from the same soaring lobby windows you could gaze out across the twinkling lights of the harbor and its shipping and ferries to an absolute fairyland scene — the island and its rising Mid-Levels and Peak and the eastern reaches of Wanchai, Happy Valley and Causeway Bay, all of it ablaze with lights as though it were a huge diamond, encrusted with millions of precious gems — many of those gems, at the eastern end of

the island, the lights of thousands of hillside squatter huts, shanty dwellings of tin, scrap timber and even cardboard, built on the hillsides by the thousands of refugees who had poured across the border from China.

In that year of 1966, Prince Charles paid a visit and the colony's British community went wild, filling the So Kon Po Government Stadium and the streets with thousands of Chinese schoolchildren waving Union Jacks. A "Buy British" trade drive was launched and the Union Jacks came out again, along with British food, industrial and consumer displays, British fashion shows, British beer, British pop stars and a lot of British pomp. The Australians left their mark on the colony that year too — a

ABOVE Old world grace and charm at afternoon tea in the renowned Lobby of The Peninsula..

whole team of Aussie journalists working on one of the daily newspapers abruptly picked up and departed Hong Kong en masse, taking thousands of dollars' worth of tailored suits and other clothing with them, along with radios, cassette recorders, television sets, watches, jewelry — even a brand new car — and leaving a lot of Hong Kong merchants stuck with nothing more than some hire purchase deposits.

It was that kind of year and era, the swinging era when fortunes were being made and flamboyantly shown off in public, when you could sit and work at your office desk while a man traced the outline of your stockinged feet on a sheet of paper — and come back two days later with a pair of brand new hand-made high fashion, and cheap, shoes; when the same nineteenth century free-wheeling laissez-faire principles that had guided the colony's business and prosperity since the first shot of the Noon-Day Gun were still manifestly successful.

And it was also the year of reckoning, when the special laissez-faire license and "borrowed time" that had built the colony's fortunes suddenly ran out.

RED GUARDS AND REALITY

Two calamities hit Hong Kong in 1966 — one a natural disaster (or perhaps, in the context of that time, an act of God) and the other a momentous political act that suddenly

brought home to people the implication of all those "fairyland" shanty lights in the squalid squatter areas that spilled down many of the colony's hillsides.

In June, one of the heaviest unbroken monsoonal storms in Hong Kong's history dumped so much rain that parts of the slope of The Peak and Mid-Levels, and the hillside above Causeway Bay, collapsed. The mudslides caused incredible damage, and even loss of life, at one point smashing into the foundation pillars of a high-rise block of flats and tearing the building to the ground. I remember walking down Tin Hau Temple Road to the Causeway Bay harbor front in the pounding rain and watching people trying to leap from their apartment house entrances over torrents of water that were

raging down the gutters and footpaths to the harbor. At the bottom of the street lay a huge junk yard of cars that had been washed down in the night and piled up on top of each other at a pedestrian barrier. On that same night two British journalists had tried to get across a flooding viaduct and one had been carried away and drowned in the Mid-Levels.

It wasn't that disaster of that scope was particularly new to Hong Kong — landslides were a regular occurrence in monsoonal storms, and so too were violent and destructive typhoons, which boil up out of the Pacific to smash against the South China Coast from July to October every year. But what the 1966 tragedy showed was that Hong Kong could no longer go on

violent riots in the teeming, tenement-packed streets in the urban hinterland of Kowloon.

For two weeks, in the interminable rain, the tourist mecca of Tsimshatsui and the deeper districts of Mongkok and Shamshuipo looked like an urban battleground. Police and army Land Rovers veered through the almost deserted streets with riot-clad crews and anti-missile metal grids over their windscreens and doors. The stately colonial stone and glass façade of the Peninsula Hotel was boarded up, and riot shutters guarded the hotels, stores, banks and money-change kiosks along Salisbury and Nathan Roads.

In the backstreets, fires blazed in the night, casting a hellish glare over huge mobs of screaming, chanting, rock-throwing rioters and, confronting them, deep, heavily-armored and shielded ranks of police and Gurkhas — the British Army's long-standing strike force of Nepalese mercenaries — advancing under big banners emblazoned with Chinese characters warning the crowds to disperse or be gassed, or even possibly to be shot.

Again, Hong Kong was no stranger to civil unrest — there'd been labor strikes in the 1920s and riots in 1952. But, like the rains and mud slides, the 1966 outbreak exposed the bare bones of social neglect, exploitation and discontent that lay under Hong Kong's swinging image. When, in the following year, there was another natural calamity — this time a crippling drought — and even more violent and prolonged riots, including an incident in which a mob besieged Government House chanting slogans from Mao Zedong's "Little Red Book", it was obvious that radical and fundamental reforms had to be made to the way in which Hong Kong conducted its business and its community.

simply making money and ignoring its own infrastructure, safety and welfare. The immediate lesson of 1966 was that a huge and costly public works program was needed to shore up and strengthen all hillside places where land slips were likely to occur.

The second calamity was the launching by Chairman Mao Zedong (Mao Tse-tung) of his Great Proletarian Cultural Revolution and the unleashing of the Red Guards, some of whom immediately began denouncing the imperialist regimes of Hong Kong and Macau. The Cultural Revolution ignited just as public outcry and unrest were coming to a head in Hong Kong over a proposal to hike up the fares on the Star Ferry. Both fire and tinder came together in

Thousands of its people were without homes, and many of those who were crammed into the packed tenements of back-street Kowloon were without adequate

ABOVE: The Star Ferry — the proposal to hike up the fares attributed to an unrest in Hong Kong in 1966 — is still probably the cheapest sightseeing ride in the world I

sanitation, health care, education, social welfare and many other facilities and amenities. The police force and civil service had a growing reputation for corruption. Chinese salaries were ridiculously low compared with those of the British and other foreign expatriates — less than one-tenth of the *gwei lo* (foreign devil) incomes even at middle management levels (if, indeed, Chinese employees could break into middle management positions anyway).

Momentous and inevitable decisions were made at that time. Laissez-faire had

GOING FOR BROKE

By 1974, when I returned to Hong Kong for what was to become another five-year "live-in" romance with the place, it was already well into a massive building boom that was completely changing its physical character and social attitude. Suzy Wong had thrown away her stiletto heels and slinky *cheong-sam*, settled down, got an office job and joined the PTA. If the transformation aroused a twinge of indig-

to end, or at least be moderated and reformed to produce a caring, rather than exploitative, society. Hong Kong had to shed its buccaneering attitude and begin to regard itself as a serious and possibly permanent society, not a temporary dwelling and business house living on borrowed time.

And in typical Hong Kong style, it threw itself headlong into major reform — and another huge development boom began.

ABOVE: For the population of Hong Kong, every movement on the Stock Exchanges is closely scrutinized. OPPOSITE: High-rise housing sprang up in Shatin — Hong Kong's first designated New Town.

nation and regret among the hedonists, it offered a new sense of hope and inspiration to thousands of immigrant Chinese families who, only a few years before, had crept across dark, guarded borders, run the coastal waters in packed sampans and junks, or swum across Deep Bay or the inlet south of Shataukok, and now demanded and deserved a society with some permanence and sense of concern in which they could build decent lives. Also, it had not escaped the calculations of the government and business world that Hong Kong could not succeed in its next stage of development — from trade, textiles and toys to trade, international banking and finance and electronics — without a vastly improved housing and public transport infrastructure that would keep its working population reasonably happy.

So, by 1974, the first Cross-Harbour Tunnel had been built, providing speedy, direct access between the island and the mainland districts. The Lion Rock Tunnel had been blasted through the tall hills just north of the Kowloon urban sprawl to free the traffic bottleneck that had existed on this key route to Shatin and the New Territories. On Hong Kong Island, initial work had already begun on the Aberdeen Tunnel,

land — already one of the world's most thrilling examples of space-saving engineering, providing a spectacular touchdown right in the heart of a high-rise beehive. Work had started on the huge Kwai Chung container terminal, destined to become the main export conduit for China trade.

THE NEW CITIES

But all this paled against the central showpiece of the development boom — a

carving through the island's central mountain to Aberdeen, Repulse Bay and Stanley on the southern side. And an even bigger, far more ambitious tunnel system was also under way, the US$2.2-billion Mass Transit Railway (MTR), a high-speed subway that would switch the bulk of Hong Kong's public transport underground and solve the enormous "people pressure" in its urban streets.

Two other gigantic projects, the Plover Cove and High Island reservoirs, were under way in the New Territories to solve Hong Kong's chronic high-summer shortage of fresh water. Kai Tak Airport was being expanded, its harbor runway — streaking out into the harbor waters on reclaimed

multi-billion dollar resettlement scheme to develop three rustic, sleepy rural centers in the New Territories, Shatin, Tsuen Wan and Tuen Mun, into huge New Towns, or satellite cities, providing public housing and full social amenities for one million people. When the first blueprints were made public it looked like another urban nightmare the plans calling for a population of 90,000 in one gigantic skyscraping housing estate alone.

There was an echo of Hong Kong's old laissez-faire attitude in the arguments that were put up to defend this, one of the most massive, tightly crammed high-rise public housing projects on earth. The Chinese were accustomed to living this way, one argument went — they even preferred it. Its promoters were on much more realistic ground when they pointed to the space-saving factor — Hong Kong's largely hilly terrain, making it difficult to create sprawling low-rise tract housing. But even then it was apparent that one million working people were going to be poured into huge industrial dormitories, thrown up relatively cheaply on reclaimed land, while the hillsides were to be kept free for high-profit luxury private condominiums. Of all the development schemes under way in 1974–75, the New Towns had the biggest question mark over them. There were costly development projects under way on the social and recreational fronts too. New sports stadiums to be built in Wanchai and on the roof of the new Kowloon–Canton Railway terminus at Hung Hom; a new ultra-modern Space Museum and Planetarium on the waterfront at Tsimshatsui; a huge US$25-million marine playground, Ocean Park, featuring aquariums, marine zoology, wave tanks, whale and porpoise shows, a cable car system, fairground rides and cultural gardens, on the Brick Hill headland between Aberdeen and Deep Water Bay on the southern shore of Hong Kong Island.

On the island and in the tourist and commercial centers of Kowloon, the face of Hong Kong in the latter half of the 1970s was one of noise, overcrowding, stress and chaos. Whole streets were being excavated and districts ripped apart in the work on the MTR and other projects; pneumatic pile drivers shrieked and thumped on dozens of building sites right through the day and sometimes into the night; cherished landmarks of the colonial era, notably the old Kowloon–Canton Railway Station Tsimshatsui, disappeared in the frenzy of redevelopment, adding to the trauma of some of the more traditional sections of the British community. And amidst it all, some two million tourists a year poured off the Jumbo 747s at Kai Tak Airport and 70,000 Vietnamese boat people struggled ashore from leaking ramshackle sampans and junks — and cargo freighters that had rescued them at sea — to be herded into makeshift refugee camps, and, as their numbers swelled, locked up in concentration centers. Not surprisingly, the general health of the community suffered a report in 1979 claimed that between 20 and 50 percent of the population was suffering from some degree of stress-related mental sickness.

But already, the signs of a new, far more just and realistic community were beginning to appear. With the combined pressure of Beijing and local outrage, and a couple of notorious court cases, the Royal Hong Kong Police was brought to heel with the setting up of the watchdog Independent Commission Against Corruption (ICAC). The Hong Kong Festival, launched in earlier years to counteract the adverse publicity of the Red Guard confrontations and riots, had now been turned into the annual Hong Kong Arts Festival, combining public relations with a bid to lift the community out of what had been a profit-oriented cultural wasteland.

What had been a colony was now a "trading territory" — it distinctly said so in all Hong Kong Government Information Service releases. The government's Information Officers were also under distinct notice that anything questionable they wrote about Hong Kong would be discussed over tea in Guangzhou or Beijing that same day. There was a coincidental and gradual breaking of the political and commercial umbilical with the "Home Government" in Whitehall. First, a decision by Hong Kong to break away from sterling and link its currency to the United States dollar, then a certain distancing of this burgeoning enclave now one of the top 20 trading and industrial centers of the world, and potentially its third richest financial capital from the staggering, crisis ridden, and comparatively impoverished economy of Great Britain.

OPPOSITE: The entrance of the first Cross-Harbour Tunnel emerges amid a net work of highway at the Causeway Bay waterfront. The second Cross-Harbor Tunnel links Kowloon Bay with Quarry Bay while the third connects western Kowloon to Kennedy Town on the western harbor front of Hong Kong.

The "territory's" own economic structure began to change significantly, with high-tech production rising to dominate the manufacturing sector.

Its financial structure saw an even more significant change — mainland Chinese investment moving in, and "communist" corporations suddenly challenging the long-established Old Boy network of British and Western corporate powers that had enjoyed almost divine authority in the profitable property and development fields.

Another momentous change was about to take place in Hong Kong, and one that explained everything — the sudden massive social development, the slow but steady erosion of its ties with the British Crown. It was a change that would, once and for all, test Hong Kong's unique ability to turn every challenge to its own advantage. It was more than just a change, it was a crisis. Hong Kong was to be returned to the sovereignty of China.

The old-fashioned method of transportating goods — wide-beamed junk-style harbor lighter ABOVE hauls cargo from mid-harbor freighter. OPPOSITE Yaumatei typhoon shelter harbors a colorful array of lighters.

CHINA'S FRONT DOOR

When Hong Kong had been grabbed as a colony in 1841, the Union Jack had flown only over the island itself. In 1860, after the second Opium War, China's Qing dynasty government had been forced to cede the waterfront district of Kowloon up to what is now Boundary Street, and 38 years later the British took a 99-year lease on the hinterland, what is now the New Territories, and 233 more islands.

After the 1949 revolution the communist government in Beijing disowned all colonial agreements, quite rightly pointing out that they had been obtained under military duress. But, for reasons that have already been explained, Hong Kong was allowed to continue existing and serving Beijing's interests under British administration. The internal rule and day-to-day running of the "colony" were left to the British, but most key decisions on defense and diplomatic affairs required Beijing's approval — and, just in case the British were tempted to exert full colonial autonomy, Beijing occasionally demonstrated the sort of overwhelming *fait accompli* Hong Kong faced by flooding the people with thousands of "illegal immigrants".

It became apparent from the moment that Mao Zedong died, when the ultra-revolutionary Gang of Four were crushed and imprisoned and when the head of the Chinese "revisionist" moderates, Deng Xiaoping, rose to power, that the status of Hong Kong was in question. China's sudden swerve to the semi-capitalist path was accompanied by a new open, but more aggressive, foreign policy in which Deng himself made it clear where the future lay by donning a Texan ten-gallon hat at a rodeo while on a visit to the United States, during which time the Chinese military turned its jets, tanks and guns on neighboring Soviet-backed Vietnam to put it in its place, and when it was made clear that the futures of Hong Kong, Macau and even nationalist Taiwan were now to be settled.

In Hong Kong, word rippled down through the expatriate business community that it was time to begin a strategic retreat.

Outside the highest levels of government, the feeling was that Hong Kong's value to China, and thus its reason for existence, had run its course — a capitalist China flinging its door wide open to the rest of the world would hardly need a special offshore trading base and diplomatic window any more. That feeling rose to panic when, in 1982, British Prime Minister Margaret Thatcher visited Hong Kong on her way to the first talks on its transfer back to Chinese control in the year in which the lease would run out on the New Territories, 1997.

The Hong Kong stock market slumped, the hugely inflated property market took a nose-dive with it. Some of the biggest Hong Kong corporations, headed by Jardine & Matheson, let it be known that they were transferring their financial bases elsewhere. Two major property companies collapsed and had to be bailed out, and there was a temporary run on a leading bank. Capital flew out of the territory with the speed of migrating swallows. Amongst the Hong Kong Chinese there was a sudden rush for immigration to the United States, Britain, Australia and just about any other non-communist country that would take them, and up to 40,000 a year began leaving in what became a serious drain of middle-management expertise. In Britain, the "Hong Kong lobby" of parliamentarians and business chiefs, bolstered by the Falklands victory, fiercely rattled their sabers against this cowardly sell-out in the face of one billion mainland Chinese.

But in fine traditional style, Hong Kong recovered quickly from its initial panic, took a good hard businesslike look at the situation and did what it had done in the midst of all crises of the past — looked for the opportunity for profit. A new restaurant opened in Central District, for example. Its name? "Nineteen 97".

MONEY AND POLITICS

As any visitor to Hong Kong will immediately confirm today, the much-feared Anglo-Chinese agreement didn't sink the territory at all, nor did it even make a dent in its phenomenal economic growth. Hong Kong continued to boom in the face of the Beijing takeover, and is showing every sign of continuing to boom now that the takeover is history. Indeed it has taken vigorous advantage of the economic expansion that its absorption with the mainland economy promised.

The territory's economy has more than doubled as Hong Kong manufacturers, sidestepping escalating labor and property costs, have shifted their operations across the border to the Shenzhen Special Economic Zone and other key low-cost sites of Guangdong province. The Pearl River delta, embracing Hong Kong, Macau and southern Guangdong, is now regarded as

the front-runner of another wave of Asian economic "tigers". An even more powerful industrial and trading axis comprising China, Hong Kong, Macau and Taiwan is seen as a possible generator of Asia-Pacific growth and investment in the 21st century.

Chinese corporations have continued to invest heavily in Hong Kong, particularly in the property market. The huge Bank of China building, a monolithic architectural hybrid of steel, glass and Chinese imperial arrogance, has planted Beijing's standard right in the heart of the territory's business community. Despite increasingly exorbitant office rents and real estate costs, foreign corporations have continued to pour into the territory, heeding the

words of one business commentator in the *South China Morning Post* that "the only reason to be based in Hong Kong today is China".

But this new economic explosion has been underscored by dramatic confusion and confrontation on the political front, in the shaping of the territory's crucial relationship with its new landlord, Beijing. And much of it has been caused by the realization

Started off as the "laundry" port during the days of American embargo on "Red Chinese", entrepôt trade with China still accounts for the majority of cargo passing through Hong Kong. Hong Kong's conatiner port at Kwai Chung, in western Kowloon, is the busiest in the world.

that despite Beijing's pledges on its control of Hong Kong after 1997, despite its assurances on "one country, two systems" and its promise that Hong Kong's fundamental business, political and social structure will be left intact for the next 50 years, the territory may well be shedding colonial power only to face a form of rule far more authoritarian and iniquitous in the years to come.

The moment of realization was a brutal one. On the night of June 2 1989 the Beijing authorities sent tanks and troops into Tiananmen Square to crush the student pro-democracy movement. Up until that night when mass killings that took place, Hong Kong's business community and a growing number of its people took the view that despite the prospect of coming under Chinese Communist Party rule, the "Open Door" policy and rapid economic changes in China would lead to political and social liberalization as well. The Tiananmen Square massacre proved that despite all the other fundamental changes taking place in China, the Communist Party had no intention of relaxing its grip on the country.

Hong Kong's reaction was equally dramatic. Mass demonstrations of more than a million people at a time, Chinese and expatriates together, poured through the streets in protest against the Tiananmen crackdown. An underground escape system went into operation to help Chinese democracy activists on the run from the authorities to get out to the West. There was another emigration panic, with Hong Kong Chinese — again mostly skilled middle-management people — seeking citizenship in, predominantly Canada, Australia, Britain or any other country that would admit them. Beijing's view of Hong Kong perceptively shifted: while it was still a much-coveted political and economic asset, come 1997, it was now also a potential hotbed of resistance and possible insurrection against authoritarian rule.

Since Tiananmen Square, Hong Kong's relationship with its new masters has followed two distinct tracks. On the economic track, even the horror of Tiananmen and a subsequent hardening of communist party

rule have been largely ignored in the clamor to take advantage of business opportunities in China. On the political track, the collapse of world communism, leaving China and North Korea as the last bastions of Marxist authoritarianism, produced a British-led administration in Hong Kong, with wide domestic and international support, which, far from being the caretaker government that one might have envisioned diligently putting the books in order for Beijing's triumph in 1997 — actually began redefining and reforming Hong Kong's political institutions to strengthen its hand in the inevitable power-play with Beijing after the takeover.

The appointment of Chris Patten, a tough British Tory Party strategist and former MP, as Governor of Hong Kong in 1992 brought to an end a tradition of British Foreign Service mandarins who tended to bow to China's demands as though it was still the fashion to bear tribute to imperial Beijing. In a sense, they were right: first Mao Zedong, then Deng Xiaoping, both elevated to cult status at the tip of the Communist Party pyramid, simply copied the imperial structure of authority and administration that had existed for many centuries before the 1949 revolution.

But under Patten's governorship, the scholarly myths of 5,000 years of Chinese history and culture were swept away. Far from being the Middle Kingdom, endowed with innovation, wisdom and exoticism that have fascinated China scholars for years, China was seen as a politically and socially backward, over-populated, under-educated Third World monolith with a brutally self-protective ruling structure that lacked the worldliness, experience and insight required to safeguard Hong Kong's basic freedoms after 1997.

It was Governor Patten's most fundamental step to safeguard those rights — a move to reform and shore up democratic rule in Hong Kong through expansion of elected representatives in the Legislative Council that finally tore Beijing's veil away. The Chinese unleashed such a ferocious, vilifying campaign to personally undermine Patten and to rein in all major political and economic development in

Hong Kong particularly the new International Airport project at Chek Lap Kok — that the territory saw for the first time how radically life could change after Beijing's administrators and public security people strode in.

There were other more immediate changes that altered the public view of life after 1997. Major crime spiraled in Hong Kong during the early 1990s as armed gangs from Guangdong, alleged to have the tacit support of corrupt provincial officials, launched a spate of raids on banks and jewelry stores, fighting deadly gun and grenade battles with the Hong Kong police. A wave of car thefts, in which mainly luxury vehicles in the Mercedes Benz class were stolen and smuggled across into Guandong, was followed by a surge of cross-border thievery involving luxury yachts and cabin cruisers some of which were later found operating as public ferries on the Guangdong river network. Hong Kong's Independent Commission Against Corruption (ICAC) reported an alarming 40 percent rise in commercial corruption, most of it committed by mainland Chinese interests. Indeed, in a scenario published by one Hong Kong magazine of life after 1997, the analysts who contributed to the article generally agreed that increasing lawlessness and corruption were two prime epidemics to be expected after the takeover — spurred by mainland officials and business interests whose interpretation of capitalism was simply the means to get rich quick.

But for all this, Hong Kong has continued to prosper, and in development terms has outshone even the great social and commercial booms of the 1970s and 80s. The prospect of enormous wealth in the economic partnership with China has far outweighed the real and nagging fears of post-1997 rule. The thousands who fled the territory in search of foreign citizenship after the Tiananmen Massacre have been drifting back, weighing up any fears that they still may have against the lack of qualified jobs and aggressive Hong Kong-style business opportunities in the recession-hit West. Hong Kong's endemic pragmatism and flexibility has triumphed again. And while

that is both its drawback and its strength, depending on one's own moral view, it cannot be denied that much of this tiny, ultramodern, ever-burgeoning territory's special allure is its belief that nothing short of catastrophe should stand in the way of a fast buck.

Not even a nagging desire for democracy or political freedom has dented this belief. In the last years of colonial rule, it became obvious that Beijing would have nothing to do with Patten's political reforms that had finally — and very belatedly — sowed

the seeds of political awareness in Hong Kong. It announced that on the day of handover it would disband Patten's Legislative Council, which was mostly directly elected in 1995, and hold fresh elections, under new rules, in 1999. In 1996, it appointed a 400-member Selection Committee of pro-China Hong Kong people to choose not only the SAR's new Chief Executive but also a 60-member Provisional Legislature which would take over power from the Legislative Council until the 1999 elections.

Britain and many other countries at once criticized this step back from democracy but there was little they could do. In December 1996, the chosen 400 picked Tung Chee Hwa as Chief Executive-designate and went on to select (mostly from their own ranks) the controversial Provisional Legislature which immediately began to act

"One country, two systems;" neon signs will continue Hong Kong's capitalist style, for 50 years after 1997.

like a shadow government. Hong Kong's small band of Democrats demonstrated, criticized and appealed to the world to speak out on their behalf. But most of Hong Kong's remaining six million people took the events for granted, and went back to work. A survey taken four months before the handover revealed that most of the respondents simply did not believe that Hong Kong's new political leaders could or would protect them against interference from China.

THE FUTURISTIC CITY STATE

The Hong Kong that now welcomes more than 11 million visitors a year, including over two million business travelers and package tourists from mainland China, is a thriving, highly efficient city-state. Where the great social programs of the past two decades have given it an ultramodern infrastructure — public transport, telecommunications, parks and playgrounds, social services and business facilities — the most visual development trend of the 90s seems to be to transform, once again, the territory's commercial skyline.

They're calling it ego architecture a multi-billion dollar scramble by the territory's new tycoons to outdo each other in the scale, design and sheer audacity of new skyscrapers and commercial malls. No sooner had the 70-story Bank of China thrust skyward over Central District than an even bigger, architecturally grander monolith, Central Plaza, streaked upward out of the new harbor front business district of Wanchai, this one setting a new trend for Hong Kong in early Manhattan neo-classicism combined with an after-dark look of something reminiscent of the movie *Ghost Busters*. It's a design trend that you'll see right along the Central–Wanchai–Causeway Bay commercial corridor in new high-rise creations like Number Nine Queen's Road (The Galleria) and the Entertainment Building in Central District, the giant Times Square in Causeway Bay and a host of other smaller commercial and office complexes that have sprouted up on both sides of the harbor. The next giants to emerge will be the 108-story, 468-m- (1,560-ft)-high Nina Tower in Tsuen Wan, billed to be the world's tallest when completed in 1998; and two 400-m- (1,310-ft)--high towers, planned by the Mass Transit Railway to be completed soon after 2000, which will stand at the entrance to the harbor, one at the Airport Railway Hong Kong Station in Central and the other in West Kowloon at the Kowloon Station.

While Hong Kong has been roundly accused of ripping up its history, it is creating a new architectural heritage that is evident in the landmarks of the past three decades buildings like Jardine House near the Star Ferry and the cylindrical 66-story Hopewell Centre in southern Wanchai representing the first great burst of growth in the 1970s, supplanted in the 80s by the enormous steel and glass citadel of Exchange Square and the novel futuristic architecture of the Lippo (formerly Bond) Centre and the main headquarters of the Hongkong Bank, and now all of them giving way to the granite towers and turrets of the neo-classic 90s. Where shopping malls like The Landmark, with its vast atrium, in Pedder Street Central was the last word in a luxury, multi-functional shopping environment in the 80s, now the huge Pacific Place complex, with two lofty atriums, three sprawling levels of shops and department stores, restaurants, office towers and three hotels — the Marriott, Conrad and Island Shangri-La and the equally dramatic Times Square have become the new showplaces.

In infrastructure, too, the second Cross-Harbour Tunnel linking Kowloon Bay with Quarry Bay has recently been joined by a third from western Kowloon to Kennedy Town on the western harbor front of Hong Kong Island. This is one of the world's largest civil engineering projects which includes a complex and costly highway, a new MTR system and the world's heaviest

---

OPPOSITE: The 78-story monolith Central Plaza streaked upward out of the harbor front business district of Wanchai, setting a trend for Hong Kong in early Manhattan neo-classicism, combined with an after-dark look of something reminiscent of the movie *Ghost Busters*.

and longest road-and-rail suspension bridge — the 2.2 km (1.4 mile) Tsing Ma bridge, part of Lantau Island's first "fixed crossing" to the mainland. All of this is to support the most ambitious new development in Hong Kong's history, the new Chek Lap Kok Airport off Lantau island (see page 227.) due to take over from the old Kai Tak Airport in April 1998. Designed to cope with some 35 million passengers and three million tonnes of cargo a year, Chek Lap Kok Airport features a dramatic 1.3-km- (0.8-mile)-long aircraft-shaped passenger terminal (designed by Sir Norman Foster of Hongkong Bank fame), 2.5 km (1.5 miles) of moving walkways, 288 check-in counters and a vast shopping mall.

Meanwhile, the world's longest covered outdoor escalator system has been built up to the Mid-Levels from Central District, a distance of 800 m (2,620 ft) — to make getting up and down the steep streets easier for walking commuters. It also tries to reduce Mid-Levels traffic congestion. If anything, it is a testament to Hong Kong's role as a wealthy, ego-driven super-city, and it reflects the corresponding change that has taken place in the role that Hong Kong sees for itself as a tourist attraction as we approach the 21st century.

Where the contrasting lion and dragon of colonial and Chinese culture was the main tourist draw card for many years, now it is simply the fascination of a rich, spectacular, hard-driving major Asian metropolis.

THE MASS TRANSIT RAILWAY

Nothing has revolutionized Hong Kong's public transport system more than the underground Mass Transit Railway (MTR). It's taken the people-pressure off the streets of the main tourist districts on both sides of the harbor and also considerably reduced what was once a costly and aggravating travel problem caused by the territory's island-mainland geography. This fast, clean and constantly growing MTR system carries over two million passengers a day on three routes — one running along the east–west corridor of the Hong Kong Island harbor front from Sheung Wan to Chai Wan, the second linking the island with mainland Tsimshatsui and western Kowloon and the other running through the second Cross-Harbour Tunnel between Quarry Bay and eastern Kowloon. The MTR's latest line is the Airport Railway, opening mid 1998 to link the new Chek Lap Kok Airport with Kowloon and Hong Kong Island. In fact, it will provide two separate services: the Airport Express, a fast passenger link to the airport (just 23 minutes between the new Hong Kong Central station and the airport); and a domestic service called the Lantau Line, linking Central with west Kowloon, Tsing Yi and Tung Chung (the new town opposite Chek Lap Kok) and providing a much faster service between Tsuen Wan and Central than the current Tsuen Wan Line.

One warning about traveling on the MTR in general: try to avoid it at peak travel times, when demand is so fierce that Japanese-style "people-pushers" have been employed to pack passengers on to the trains.

THE NEW TOWNS

Gigantic clusters of high-rise housing estates, shopping malls and manufacturing zones have transformed former mainland and New Territories market and fishing centers like Shatin, Tsuen Wan and Tuen Mun into self-contained satellite cities. Built to resettle squatter populations and boat people who poured into Hong Kong in the 1950s and 60s, they've also taken some of the pressure off the urban beehives of Kowloon and Hong Kong Island. And at night they are awesome to behold — glittering mountain ranges and soaring peaks of light, an astonishing mixture of Disney castles and the extraterrestrial visions of *Star Wars*. They've decentralized shopping, too, with vast commercial malls like Shatin's New Town Plaza and a series of malls at one of the later residential developments, the huge Whampoa Gardens complex near Hung Hom, rivaling anything found in Tsimshatsui or Hong Kong Island.

TSIMSHATSUI

This bustling commercial center right on the tip of the Kowloon Peninsula has long been Hong Kong's main tourist district, the site of most of its tourist hotels and the key shopping area for visitors. During the 1970s and 80s, the area expanded on to reclaimed land in the harbor. This formed a completely new tourist area, Tsimshatsui East — the area where hotels like the Royal Garden, Regal Meridien, Holiday Inn Crowne Plaza Harbour View and Nikko are now situated.

But for all its reputation and growth, along with its famous Golden Mile of shops and department stores, Nathan Road, Tsimshatsui has never really matched the high-rise architectural drama of Hong Kong Island's Central District and other harbor front locations. The reason: a long-standing restriction on building heights to ensure a safe passage for aircraft landing and departing at the Kai Tak International Airport.

All this is changing. With the new airport at Chek Lap Kok and with the vast area of ready-formed flat, open land at Kai Tak already slated for massive redevelopment once the airport here closes down, building restrictions have already been relaxed and Tsimshatsui is starting to mushroom with new skyscrapers.

The new tower wing at the famed Peninsula Hotel, opened in 1994, reflects something of the skyward explosion that's going to take place right through Kowloon in the coming years. Until the tower was built, this grand dame of hotels was almost lost in the welter of new (if low-rise) business and recreational development that transformed the Tsimshatsui waterfront including the spherical dome of the Space Museum and Planetarium, the sweeping roof of the Hong Kong Cultural Centre and the giant Regent/New World hotel and commercial complex.

Meanwhile, a wide swathe of reclamation off Yaumatei, west of the peninsula, has extended the waterfront of what used to be a typhoon shelter so deep into the harbor that old Hong Kong hands joke about the days to come when you'll be virtually able to step back and forth from Kowloon to Central.

HONG KONG ISLAND

If you think the image of the Incredible Shrinking Harbor is a bit beyond the pale, take a look at the new reclamation and development that's going on in the harbor front in Central District. It's only 20 years since the Mandarin Oriental Hotel on Connaught Road was virtually at the water's edge. Then it somehow shrank amid a burst of new development that saw the waterfront extended and buildings like the Shun Tak Centre, Exchange Square, the GPO (General Post Office) and City Hall, the Ritz-Carlton Hotel, the giant Admiralty, Lippo and Far East Finance centers, the avante-garde Hongkong Bank and adjacent Standard Chartered Bank, the Bank of China and nearby Citibank buildings, not to mention the huge Pacific Place complex to the east, turn the area into Hong Kong's Wall Street.

Now, all this new high-rise expansion is receding into the urban hinterland of Central as the new waterfront reclamation is prepared for new office blocks, government buildings, parks and recreational centers and the cross-harbor Star Ferry trip, surely one of the last touches of tranquillity in this booming city, gets shorter again. The entire length of the harbor between Central and Wanchai will eventually be reclaimed to create 123 more hectares (303 acres) of land, used for the new Hong Kong Central station of the Airport Railway and expansion of the business district. Further reclamation plans — another 480 hectares (1,185 acres) to be created between the western tip of Hong Kong Island and Green Island and around Kai Tak in southeast Kowloon — will mean that in some places the harbor will by reduced at some points to as little as 800 m (2,624 ft) wide. Opponents of the land-hungry planners, united under The Society for the Protection of the Harbour, warn that Victoria Harbour will eventually have to be renamed Victoria River.

As for Wanchai, once famous for its bars and brothels, I can remember the time in the late 60s when Queensway ran right alongside the harbor waters. Now, the great towers of the Lippo Centre and the office blocks and hotels of Pacific Place provide a kind of triumphal introduction to a district that's not only streaked right out into the harbor on reclaimed land but has also become a financial and business hub rivaling Central.

On this harbor frontage, Central Plaza building stands like an architectural champion, challenging Central District, amid development that includes the Hong Kong

Academy of Performing Arts and Arts Centre, the vast Hong Kong Convention and Exhibition Centre — flanked by the deluxe Grand Hyatt and New World hotels — three towering government offices, including the new Immigration Department head-quarters — and the China Resources complex. If you knew Wanchai in the past, go to the 62nd floor revolving restaurant at the top of the Hopewell Centre, which once dominated this district, and take a look at all the breathtaking changes that have transformed Suzy Wong's old neon-lit beat.

Further east, Causeway Bay is now another small city in its own right. In the 1970s and 80s, the Excelsior Hotel and

adjacent World Trade Centre (which itself may well have been demolished and replaced by now) rose up to dominate harbor front development overlooking the typhoon shelter and Hong Kong Yacht Club. The big Japanese department stores — Matsuzakaya, Daimaru and Sogo — moved in to turn what was once a series of street markets and teeming tenements into a major shopping center. Now, Times Square, thrusting up out of the former tram depot, has added a nine-floor mega-mall full of shops, restaurants and cinemas, a cavernous piano-shaped atrium and commercial skyscrapers to the Causeway Bay/Happy Valley skyline.

From there, the Island Eastern Corridor, a long table-top expressway, streaks right along the waterfront to Chai Wan at the eastern end of the island. And, all along the route, Further on, some of Hong Kong's most famous old sea front landmarks — old residential tenement districts and fishing ports like North Point, Quarry Bay, Fortress Hill, and Shaukeiwan — have burgeoned into high-rise housing estates and commercial centers every bit as dramatic as the mainland New Towns. One huge development along the way, Taikoo Shing, once an ugly industrial and warehouse district, is built around one of Hong Kong's biggest multi-story shopping malls and includes an indoor ice-skating rink.

All this has made Hong Kong an exciting and efficient place to live and work in, even if it is overcrowded, hyperactive and surely one of the most exhausting environments on earth. For people like me, who've watched it go through a succession of building booms since 1966, it sometimes feels as though there's finally no more room, no more greed and vision, no more energy left, and that it cannot possibly expand any further. There must come a day, I keep telling myself, when, with a vast sigh, Hong Kong decides that whatever it decided to build itself into, the work is finally done.

But of course, that's not so. If anything, the territory has simply been preparing the ground for yet another momentous development boom, fueled by new vision and greed, when China's new capitalists have moved in.

The southern side of Hong Kong Island has undergone a similar development boom. With the Aberdeen Tunnel now virtually jetting traffic right through the island's mountainous central spine Aberdeen has been transformed from the crowded, rustic fishing port that it once was packed with fishing junks and floating homes — into a new satellite city. The small island of Ap Lei Chau, right across from the main Aberdeen waterfront, has also mushroomed into a high-rise residential estate.

All this has robbed Aberdeen of much of its former exoticism. But the harbor is still a fascinating sight — squadrons of new sleek-hulled, deep-sea fishing trawlers, some of which fish as far away as the Gulf of Tonkin off Vietnam, moored in neat rows where a pandemonium of junks and sampans once reigned. The Ap Lei Chau Bridge now separates the port into two sections, fishing craft at one end, and the city's most famous attraction, the huge floating restaurants, along with a marina of luxury yachts and private cruisers at the Aberdeen Boat Club at the other.

To the east, a looming headland provides the stage for one of Hong Kong's biggest cultural and recreational attractions, Ocean Park. This sprawling playground, with one of the world's longest cable-car systems linking its lowland and headland sites, includes an Ocean Theatre, a Wave Cove with an artificial wave tank full of seals and other aquatic creatures, a vast shark aquarium, the world's largest reef aquarium, the Atoll Reef, a funfair with one of Asia's biggest roller coasters, a 3.5-hectare (8.6-acre) walk-through aviary featuring some 2,500 exotic birds, a step back into old China at Middle Kingdom and a Disney-style Water World.

Beyond Aberdeen, Repulse Bay — once a rather sleepy bay where the famous Repulse Bay Hotel recalled Asia's more graceful days — is a high-rise citadel of luxury apartment blocks overlooking a beach which has been extended and widened with sand dredged from the sea. The hotel isn't there any more, but a public

outcry managed to save its famous Verandah Restaurant, which is now incorporated into a residential and commercial development. In front of the beach itself is a sprawling complex of fast-food restaurants, including McDonald's, and a rather hideously designed "theme park" of traditional Chinese statues and shrines. This has turned Repulse Bay into something quite tacky. But the view of the bay is still exciting.

The village of Stanley, once a peaceful fishing haven, then a popular tourist market for cheap jeans and factory "seconds", is now

an even bigger, far more crowded tourist shopping spot, mushroomed with luxury apartment blocks and condominiums, with an entirely new up-market residential estate spilling down to its beach front from nearby Chung Hom Kok. Stanley has gone the way of Repulse Bay, and at weekends it's a struggle to get through the shopping crowds and invading hordes of barbecue picnickers. But like Repulse Bay, it still has fantastic views, even if you're likely to find reclamation barges and pile drivers blocking the way.

OPPOSITE Opera singer entertains while ice skaters twirl in City Plaza, Taikoo Shing. ABOVE: Aberdeen waterfront.

For an impression of what Stanley and Repulse Bay were like in calmer days, go even further south to Shek O, which features one of Hong Kong's best beaches. This seaside town, also once a little fishing port, hasn't yet come under the developers' jackhammers, and it's spending its last days of peace as a mecca for day-trippers and an off-the-track residential spot for young foreign expatriates. The Shek O Golf and Country Club, and another nearby beach community, Big Wave Bay, add to this area's resort potential (see THE OPEN ROAD page 35 for more on Shek O).

THE OUTLYING ISLANDS

Even Hong Kong's biggest outlying islands are under development, with Cheung Chau now more of a New Town housing estate than what it traditionally was — a bustling fishing community with a bay packed with junks and its waterfront cafés providing rustic salons for its expatriate and Chinese community of artists, photographers and media people. But the biggest offshore development has taken place at Discovery Bay on the southern tip of Lantau Island — a largely undeveloped island that's actually one and a half times the size of Hong Kong. Discovery Bay has been turned in to a vast, constantly growing residential resort of high-rise apartment blocks and beach front condominiums, with its own shopping center, sports and social club, fire station and 24-hour hovercraft service linking its largely executive community with Central District.

A decade ago, the plan was to retain Lantau as Hong Kong's biggest parkland and nature reserve, but the pressure for new development particularly in middle-and upper-class residential property — and the advent of the new airport at Chek Lap Kok off Lantau's northern coast, has put paid to that. While Lantau is still a comparative wonderland of soaring, untouched hillsides and mountain peaks, with tremendously inspiring views and hiking trails, it's days are numbered as a parkland. It is now the site of the next big property boom.

The very prospect of all this development seemed daunting and even unnerving back in the late 70s. Even then, Hong Kong seemed to have crammed just about everything into one solid monolith of concrete and glass. It was feared that another development boom could only worsen what was already a deteriorating and stressful environment.

It has certainly caused a grave pollution crisis affecting the harbor, surrounding waters and most of the best beaches; and whether this will be tackled and eventually repaired depends on how the mainland Chinese view environmental matters now that they have the key to Hong Kong. On past performance, there's very little reason to feel optimistic about it.

But to objectively consider Hong Kong today you have to look at what all this development has done for its people. It has given them a sense of community and permanence that did not exist in its more anarchistic days as a colonial emporium. It has given them comfortable, if pressure-packed, housing. They now enjoy one of the finest integrated transport systems anywhere in the world and an exciting range of cultural, recreational and educational amenities. Their business world has been streamlined, computerized, coordinated and fitted neatly like a microchip into a social infrastructure that already anticipates the demands of the 21st century.

Thirty years ago a great many of these people were living in rude tin-roofed shanty towns where the huge apartment blocks, office towers and shopping malls now stand. From their point of view, this is indeed progress.

ABOVE Your can still enjoy fresh air and open spaces on Hong Kong's outlying islands — this one is Lamma, before such peaceful spots catch the eye of developers.

The
Colonial
Past

THE "BARREN ROCK"

When Commodore Sir J. J. Gordon Bremer rowed ashore with a party of Royal Navy officers and ratings to plant the British flag on the Hong Kong Island foreshore on January 26, 1841, he can be forgiven if he thought he was adding a priceless new colonial jewel to the wealth and glory of the British Empire.

At that time of the year, Hong Kong would have looked its best. The sky would

cannon-packed sailing workhorses of the China and Far East trade, and the new faster slim-hulled American clippers which were beginning to slash days and even weeks off the long, highly competitive race from Baltimore and Liverpool to the South China Coast. With the mainland foreshore to its north and the mountainous island protecting it to the south, it was simply one of the finest harbors that Commodore Bremer and his men had seen anywhere.

Although it lay not much further than a cannon shot from the mainland, the island

have been clear and the weather relatively dry and sunny. Being winter, a faint gossamer of early morning mist may well have lingered over the harbor waters, an echo of the mild seasonal chill of the night. The island itself would have loomed over the naval whaleboat in wooded slopes rising upward to the lofty 552-m- (1,811-ft)-high peak of a central mountain spine running along the island to the east sunbathed and serene and lush, and no doubt achatter with bird life and possibly a troop or two of monkeys.

The anchorage itself would have excited Commodore Bremer's nautical appreciation wide and deep enough to take three or four huge fleets of East Indiamen, the

was virtually bare of human presence. It had been uninhabited until the fourteenth century, and even then had become only an occasional stopover for roving fleets of *Hoklos*, the "sea gypsies" of southern China. At some point in the century before Commodore Bremer's sea boots trod triumphantly along its sandy shore, small bands of mainlanders, driven by famine, had crossed over to it and established small fishing settlements on its eastern and southern foreshores in what are now Shaukeiwan and Aberdeen. Pirates had also used its sheltered bays as lairs, but even they had not regarded the island as a permanent base. Until the British arrived, the island and its "Fragrant Harbour" lay off the main trade route, ignored by all except an occasional junk on its way to or from Canton (Guangzhou).

As the Union Jack unfurled in the light breeze and prayers were said and the island claimed in the name of Her Britannic Majesty, little did Commodore Sir J. J. Gordon Bremer know that official wrath would ignite back in Whitehall, careers and reputations would be destroyed, contempt would be heaped upon the island and all involved in its seizure and the Crown would even refuse to accept it before it finally took its place on the official map of British colonial possessions.

It may also be that the Commodore had little idea of exactly what it was that he was committing brave red-blooded British men and fair womenfolk to. While the island lay in a pristine setting of clear dry skies and balmy winter sunshine on that historic January day, within a matter of months it would be like a steam bath, a furnace soaked in dense mist and incredibly high humidity, then hammered for days on end by strong torrential monsoon rains, and then, lashed and torn time and time again by the terrible *tai fungs* or typhoons, that boil up each high-summer out of the northern Pacific.

If ever there was a more unlikely place for the birth of a huge, densely populated, highly prosperous trading and manufacturing city-state, it was this desolate, hump-backed island. When the news of its acquisition reached London, back came the imperious and indignant response which, to this present day, has been a catch-phrase of Hong Kong's incredible survival and development in the face of immense odds. Lord Palmerston, Queen Victoria's Foreign Secretary, dismissed it as nothing more than "a barren rock with hardly a dwelling upon it".

FOREIGN MUD

It had been a far more dramatic and historic chain of events that had culminated in Commodore Bremer's flag-raising ceremony on the island's foreshore. Britain and China had gone to war in one of the most

sordid conflicts of all time — one that was to end eventually in the total collapse of China's 5000-year-old tradition of imperial and dynastic reign.

The struggle had begun from the moment that the British, following on the heels of the Portuguese and Dutch, had first broken around the Cape of Good Hope and across the Indian Ocean to join in the rich trade pickings that were available along the China coast. The trouble was that, the trade was all virtually one way — there was a fierce British demand for two prized

products, silks and tea, but there was nothing the British could tempt the Chinese with in return. As the Manchu Qing dynasty emperor Ch'ien-lung (Qianlong) bluntly informed King George III: "I set no value on strange or ingenious objects and have no use for your country's manufactures." Not only that, but the British "merchant princes" were banned from all Chinese soil except for a confined, segregated trading depot in Canton where they were at the mercy of

---

OPPOSITE: Before the emporium — a view of the modest skyline of Wanchai and almost barren Mid-Levels photographed around the year 1890.
ABOVE: Chinese artist in Wellington Street studio specializing in "photographic" portraits.

a Chinese trading monopoly called the Co-Hong.

The Chinese would accept only one thing for their trade, and that was silver bullion. By the turn of the nineteenth century, the British taste for tea had reached the level of a national craving, and so much silver was being committed to tea imports that the treasury was close to bankruptcy. A commodity of some sort had to be found that the Chinese simply could not resist, and, as it turned out, there as one product that proved irresistible to thousands upon thousands of Chinese, from the most lowly, back-breaking, debt-ridden level of the peasantry to the effete, languishing refinement of the mandarins and aristocracy; and that product was opium from British Bengal.

By 1834, the Chinese were well and truly hooked. Opium was being shipped in through Canton at the rate of 16,000 chests a year. Five years later it had increased to nearly 40,000. Also, the silver flow had now completely reversed, and it was this threat of Chinese bankruptcy as much as the growing addiction to opium that finally galvanized the Qing Government into action. It imposed a ban on the opium imports and, when the British and other European traders tried to break the ban by smuggling the stuff in, it ordered its commissioner in Canton to blockade the foreign depot and confiscate their opium stocks. To the bitter chagrin of the British traders, some 20,000 chests of "foreign mud" went up in smoke right before their eyes. And they promptly declared war.

The officer who led the attack was Britain's Superintendent of Trade in China, Captain Charles Elliot. He did a simply splendid job of it, leading a naval squadron up the Pearl River to Canton, blockading the city and forcing the Chinese to come very smartly to heel. He then sat down with the Qing emperor's negotiator, a Manchu viceroy named Kishen, and demanded trade concessions as compensation for the loss of the 20,000 chests of opium.

In hindsight, both men acquitted themselves quite admirably at the negotiating table. Faced with superior military power and an aggressiveness to go with it, Viceroy

Kishen fobbed Elliot off with "a barren rock with hardly a dwelling upon it" and one that was conveniently separated from the Chinese mainland. As for Elliot, that's exactly what he was demanding, an offshore sovereign sanctuary from where British trade could be conducted free of direct Chinese interference.

But hardly had Commodore Sir J. J. Gordon Bremer raised the flag in the sands of what was to be called Possession Point than the roof fell right in on the deal. Elliot was lambasted by Whitehall for allowing

himself to be conned into a virtually useless piece of real estate, and quickly transferred to an uncivilized backwater of the British foreign service as Consul-General in Texas. Kishen was similarly berated and punished for giving away sovereign Chinese territory, and was hauled to Peking (Beijing) in chains and then banished to Tibet.

EARTH, WIND AND FIRE

Even though the luckless Elliot's successor, Sir Henry Pottinger, was also in favor of establishing Hong Kong as a major trading depot, for all of two and a half years the British Government dismissed it as a worthless embarrassment and unworthy of even being regarded as a British possession. And the island itself certainly offered nothing that would endear it to anyone, let alone the mandarins of Whitehall. In fact it gave the initial impression of being absolutely unsuitable for human settlement.

Within a few months of the flag-raising ceremony a severe fever epidemic gripped the tiny community, forcing it to embark upon its first public works project—a cemetery. Then a violent typhoon roared in and destroyed all its makeshift housing and tore

complete the task that Elliot had failed to do—force the Chinese to open up mainland ports, or a more suitable island, for free trade and compensate. Government for the confiscated opium.

By August 1842 his guns were trained on the key Yangtze River city of Nanking (Nanjing), and the Qing Government was cowed into signing the Treaty of Nanking which gave the British five Treaty Ports, including a rather nondescript coastal weaving and fishing township called Shanghai. Almost a year later, on June 26,

huge merchant men from their moorings in the sheltered harbor. A few days later another typhoon struck, and this one caught Captain Elliot himself — not yet dispatched in disgrace to Texas on a journey from Macau. He narrowly escaped with his life after taking control of the small ship and beaching it on an island. A month later, fire raged through the island's first squatter community built along its western foreshores by Chinese traders, craftsmen and laborers who had already begun pouring over to the island.

Despite these setbacks, Pottinger allowed surveying and land sales to begin as soon as he replaced Elliot, and then sallied north with a British expeditionary force to

1843, Whitehall declared Hong Kong a British colony with Pottinger as its first governor. But it was still a rather reluctant gesture — the assigned role of this new British possession was simply to provide a port "whereat they may careen and refit their ships."

THE COLONIAL GEOGRAPHY

This early history of Hong Kong not only explains its birth, and the struggle, pain and

Tea making OPPOSITE a 5,000-year-old tradition and the indulging of opium ABOVE — the core of the Anglo-Sino trouble in the nineteenth century.

humiliation that accompanied it, but also its geography — for the Hong Kong that exists today is really what those piously aggrieved nineteenth century merchant-soldiers made of it. They first took an island that covered only 68 sq km (26 sq miles) of landspace, with most of that space unsuitable for large-scale development, its 552-m (1,811-ft)-high backbone rising virtually from the water's edge. It had absolutely no natural resources beyond its 44 sq km (17 sq miles) harbor — but the harbor was immediately its most prized and potentially powerful asset.

harborfront through Wanchai and another indent of reasonably flat land at Happy Valley — where another fever epidemic struck its first settlers, driving the British back toward Victoria and instilling all sorts of fears and superstitions in the Chinese. Above Happy Valley, a natural pass through the steep hills provided a vital road through what was named Wongneichong Gap to the island's southern beaches at Repulse Bay and Aberdeen.

As the first road cut through the ocher-colored soil of the hillside the Chinese

Early *gwei lo* development took place along the waterfront of Victoria, or what is now more commonly known as Central District, on the only immediately available skirt of reasonably flat land. Their Chinese camp followers erected their raucous, sprawling, densely packed shanty town further to the west, in what was for many years marked on the maps as Chinatown but is now known as Western District.

As development gathered pace it pushed in two directions, up the steep slopes, or Mid-Levels, of the tallest hill overlooking the harbor, The Peak, and east along the

protested that the British had severed the spine of a dragon that reposed in the hills, destroying the island's *fung shui*, or natural harmony of spirits and elements, and laying the settlement open to great misfortune. They didn't have to look far for the evidence of the dragon's wrath — successive epidemics continued to cut like scythes through the merchant and military ranks, and lawlessness reigned throughout the infant colony, with constant violence, burglary, robbery and piracy. Hong Kong's second major geographical development came in 1860 when, as part of the final settlement of the first Opium War of 1841, the Qing Government ceded Kowloon Point, the mainland wedge of what is now Tsimshatsui, and

The imposing Government House in Upper Albert House, built in 1855.

The Colonial Past

the strategic Stonecutter's Island. This not only gave the colony a bit more elbow room and a mainland foothold but also more effective control of the harbor.

In 1898, having fought the second Opium War to force China to open her doors to trade, the British dictated another deal, this one a 99-year lease in which the present-day geography of Hong Kong was established — the island, the main-land Kowloon district, the hinterland New Territories stretching up to and slightly beyond the Shumchun River, now called the Shenzhen River, and 233 more islands. It gave the colonial government a total 850 sq km (328 sq miles) of territory.

THE HUMAN GEOGRAPHY

Nowadays, it is this aspect of Hong Kong which is the most little-known to outsiders and a constant surprise to them when they get here. Most think of it as simply one island — the bargain-shopping, joss-reeking offshore world of Suzy Wong. Often it's not until they arrive there that they realize how big Hong Kong really is. Aside from the main island and the large rump of territory across the harbor, two of the myriad other islands, Lamma and Cheung Chau, are big enough to support large mixed Chinese and foreign expatriate communities, while Lantau Island is a huge, relatively undeveloped opportunity for future expansion, twice the size of Hong Kong Island itself.

The tenacity with which the early British traders and settlers clung to this "barren" place can be understood when you consider the territory's position within the geography of southern China. It lies at the eastern side of the mouth of the Pearl River, the major access to the sea for the key river of the south, the Xi Kiang, and part of a vast network of waterways that reaches right up into the heart of China. Canton (Guangzhou), the southern gateway to China and its most rapidly modernizing city, lies just over 100 km (66 miles) to the northwest — and this doorstep proximity is now of considerable value to both cities, giving Hong Kong a close, reasonably efficient trading and investment partner, and a source of food, and Guangzhou a ready supply of capital and much-needed consumer technology.

But it is the human settlement of Hong Kong that has really established its present-day geography. Just as the prospect of one billion people confined in 15 percent of the land-space can be regarded as the most fascinating topographical feature of China, Hong Kong's six million population crammed into 10 percent of a relatively infinitesimal 1,070 sq km (328 sq miles) pimple of land has never ceased to amaze the outside world. A decade ago, the urban beehives of the island waterfront and Kowloon were so overcrowded that three square meters (32 sq ft) per person was considered to be an acceptable living space, and the district of Shamshuipo had a population density of 165,000 people per square kilometer (427,000 per square mile) — the highest the world has known.

It is this struggle to fit all its people in that has given Hong Kong its dramatic human topography, the massive high-rise development of its two main urban centers and the satellite towns of the New Territories. And, just as dramatically, the geography has been changed and re-sculpted over the past century in another continuing thrust for more living space — large-scale reclamation of harbor side and seafront land.

ENGULF AND DEVOUR

When the first traders, merchants and soldiers began building the colonial settlement, Queen's Road was their first main thoroughfare on Hong Kong Island, and it ran right along the harbor foreshores. Before the island had even been officially declared a colony, trading depots, warehouses and wharves were being built on reclaimed land on the northern side of the road, and from that point on the waterfront was steadily devoured and the harbor gradually narrowed — by successive waves of development.

As early as 1851, when a fire virtually destroyed the "Chinatown" settlement to the west of Victoria, new land was claimed from the harbor around what is now Bonham Strand to build a new community. Four years later the first reclamation work began along the eastern harbor front, extending the Happy Valley district into the sea. Over the next few years another reclamation project created a *praya* along the Victoria harborfront that pushed Queen's Road back from the water — but by 1890 this new land-space had become so overcrowded and unsanitary that it was overtaken by another big reclamation scheme, and the old *praya* is now Des Voeux Road, deep in the heart of Central District. Successive reclamation schemes extended Kennedy Town and Wanchai into the harbor waters, and "pestilent swamps" on the foreshores of Causeway Bay and the mainland Yaumatei were filled in and quickly turned over to commercial development. Right into the 1920s, the scramble for new land continued — the Wanchai waterfront was pushed further into the harbor, creating the teeming urban tenement area between Hennessy and Gloucester Roads; Kai Tak was extended into the harbor on the mainland side to create room for the colony's early land-based airstrip; and other reclamation work created new harborfront space at Shamshuipo and Laichikok. In the most dramatic reclamation project of all, the runway of Hong Kong International Airport, Kai Tak, was later built entirely on reclaimed land, creating what is virtually a fixed flight-deck in the harbor and, for travelers, one of the world's most awesome arrival and take-off experiences.

By the late 1950s, so much of the harbor front of Hong Kong Island was earmarked for reclamation that engineers began to worry about the effect it would all have on the harbor currents. It took a major research project to settle the fears — a 23-m (75-ft) scale model of the harbor, with electronically operated weirs creating "tides," was constructed at a hydraulic research plant in England. Tests showed where the land could be extended without damaging the colony's most valuable asset.

Since then, the harborfront around Central District has marched on beyond Connaught Road, creating landspace for the General Post Office, City Hall, the former British Forces headquarters, Mandarin and

Furama Hotels and the soaring Jardine House and Exchange Square. In Wanchai, another massive reclamation scheme has doubled its area, creating the harborfront area on which the Academy for the Performing Arts, China Resources Building and Wanchai Stadium now stand. To the east, the Island Eastern Corridor streaks across reclaimed land that has doubled the land-space of North Point, Quarry Bay and Shaukeiwan.

On the Kowloon side, the Kowloon-Canton Railway Terminus, Kwai Chung container port and the huge Tsimshatsui East development all stand on land that was once harbor waters. Out in the New Territories, reclamation has provided much of the land-space for the huge New Towns of Shatin, Tsuen Wan and Tuen Mun. In all, more than 220 sq km (85 sq miles) of extra land has been squeezed from the sea bed over the past century and a half.

And there's more to come. As Lantau Island is developed, easing pressure on the rest of the territory, more land will be reclaimed around its hilly coastline for more high-rise residential and commercial centers. And the geography of Hong Kong will change again. In addition to the Central to Wanchai reclamation already mentioned, a broad strip of reclaimed land west of the Macau Ferry Terminal is radically altering the harbor front face of Western District.

BETWEEN THE MONSOONS

If the struggle for living space has molded much of the topography and character of Hong Kong, the struggle with its distinctive climate has been just as dramatic. The island lies just south of the Tropic of Cancer, which makes it sub-tropical. But it also lies virtually at the point where the southern and northern, or summer and winter, monsoons collide over Southeast Asia — and that has made it a place where only mad dogs and Englishmen could probably have envisaged settling, survived, and developed the huge urban society that it is today. It was Hong Kong's position between the monsoons that brought the British and European traders in the first place. In the days of sail, the huge canvas-laden merchant ships rode the

Hakka women dressed in their traditional headdress are still a frequent sight in the New Territories countryside.

summer monsoons north to the China Coast, stopping over in the "Fragrant Harbour" to take on fresh water and repair any damage before continuing up the Pearl River to Guangzhou. The winter monsoon, its winds originating in the frigid reaches of the Siberian steppes and blowing south right down through China and into the northern Pacific, carried the fleets on their first stage home to the West.

Around March each year, as these mighty wind systems change, the warm southern monsoon meets the cooler, waning

winter monsoon over the South China Coast, and the result is muggy moisture-laden air that blankets Hong Kong, settling in thick clouds over The Peak and the mid-levels of the mountains and drenching everything it touches. The summer months — May through September — see regular and sometimes torrential rains and, during the hottest months in July and August, temperatures soaring to between 27°C and 34°C (81°F and 93°F), along with humidity in the 90s.

Not surprisingly, Hong Kong is the answer to every airconditioning salesman's dream, and its newest urban development, particularly in Central District and Tsimshatsui, seems to reflect the enervating climatic conditions — enclosed walkways and pedestrian flyovers connect many of the big shopping plazas and hotel arcades so that you can scurry from one frosty, blissful air-conditioned haven to another with only an occasional exposure to the sauna outside. From October through December the northern monsoon takes over, its icy winds abating and softening by the time they reach this far south, moderating the climate to pleasant sunny days with 21°C to 25°C (70°F to 77°F) temperatures and a relatively parched 70 percent humidity. From there, January through March is cool, about 14°C to 21°C (58°F to 70°F), and April in the mid-20°C (70°F) range.

But the most fearsome climatic feature that the territory has had to face, and still faces each year, is the typhoon season. These powerful cyclones rear up out of the Pacific south of the Philippines each summer and surge northwards to hurl themselves one after the other at the Chinese mainland. They carry tremendous volumes of rain and winds of up to 200 km (125 miles) an hour and they usually cross the China coast to the east of Hong Kong, lashing the territory with their stormy outer bands. Mercifully, it's only on occasions that they hit Hong Kong head-on.

Two typhoons scored direct hits within months of Commodore Bremer's historic landing in 1841. On Tuesday September 22, 1874, a particular violent one almost devastated the colony, the *Hong Kong Times* recording this vivid description of the disaster: "The rain descended in torrents: the wind blew with the violence of a tempest, the rage of a whirlwind. Vessels staunch and strong were driven about the harbor or on to the shore like children's toy craft. Roofs were torn off as by the hand of a mighty giant; trees were uprooted by the hundreds; rows of buildings were blown down in a moment, many of the inhabitants beings buried in their ruins. The harbor water overflowed on to the Praya dashing aside and carrying away coping stones of tonnes weight. The work of destruction went on without intermission for hours; and it maybe said that there is not a single house in the Colony but what has suffered."

Altogether, 35 huge merchant men were either sunk, driven ashore or badly damaged, along with hundreds of junks and sampans. More than 2,000 lives were lost in Hong Kong and Macau. In the hinterland of Guangdong province, the death toll was an horrific 100,000. And in September 1906 an even more destructive typhoon hit — this one killing 10,000 people in just one and a half hours, sinking or crippling 141 British and European ships and destroying more than 2,000 Chinese craft.

The most recent destructive *tai fung* (big wind) was Typhoon Rose in 1971, which hit the territory head-on with 150-knot winds that actually broke the anemometer and dumped 288 mm (11.23 in) of rain in just a single day. In 1979, when I was living in an apartment block on the seafront at Stanley, Typhoon Hope roared in and I was able to witness firsthand the full fury of these tropical hurricanes.

The winds were so fierce that they shook the nine-story building. The view from the windows was, on the one hand, frighteningly bizarre — a howling, shrieking green blizzard of leaves stripped from the surrounding trees. On the sea front side of the apartment, the view was of raging seas, huge waves crashing over the sea-wall — and a beautiful "staunch and strong" pleasure junk belonging to one of my friends being torn from its mooring and hurled right up on to a beach and dashed to pieces against a brick and concrete public toilet.

But by 1979, Hong Kong had long been dealing with typhoons as an irritating but not necessarily dreaded annual weather disturbance. The territory now has a very advanced and effective early warning system that gives the community plenty of time to batten down for a "big blow". As a typhoon or tropical storm is spawned and begins its northward rampage, it is tracked by weather satellites and reconnaissance planes, and if it looks like coming close to Hong Kong a series of typhoon signals go up.

Signal N° 1 means there's a typhoon building in the region. Signal N°10 means it's going to cross the coast close to or perhaps right over Hong Kong — and by then the entire population has gone home to sit it out. Windows are taped or fitted with storm shutters. Shop fronts and hotel façades

are boarded up. Work sites are battened down to prevent what is now the main danger of these annual visitations — flying building material and debris in the streets. The radio and television network issues constant bulletins on the strength and direction of the storm. For tourists, snug and safe in their hotels, the only danger or inconvenience that a typhoon presents nowadays is the possibility of a delayed departure from the airport or the train and ferry terminals.

Somehow, against all these political and physical odds, Hong Kong has more than

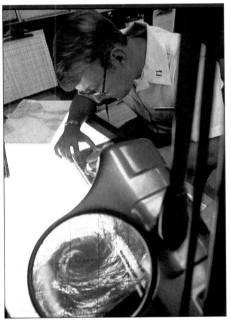

justified the faith and the colonial dream — however antiquated and piratical it may seem to be from these more honorable times — that fluttered with the Union Jack on the flag staff on Possession Point on January 26, 1841. Even more remarkably, that dream has been realized in the face of an even greater challenge — a partnership of what must certainly be the two most distinct and incompatible cultures on earth: the British and the Chinese.

OPPOSITE: Sampans hustle between moored fishing trawlers and junks in picturesque Aberdeen.
ABOVE: A meteorologist interprets radar and satellite pictures of weather disturbances to give advance warning of typhoons.

The Lion
and the
Dragon

THE CULTURAL CONTRAST

Right up until the development boom and sudden political shift of the eighties, an integral feature of Hong Kong's vivid and most unlikely cultural character went on show each Saturday afternoon on a neatly trimmed and jealously exclusive oval of green turf right in the heart of Central District.

There, in the grounds of what is now a public park, Chater Garden, British creams communism was for many years a much-photographed symbol of Hong Kong and the tenuous circumstances in which it existed — a borrowed place living on borrowed time.

But it also represented a much wider contrast, that of two largely alien cultures, British and Chinese, which had somehow managed to settle together and function side by side in Hong Kong, harness their various qualities and skills to a common goal — prosperity — and still retain their own cultural traditions and characteristics.

and white cottons flapped in the damp breezes from the nearby harbor, and the sharp thwack of stitched leather on wooden bats — along with occasional cry of "Owzat!" — gave a faint, waning echo of British imperial tradition and power amid the general downtown clamor of traffic, trams and construction site pile drivers.

This Saturday cricket match, as religious to the British community as Sunday services in St John's Cathedral and the firing of the Noon-Day Gun, took place right under the towering, austere façade and red-lettered Chinese sign of what was then Maoist Beijing's main commercial and political base in Hong Kong, the Bank of China. This striking contrast of cricket and

While the British enjoyed their sedate pursuit of maiden overs and silly mid-ons right below the bastion of Chinese communism, an antique Chinese sailing junk might have been tacking its way ponderously down the harbor, a traditional Chinese funeral might have been wending its way through the packed streets of Causeway Bay or Stanley in a cacophony of clashing cymbals and thundering tom-toms and wailing pipes; or thousands of Cantonese might have been flocking to pay their annual homage to Tin Hau, the Goddess of the Sea, pouring across the harbor in decorated sampans, fishing junks and lighters to Po Toi Island or Joss House Bay, on the southern shore of Clear Water Bay.

If there was any real measure of cultural exchange, it still placed each culture on the fringe of the other. The British and other foreign expatriate groups enjoyed the Tin Hau Festival and other Chinese cultural events just as the Cantonese enjoyed Christmas — but only as spectators, swiveling their camera lenses from the edge of the mêlée, never really to share the spiritual impulse of the occasion. If there was a point at which both cultures could actually find common ground and speak each other's language, it was in the business office or the boardroom, or in the one major "cultural" pursuit in which distinctions are blurred because it is another proving ground of the mutual lust for the fast buck — Hong Kong's paramount and incredibly wealthy gambling institution, horseracing.

Since the redevelopment of Central District and, significantly, since the gradual changing of the guard from Western to Chinese political and commercial power, the Cricket Club has moved to a more roomy but far less dominant site above Happy Valley on Wongneichong Gap Road. But the cultural contrast remains, and thankfully so, for it provides perhaps the most colorful and exciting of all Hong Kong's tourist attractions. And it also bears testimony to the extent to which the Lion and the Dragon have been able to lie down together, and each occasionally get a wink of sleep.

WIND AND WATER

In many respects, Hong Kong's colorful and often dramatic cultural character exists because of the tenacity with which the vastly predominant Cantonese population clings to its Chinese beliefs and traditions. In other respects, it prevails because of a constant and tenacious Cantonese struggle to drive a coach and horses through the slightest loophole or loose clause in the territory's British law.

In the midst of high-tech high-rise development, many Chinese cling, for example, to the traditional *fung shui* ("wind and water"), a mixture of belief, superstition, divination and geomancy which is aimed primarily at placing man in his most harmonious relationship with the physical and

spiritual world about him. When a new apartment is being furnished and equipped, a *fung shui* geomancer may be called in to position the furniture so that it conforms with the *Ch'i* or spiritual breath of the universe. Mirrors are often strategically placed in Cantonese homes to block or deflect the path of evil spirits and influences.

This 4,000-year-old science created havoc and apoplexy with Western attempts to modernize China in the early treaty port days. When the first railway line in China was built between Shanghai and Wusong it

was bought up by Chinese investors and then destroyed for fear that the speed of the trains would disrupt the *fung shui* of thousands of people living along the route. When the first telegraph line was strung between Guangzhou and Hong Kong it aroused Chinese outrage and opposition because in their eyes it would weaken the southern capital by linking it directly with the inauspicious Nine Dragons said to be residing within the earthen bowels of Kowloon.

But even today, homes and offices in Hong Kong are sometimes evacuated and

OPPOSITE: Compelling character make-up of a Chinese opera singer. ABOVE: Incense burner and Buddhist deity.

then exorcised by *fung shui* experts to get rid of "ghosts" and malevolent influences, as happened just a decade or more ago with an entire floor of the Inland Revenue Department. The movie tycoon Run Shaw is said to have consulted *fung shui* geomancers about the site of his huge production center at Clear Water Bay. When the Hong Kong Hilton rented its ballroom for a particularly important land auction, the development company conducting the sale brought in a *fung shui* man to check the ballroom's harmony before bidding began. He decided

that the sale would be a big success if the ballroom doors remained open throughout the proceedings, several windows were blacked out to block evil spirits and the cocktail bar, of all things, was rearranged in an L-shape.

Fung shui enjoyed an upsurge of popularity during the initial New Towns resettlement and development in the New Territories. Any new home that didn't conform to the most propitious *fung shui* siting brought an immediate complaint — and a demand for compensation — from its occupants. It was a constant headache for the hard-pressed planners of the government's Public Works Department, and it may have been motivated less by spiritual concern than the opportunity for base coin, but it also tended to be an effective grassroots defense against a wholesale process of uprooting and re-housing in which human comfort and needs may not on occasions have been given a high priority. It was taken seriously, nonetheless, and especially when it became known that one of the PWD's Chinese departmental

heads responsible for settling *fung shui* issues had himself brought in a geomancer to check the location and surrounding influences of an apartment that he was interested in buying.

It's difficult to say just how deep-rooted these beliefs remain in the present-day mini-Manhattan of Hong Kong, but it's estimated that there are still around 100 geomancers at large and still a fair proportion of the population that will not sign a business contract, take a trip, buy or build a home, select a grave site, bury their dead, or choose a wedding date without consulting the vital signs first.

THE BAMBOO RULE

But whatever its present-day strength, *fung shui* is an interesting cultural phenomenon for the role that it has symbolically played in the division of power in Hong Kong. Just as the British administration often found it prudent and expedient to back down and pay lip service to its beliefs, so it has had to give ground on more major cultural and political issues over the years to accommodate its vastly overwhelming 98 percent Cantonese population and to keep the essential profit-making machinery of Hong Kong running smoothly.

In fact, for an undemocratic colonial government, ruling largely through the personal power of its governor and a non-elected Executive Council (with a partially elected Legislative Council responsible for passing policy into law), the British were reasonably even-handed and non-interventionist in their dealings with the Cantonese, preferring to guide rather than govern and to bend like bamboo rather than stiffen like oak in the face of Chinese pressure. Their most obvious stamp on the society was the civil law and order that allowed the territory to develop to its present extent. They also took a hard and uncompromising line against spitting in the streets and other public places, much to the relief of visitors and young Chinese alike. They discouraged littering, at least in the most popular urban tourist districts. Quite naturally, considering their obsession with "man's best friend," they strictly banned the eating of dogs — or at least driven it underground. They even managed to encourage the Cantonese to form British-style queues for buses, ferries and other public services and facilities — an accomplishment that can only really be appreciated when you experience the mob frenzy and struggle for any essential service throughout China itself.

But for the most part the British allowed, and even encouraged, the Hong Kong Cantonese to be themselves, to freely observe their own traditions, rituals, beliefs and lifestyles. And it is this cultural freedom that has given Hong Kong its unique color and excitement on the one hand — and, on the other, preserved much of the most fascinating aspects of Chinese culture that were dealt a destructive body-blow in the Red Guard rampage of China's Cultural Revolution. The result has been a society that appears to be constructed almost entirely of steel, concrete and glass at first glance, but underneath is a constant and whirling pageant of Chinese social and spiritual life.

WORLD OF THE LIVING DEAD

Alongside the fear of spirits and worship of gods, there lies the most vital of all the spiritual impulses and disciplines of the Chinese — ancestor-worship. Its importance in Chinese culture cannot be overstated — it is the bond, or thread of continuity, that ties their remarkable 5,000-year-old civilization together and has enabled them to keep it virtually intact, and its main traditions, customs, beliefs and rites unchanged, to the present day. It is also the discipline that has maintained the ancient social codes of Confucius, keeping them firmly established as both the base and most powerful creed of the Three Teachings, setting the rules by which the society is structured and leaving individual matters like faith, hope and fortune to the two religions.

The essence of Confucianism, like many other basic Chinese traditions and beliefs, is the pursuit of social harmony. Its abiding principle is this: if people know their allotted place within a society, and are taught to accept it, they'll achieve a measure of contentment; and contentment means peace. The broad picture of Confucianism is a vast

pyramid — peasant or laboring masses at the base and the emperor or ruling elite at the topmost tip — with each teeming class or level in between submitting and kowtowing to the one above.

And there are levels within levels. Not only are wealth, birth and social role and status honored, but age is respected and even revered, filial piety elevates parents close to godliness and, most fascinating of all, ancestors are not only diligently recorded, honored and worshipped — they are placed in the realm of the living dead, an

underworld which is the mirror-image of the living society and in which their comforts and needs must be taken care of as if they were themselves alive.

This reverence for the dead adds its own color and somewhat bizarre ritual to the spiritual pageantry of Hong Kong. At any time in the city streets, people may be seen setting fire to paper replicas of jewelry, furniture, washing machines and, in the years to come, probably micro-computers too — the flames consigning these comforts and

---

OPPOSITE: Decorative lanterns in Buddhist temple. ABOVE: An shop in Western District specializing in ancestor-worship necessities — altars, a variety of incenses and all sorts of paper replicas.

luxuries to needy ancestral spirits in the underworld.

In China, a recent edition of the *Shandong Law Journal* reported the sudden re-emergence of the ancient practice of arranging "marriages" for dead relatives. Incredible as it may seem, the corpses of unmarried women were being sold at high prices in Shandong to parents whose sons had died unwed, the journal said. In one particular case, the body of a girl killed in a road accident had been sold for nearly US$1,000 to a family whose son had died before an arranged married could take place. More than 10 other cases had been reported in one area of the province.

In each instance, symbolic "weddings" had been conducted, in keeping with the Chinese belief that it would provide a marriage partner in the wonder world for a male soul who would otherwise face a lonely afterlife.

WHERE CULTURES CONVERGE

GOD OF FOOLS AND HORSES

Given the extraordinary religious fervor and exuberance of the Cantonese, and, by comparison, the orderly, reserved and almost self-conscious character of the British and their fellow Westerners, it's not surprising that while the two cultures lay quite peacefully alongside each other in Hong Kong they very rarely touched. Most direct contact between the Chinese and *gwei lo* still only takes place in the business arena, and outside office hours they generally both tend to go their own ways. East and West may indeed meet in Hong Kong, but when it comes to actually mingling, East is still East and West is still very much West.

There are some obvious reasons for this. First of all, for most Westerners Hong Kong is a transitory place, and for most Hong Kong Chinese it's a sanctuary beyond which there's no place else they can really go. There's also a history of British and Western social and economic supremacy — and a colonial superiority often expressed in the most racist terms over the years — that

the Chinese have no real inclination to forget or forgive now that they have taken over the reins of power. And when it comes to superiority, there's no civilization on earth that can quite match that of the Chinese when it comes to belief in its own pre-eminence.

In the main, business is their common language and profit their common religion. And if there's a god that embraces both cultures it is a strange Taoist deity called Wong Tai Sin, the guardian namesake of the Wong Tai Sin Temple in Kowloon City — and the patron saint of racing punters!

It says a great deal about Taoism and the Chinese perspective on religion generally that a new god could be created, only as recently as 1973 in fact, to preside over the fortunes of fools and horses. But then, Hong Kong's racing industry is no ordinary one — it is a mammoth business institution that provides the right mix of luck, leisure and profit that gives both the Lion and Dragon cultures an arena in which to meet and mingle. And it is extremely profitable, with its wealth spilling down the sides of its coffers and into various huge community projects to benefit society at large.

THE JOCKEY CLUB'S DOMAIN

The whole industry is operated exclusively by The Hong Kong Jockey Club, which is the largest private employer in Hong Kong. Membership of it is fiercely sought and highly prized. To win the right in the Jockey Club's annual ballot to buy, train and race a horse is to know that you have been decorated with full honors for your distinguished service to Hong Kong.

The Race Tracks
Everything about the Jockey Club's vast domain is bigger, richer and more streamlined than anything like it anywhere else in the world. It operates only two racecourses, one at **Happy Valley** on Hong Kong Island and the other at **Shatin** in the New Territories, but the US$7.6-million Shatin course covers an area of 100 hectares (250 acres) — all of it reclaimed land and — has a capacity of 83,000, the biggest on earth. The equipment and facilities at both tracks are pure state-of-

the-art, featuring fully computerized betting, closed-circuit television and huge in-field video screens which flash late information for punters on the condition of the track, jockey changes and anything else that could possibly shave a half a nose off the anticipated outcome of a race.

Betting

Outside the tracks the club operates 125 off-course betting shops and a telephone betting system that covers 643,000 accounts. There are so many betting combinations available that anyone putting money on a straight win place would be recognized immediately as a rank outsider. There are about 71 race meetings a year — the horses are stood down in the summer months because of the heat, humidity, rainstorms and the threat of typhoons — but the turn-over is enormous. During the 1995/96 season, for example, punters laid HK$80.6 billion in bets with more than 45,000 attending each meeting. An average of HK$1.13 billion was bet on each race meeting and HK$147.2 million per race — a record HK$1.84 billion (over US$235 million) was bet on one day.

Of course, the mainstay of all this wealth is the Hong Kong Chinese — no less than one million of whom are dedicated and devout gamblers who would bet on two flies walking up a wall, and go for the quinella. And this passion for gambling is, in effect, simply an extension of their peculiar interpretation of the term "religion", in which the various gods and goddesses of Taoism and Buddhism and the mystic codes of folklore are thrown in with incense, ancestor-worship, fortune-sticks, calendars, geomancy, drums and gongs to conjure up blessings that are not so much spiritual as purely down to earth — health, happiness and good luck, with the accent on luck.

It is this frantic pursuit of luck that has created the huge racing revenues that, year by year, make an absolute mockery of a report once issued by the Hong Kong Government claiming that gambling was "not conducive to the basic Chinese character." The comment still triggers howls of laughter as the bulging, straining breadths of the racing industry continue to spread.

Among the Jockey Club's current expansion schemes there's a plan to greatly increase the number of telephone accounts, then to introduce accounts to anyone who wants one — all they'll need is a bank guarantee to cover defaults, something like a personal loan account, a banking concept that would probably have you thrown out on your ear if you suggested it to your friendly branch manager back home. The club has introduced a service that just about translates the whole cultural impetus of Hong Kong into one symbolic form — automatic hole-in-the-wall betting machines, very much like banking cash dispensers, into which punters feed their account cards, key in their wager, and then go have a coffee and await the result without actually ever setting foot on the hallowed turf of the Sport of Kings.

Seals and Symphonies

The profits that the Jockey Club makes are so embarrassingly high that millions upon millions of surplus dollars are fed back into the community in the form of donations to medical and health facilities, community service organizations, educational and training institutions and sporting, recreation and cultural facilities. It's another testament to Hong Kong's new awareness of its social role that instead of all the betting losses being blatantly creamed off, as they would have been in the bad old days of *laissez-faire*, the money now pays for seals and symphonies, sports meets and students, and a lot of other things that spell the difference between a society and a ledger sheet. Among the major amenities that the Jockey Club has given Hong Kong are the magnificent Ocean Park complex between Aberdeen and Deep Water Bay, the Olympic standard Hong Kong Sports Institute near the Shatin Racecourse, the Hong Kong University of Science and Technology in Clearwater Bay and the highly successful Academy for Performing Arts at Wanchai. And, without a doubt, endowments like these have added a new richness and variety to Hong Kong's cultural life.

OVERLEAF: Night racing at Happy Valley race-track.

A CULTURAL BALANCING ACT

While the brightly costumed emperors, mandarins and courtesans of traditional Cantonese Opera glide and pirouette about the stage to the accompanying howl and crash of traditional Chinese music, a Beethoven sonata or Bach suite provides the cultural counterpoint in the **Hong Kong Cultural Centre** complex in Tsimshatsui and at City Hall, the **Arts Centre** and the **Hong Kong Academy for Performing Arts**

Crufts-style dog and cat shows, pseudo-English pubs, cricket and rugby football matches, bone china, sterling silver and Home Counties twin-sets in the almost institutionalized Lane Crawford department stores, and many other instances in which Hong Kong's Western cultural whims and fancies have been maintained amidst the sweeping, boisterous, multicolored wash of Hong Kong Chinese life.

The energetic and very efficient Hong Kong Tourist Association (HKTA) puts out regular guides to cultural events in Hong

on Hong Kong Island — and all are freely available for visitors' enjoyment.

For every Chinese folk-dancing display, a whirl of traditional costume and billowing silk, there's a Western ballet performance. For every Chinese puppet show or display of traditional martial arts there's a Western-style cabaret or theatrical drama, the latest Western movie (with Chinese sub-titles) and, occasionally, a locally produced revue sending up the more amusing and bizarre aspects of Hong Kong life and its expatriate community — and the encompassing clash of the Lion and Dragon cultures.

There are Western art and photographic exhibitions, displays by local expatriate batik designers, potters and weavers,

Kong, and for easy day-by-day reference there's the "What's On" section in the South China Morning Post and HKTA's *Hong Kong Diary* and *Hong Kong This Week*, free of charge at their Information and Gift Centres. You can also try the weekly *Hong Kong Magazine*, distributed free at outlets such as book stores, restaurants, bars and cultural centres such as The Fringe Club and Arts Centre which lists anything from belly-dance classes and Shiatsu massage to concerts and theater shows, as well as reviews of restaurants. The free monthly *bc Magazine* has similar listings. If you've got your computer at hand, you can check out bc's website on http://www.netvigator.com/bconline. There are also a couple of other useful websites for information on events and sights to see and much else besides: the HKTA's Wonder Net is on http://www.hkta.org and an 'all-encompassing interactive entertainment guide to Hong Kong' on http://www.webhk.com.

THE SPORTING LIFE

The point at which the two cultures really meet and mingle is in the wide range of leisure sports that are available in Hong Kong — most of them modern and Western and

suits are waterskiing, sailing, windsurfing, snorkeling and skin-diving — all of which are available for the tourist or short-time visitor. Windsurfing, for instance, the new boom sport in Hong Kong, can be arranged by hire at most beach resorts.

Tennis, squash, badminton, snooker and, of course, golf are other Western sports which have become almost a status symbol among the emerging legions of executive-class Chinese and are therefore easily available to visitors. For details, see SPORTING SPREE on page 32–34).

therefore pursuits that have no real link with traditional Chinese life. Hong Kong's teeming beach life, for example, is a Western form of leisure and sun-worship that the Cantonese citizenry have taken to in their many thousands — turning away from their own long-standing tradition in which it was considered quite base and "coolie-class" to be exposed to the sun long enough to get a tan.

The territory's 50,000 or so pleasure craft, ranging from luxury ocean-going yachts and cabin cruisers to small pleasure junks and power boats, are another popular leisure activity to which middle and upper range executive families of both cultures have taken like ducks to water. From there, the main cross-cultural fun-and-sun pur-

So, as with its people, Hong Kong manages to pack a vast amount of culture, leisure and sport into a relatively minuscule area. For the visitor, it means variety, excitement and interest — all the more fascinating for the fact that it all goes on in the shadow of a huge high-tech high-rise metropolis. For the people of Hong Kong themselves, it is another testimonial to the governing spirit of their society: it is living proof that even the Lion and the Dragon can lie side by side if there's profit in it for both of them.

OPPOSITE: Away from the urban clamor and thrusting skyline of Hong Kong, there is a contrast in the tranquillity of some of the best beaches in Southeast Asia. ABOVE: A snooker hall.

The Obsession with Cuisine

TO MOST CHINESE, food is more than just simple taste or sustenance — it is an obsession bordering on religion. Its creed is more than just sensation or indulgence, it is part of a general worship of the body and soul in which diet and certain health-promoting ingredients and tonics are combined with traditional herbal medicine, massage and acupuncture and muscular and breathing exercises to establish a regimen that goes back several thousand years into Chinese history but which we in the West are only now recognizing as the

And like gambling on the horses or windsurfing on the waves, the love of eating well has brought Hong Kong's two cultures happily together at the same table.

If the creed of Chinese food is health, its gospel is variety. It is generally acknowledged that Chinese food is a famine cuisine, its origins going back to the nation's perennial experimentation with all things animal, vegetable and even mineral in the search for enough for its many millions to eat. This gospel, according

"whole treatment" of the physical and mental condition.

This dedication to food — some would say religion — has ensured that Hong Kong has so many restaurants, offering every kind of cuisine, that no visitor or resident can fail to get caught by the culinary attraction.

to the Hong Kong Cantonese, goes like this: "If its back points to heaven, you can eat it." Put a little less reverently, it is the proverbial "seefood" diet: everything you see, you eat.

FROM BRONZE *TING* STEWS TO DRUNKEN PRAWN CAULDRONS

The very earliest preparation of food in China was very much like that of the fur-clad cave-dwelling West — first roasted and then boiled or stewed legs and haunches of meat. But while Western man continued to roast his food over fires, and developed the knife and fork to spear and

Faces of Cantonese culinary extravaganza — the traditional Chinese hot pot ABOVE served in cold weather; and Winter melon soup OPPOSITE LEFT, a popular light soup in summer. Grades and brands of rice — an irreplacable staple in the majority of Southeast Asia and Southern China — are offered in graceful polished casks OPPOSITE RIGHT in typical Hong Kong rice store.

slice the meat from the bone, the Chinese refined the stewing process — casting heavy three-legged bronze pots and cauldrons called *Tings* in which to do it — and arrived at meat that was so tender that it virtually fell away from the bone, requiring only two twigs and nimble fingers to pick it away. Hence the origin of those most unlikely and the most infuriating of all Chinese eating implements, the chopsticks.

While the nets of the food-gatherers were cast wide for more and more ingredients, the cuisine was gradually refined

process of speedy stir-frying. It also meant that food had to be cooked in small, fuel-efficient bite-sized portions, which made the use of chopsticks all the more inevitable.

The generally hot summer climate, and the all-round heat in the south, meant that food could not be kept for long without going bad and perishing, and that meant that the first consideration of the Chinese cook was that the ingredients should be as fresh as the new day. Despite modern-day refrigeration, deep-freezing

by experimentation in the kitchens. If it was possible to eat a snail or a seaslug, it was another thing altogether to actually make it enjoyable, and the cuisine's characteristic refinement of textures, sauces and condiments evolved. The imperial courts and wealthy aristocracy added their important culinary stamp too, encouraging their master chefs to perform great feats of creativity and ingenuity to keep their tastebuds quivering and their senses wallowing in indulgence.

As the cuisine expanded, the harsh limits of the Chinese environment added their say to the way in which it developed. The country's chronic shortage of cooking fuel, for instance, led to the

and chemical preservatives, that principle is still so sacrosanct among the Chinese that it is essentially why fish are kept alive in tanks in the Hong Kong restaurants, right up until it's time for the wok, why tortoises, eels, shrimps and prawns also huddle and twitch in baths until the moment of truth. And if you venture into the incredible hullabaloo and pungent aromas of the Chinese Central Market off Queen's Road Central, right across from the Chinese Merchandise Emporium, you'll see the ultimate in fresh-food preservation — live fish laid out on display for the discerning shoppers, skillfully, surgically scaled, skinned and filleted, with their hearts still beating to prove that as far as fresh goes, there's nothing fresher.

CREATURES GREAT AND SMALL

In all the distinctive cuisines of the world, the tastes and demands of the aristocracy elevated the food from the kitchen to the realm of the gourmet and connoisseur by keeping the best chefs hard at work dreaming up new and more exotic ingredients and more extravagant

ders of culinary courage and discretion and deep into the wild and wonderful animal world about us that television networks spend millions nowadays to present in all its natural, fascinating and endangered glory.

Snakes, eels, civet cats, pangolins (a type of ant-eater), bears, mice, sharks, lizards, rice-birds, sparrows, pigeons, sea-slugs, monkeys, dogs, cockroaches, even elephants — they all filed into the enormous ark of doom of Chinese cuisine. Some were prepared and eaten entirely, others con-

ways of cooking and serving them. But what was honeyed larks' tongues to the French and Italians was kid's stuff to the Chinese.

In China, the exceptionally jaded tastes of the emperors and their courts, and the abiding search for new things to eat, took the cuisine way beyond the normal bor-

tributed certain organs and appendages to particular dishes — the shark its distinctive fin, the elephant's trunk and the hapless bear's paw. In one renowned dish, now strictly banned in Hong Kong and unlikely to be found even in China, the brains of monkeys were spooned straight from their opened skulls in a particularly uninviting repast that was supposed to boost, among other things, the sexual potency of the banqueters.

This distinctive Chinese passion for all things wild and wonderful reached such outlandish proportions that at one latter-day stage a Chinese professor in the United States satirized it with a list of eight ultimate delicacies without which

ABOVE: Dried seafoods on sale in "Chinatown" at the Western District — shark's fin, scallop, fish maw, squid, shrimp and oysters — the essence of traditional preserved foods that have survived the modern-day development of home refrigeration. Live offering from snake shop OPPOSITE in back-street market, for the bile duct or preparation of "hot" snake soup.

The Obsession with Cuisine

no gourmet banquet of ancient times was worth the tablecloth it was served upon. He came up with deer's tail, ape's lips, unborn baby jaguar, camel's hump, bear's paw, elephant's trunk, fish tail and monkey head.

In the close bonding that developed from their earliest days between Chinese food and traditional medicine, a vast zoology of other animal life contributed to tonics, restoratives and aphrodisiacs aimed at the essential principle of both diet and medicine — balancing deficiencies in the vital yin and yang, or aggressive-passive male-female influences within the physical constitution. Fox's bezoar, deer horn and powdered rhinoceros horn are among the more well known ingredients of traditional medicine, not only for their use but for the toll they've taken of wildlife around the world. Even among the more acceptable, domesticated food-giving animals, the organs were treasured as much as the meat itself for their health-giving properties. The bull's heart helped promote cardiac strength, for instance. Its testicles were said to do wonders for the flagging virility. The bile duct of the snake, taken warm from the newly slaughtered body and emptied into a glass of wine or brandy, is said to help cure eye disorders and improve vision.

The snake is among certain creatures whose flesh is said to have "hot" as opposed to "cooling" properties, and is still eaten in winter-time in Hong Kong as an invigorating tonic food. It's among a considerable number of meat-giving creatures that are shunned by the more fastidious, and traditionally better-fed Westerners, who tend to regard it as the sustenance of savages. Dog-meat is also a warming food and can be found on market-stalls throughout southern China. Here in Hong Kong, the British and European community, infatuated with "man's best friend" and staggering under the weight of their heavy beef roasts, have strictly forbidden this outrageous practice, but it goes on in secrecy all the same.

To give the Chinese chefs their due, creativity and experimentation have not atrophied in this age of chain restaurants

and fast-food fads. Every once in a while, a new culinary technique or dish appears on the tables somewhere, is quickly copied through-out the restaurant world and adds to the vast 5,000-year-old compendium of the Chinese cuisine. In the 1970s, the new culinary craze was "sizzling" dishes — both Chinese and Western recipes served up spitting and spluttering on super-hot iron pans, with the diners lifting the skirts of the tablecloth all around the table to screen themselves from the flying oil and fat. In the 1980s, another

new culinary delight called "drunken" prawns hit the scene, and one that embraces the most cherished principles of Chinese food — absolute freshness, taste sensation and a touch of the bizarre.

The prawns, huge ones, are brought to the table live and twitching in a lidded glass bowl. A bottle of Chinese dark rice wine is poured in through a hole in the lid. The prawns cavort about in it, getting riotously sozzled and then monstrously so — leaping and threshing so violently that you fear they're going to smash their way right out of the bowl. Finally, they succumb, as all hopelessly inebriated drinkers do, to supine unconsciousness, and are then lifted out one by one and dropped

The Obsession with Cuisine

into boiling soup stock. If your nerves have been sturdy enough to follow the process to its end, the result is a juicy, deliciously marinated taste.

GOD LOVES A GOURMET

If food is a religion to the Chinese, restaurants are more than just an occasional place of worship, they are a devotional way of life. The Hong Kong Cantonese spend nearly as much on eating as they do on

no-one else around. In Hong Kong it performs yet another very important social function — with living space so limited, and most Chinese apartments so cramped, the restaurant is the obvious place in which to entertain family and friends. With business the other major religion, it's inevitable that the restaurant will provide the main entertaining and even negotiating forum.

Compared with most Western restaurants and the Western etiquette for dining out, all but the most high-priced Chinese

housing, and this in a relatively confined property market in which the lack of space keeps apartment rents and prices at an astronomical level, possibly the highest in the world outside New York's Manhattan. More than that, they spend most of their money eating out.

The restaurant satisfies many distinctive Chinese needs. It is the cathedral wherein the great cuisine is paid homage — and, naturally, there's a Chinese saying that sums up this point: Heaven loves the man who eats well. It is also a community meeting place in which another of their racial characteristics is taken care of: if you ask a Chinese to define loneliness, he'll tell you it's when there's simply

eating places are a natural extension of the home. Most Western establishments are for adults only — the average Hong Kong Chinese restaurant is for the whole family. On Sundays, particularly, when most Cantonese businessmen and office workers shrug off their suits and ties and devote their entire attention to family life, their grandparents and their smallest children crowd with them into the casual carefree bedlam of a *dim sum* dining hall or a full-blown multi-story eating palace. While most Western restaurants follow the bistro style of quiet dignity and taste, in keeping with the characteristic Western need for social privacy, the Chinese restaurant is a place in which the ambiance is measured in terms of the number of people who can be packed in at any one time, the noise they make, the gusto with which the food is consumed, the number of children darting and laughing between the tables, the mess that's made and the number of staff who are worn off their feet trying to keep up with the clamor.

Amid the pandemonium, the most sober and conscientious decisions are made, for no Chinese worth his birthright will order a dish without first discussing it with everyone around him, then the waiter,

mentation began, developing three main categories of the beverage plain unfermented green tea, semi-fermented and "fruity" olongs and stronger, Indian-style black tea. Add to these the various herbal blends jasmine, chrysanthemum etcetera and the range is as wide and exotic as that of wine and liquor.

As for hard drink, the Chinese prefer beer, rice wine and cognac with their meals, and they observe a fairly strict control and etiquette in which alcohol complements a meal but very rarely becomes the main

then the manager if need be, and even the chef if it comes to that. No dish is ordered without consideration for the others that are to go with it, for while the cardinal feature of the Chinese cuisine is its variety, the cardinal rule is the right combination of foods, recipes, tastes, textures and even colors that make up a perfectly composed meal.

Tea is the main beverage, with myriad tastes and blends of its own that have evolved over some 5,000 years — a history as long as that of the food itself. Again, Chinese tea has medicinal origins; the stimulative properties of the lusty leaf were first regarded as a tonic. It was centuries after its discovery that experi-

course. Although Chinese history celebrates the inebriated poet and writer, and the artist's propensity for strong drink as something quite understandable, extreme drunkenness is frowned upon and you will not often see a Hong Kong Cantonese in his or her cups. You'll know they've had a drink — their faces usually go blood-red on two glasses. But the drinking is done in concert with the food, glasses raised in toast in a dozen different celebrative excuses as each course reaches the table, the food effectively absorbing and neutralizing much of the

The incredible variety of fresh fish OPPOSITE, myriad vegetables and fruits ABOVE at Hong Kong's markets.

alcohol intake. Boisterous drinking games are sometimes played, but they rarely go beyond the happy-go-lucky upswing of drinking. When the meal is finished the evening is over. The games cease, the laughter ends and everyone almost abruptly gets up and goes home.

THE REGIONAL TASTES

The main contributions to Chinese cuisine have come from the imperial courts and the

Dowager, Ci Xi, the last effective imperial ruler of China, is said to have dreamed one night of steamed buns filled with pork. They appeared on the imperial menu the next day and have been popular ever since. As the expanding Moslem empire pushed the Islamic faith down the Silk Road into northwest China, destroying the idolatry face of Buddhism as it went, the Moslem cuisine, which included lamb and beef kebabs and its flat, unleavened bread, joined the Chinese table. The Mongolians, sweeping down through the Great Wall to

country's principal ethnic groups and regions. The emperors themselves had immense kitchens manned by anything up to 4,000 chefs, assistants and service staff to feed and banquet their legions of retainers, courtiers, administrators and advisors, extended families and concubines. Pony express teams rushed fresh seasonal fruits and delicacies from all parts of the country. Occasionally, the imperial whim added new recipes to the burgeoning compendium of the cuisine: the infamous Empress

Traditional herbal medicine shop ABOVE offers tonics and cures that call upon thousands of years of medical research. OPPOSITE: Dried sea horses feature among range of traditional products of herbal medicine store.

wreak the most terrifying destruction and wholesale slaughter that China has ever known, introduced the hot-pot dishes that have also been part of China's regional tastes since the reign of the powerful but short-lived Yuan dynasty.

But it is the culinary customs and creativity of the various regions, based on distinctive regional foodstuffs and local climates, that has contributed the most character to the vast variety of the cuisine. Nowadays, the cuisine has been categorized under four main regions or schools — the North (Hebei, Shandong and Henan), the East (Jiangsu and Zhejiang), the South (largely Cantonese) and the West (Sichuan and Yunnan).

The Northern, or Beijing style is based largely on wheat-flour breads, dumplings and noodles, the staple of the comparatively austere temperate-frigid climate, and features the barbarian foods of the northern and northwestern tribes — the mutton, lamb and beef of the Moslems and Mongolians, served with scallions, leeks, pickled cabbage and cucumbers. But against this rather mundane culinary backdrop, the richness and variety of Shandong cooking adds regional splendor. The Shandong chefs were the maestros of the imperial courts in

juices, and so rich that at one stage in its history its leading chefs were accused of preparing "unnecessarily elaborate dishes and overly opulent banquets." Although Shanghai itself was only a small, non-descript fishing port until the British forced it open as a trading concession, Hangzhou had a far more illustrious history as the capital of the hard-pressed but culturally glorious Southern Song dynasty, and its contribution to the Eastern cuisine has been aristocratic and quite considerable. Nanjing (Nanking), west along the Yangtze River,

Beijing, famous for their delicate sauces and ingredients stir-fried with vegetables, crab, shrimp, chicken or meatballs. Of all the ingredients, none rank in stature or popularity with that abiding star of the Northern cuisine, the Beijing duck, with its golden brown crispy-thin basted slices of skin and flesh wrapped in unleavened pancakes with salty plum sauce and fresh scallions.

Eastern, or Shanghai cuisine is noted for its chicken and seafood dishes, especially fish, shrimp and crab, its rich tastes and its extravagant use of garlic and sesame oil. In fact, it's the richest and oiliest of the regional culinary styles, so oily that steamed bread is served instead of rice to soak up the

has added its famous smoked meats. As for Shanghai, it has contributed an annual culinary fever, triggered in the autumn months, when gourmets and common diners go wild over seasonal Shanghai hairy crab.

The Western cuisine, originating from the mountainous, misty Sichuan province, is the spiciest of all the regional types, reflecting both the need for "heating" foods in the damp and comparatively chilly climate and the character of the people. The citizens of Chongqing and Chengdu like to describe themselves as the fiery "Latins" of China. The cuisine is certainly hot — as one noted expert on Chinese food described it, the "poor sister of the lot, but one with a slightly vicious tongue." Green and red chillies, garlic, ginger and peppers are liberally used to spice up the food. A lot of oil is used too. The effect with most dishes, Sichuan prawns and pork and wind-dried beef recipes for example, is a reasonably mellow jolt to the senses. But anyone who's had the courage to try the province's common *pièce de résistance*, Sichuan Hotpot, will tell you that for much of the meal you can only nod your appreciation (or mute shock) — you're too speechless and tear-stricken to do anything else.

It is Southern, or Cantonese food that is the widely known, most popular and undoubtedly the supreme regional cuisine of China. It is born of the crowded, richly fertile sub-tropical lands and waterways of the south-eastern provinces, and it offers an absolute wealth of foodstuffs and ingredients — chickens, ducks, pork, geese, pigeons, prawns, crabs, lobsters, along with a similar variety of vegetables, tropical fruits and melons. It is recognized as the lightest of the regional cuisines, with particularly wide use of the stir-fry technique; and it's also noted for its combinations of meat and fish and other seafood, and meat dishes pepped up with oyster or lobster sauces.

Another specialty is red roast pork, comparable with the finest and tastiest cold cut recipes of the West. But its most renowned specialty, a sub-cuisine of its own, is its *dim sum*, or "touch the heart" delicacies, mainly light bite-sized steamed or fried pork, prawn, beef or squid recipes usually cooked in pasta jackets or bean-curd skin and taken with tea from breakfast time, through lunch and into the early afternoon.

Dim sum tea-houses are among the biggest, most ornate, most popular and most packed of all the restaurants in Hong Kong. To lunch at one of them you have to get there very early not long after 11:00 AM — otherwise you'll join crowds of hopefuls standing around in the raucous dining rooms pressing against the crowded tables and waiting for the lucky ones to finish their meals and leave. When you finally manage to grab a table, the various delicacies are brought around on trolleys, many of them in bamboo steaming baskets. You choose whatever catches your fancy and when the meal is over the check is calculated from the number of empty baskets. In some more modern *dim sum* palaces the dishes are ticked off a card.

Some of the *dim sum* teahouses, depen-doing on locations, offers discount on *dim sum or* tea free of charge, sometimes both, after 3 PM up to 5 PM. For a list of recommended restaurants, refer to THE GAL-LOPING GOURMETS in YOUR CHOICES chapter starting on pages 86.

Chinese cuisine includes the preparation of traditional delicacies like bird's nests ABOVE here meticulously cleaned in a Western District restaurant. Ornate brass urns OPPOSITE offer herbal teas that are taken as much for restorative as stimulative effects.

Hong Kong Island and Kowloon

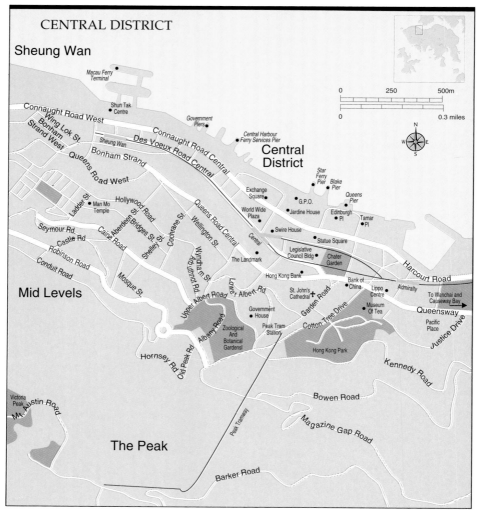

CENTRAL DISTRICT

Sheung Wan

Central District

Mid Levels

The Peak

HONG KONG ISLAND

CENTRAL DISTRICT WATERFRONT

All roads in Hong Kong lead from Central District, the financial and bureaucratic hub of the territory.

All the important action takes place there, the major board rooms of the business world clustered around this humming powerhouse of key banks, the combined stock exchanges, the huge office blocks and the most established of the big business hotels.

Central District begins on its waterfront, at the foot of its high-rise office skyline, at the Star Ferry Terminal from where the packed harbor ferries have labored faithfully for nearly 50 years to and from the "other side." Since the Cross-Harbour Tunnel and MTR went into operation, the harbor ferries have become more of a sedate and scenic short harbor cruise than a vital transport link, but they're still packed on each trip and they give visitors and residents alike a chance to relax and catch their breath in the constant urban clamor. And a first-class trip still costs only HK$2, the cheapest scenic cruise in the world.

OPPOSITE Junk passes Exchange Square providing a contrast to Central District's stark architectural wonder.

Alongside the ferry terminal stands the General Post Office, a huge edifice that is nonetheless dwarfed by the towering **Jardine House,** Hong Kong's pioneer skyscraper which, when it was first built, sank slightly on its reclaimed harbor foundations, and with startling results — the minute shift made thousands of small tiles decorating the building's façade pop off and endanger pedestrians below. Protective nets had to be strung around the tower to avoid people being brained. It has since been safely reclad.

Adjacent to Jardine House, **Exchange Square**, home of the nerve-center of Hong Kong's business world, the Stock Exchange of Hong Kong, soars up in a spectacular cliff-face of curved glass — and here you can start your tour of Central District, which is compact enough to be explored on foot.

As already mentioned, the covered pedestrian overpass alongside Exchange Square will take you in two directions—one going straight ahead across the roaring stream of traffic on Connaught Road into **World-Wide Plaza** and **Swire House** and to the temperature-controlled shopping atrium of **The Landmark,** and the other west along the harborfront side of Connaught Road passing the vast Central Reclamation area, site of the new Hong Kong Central MTR station (linking Hong Kong Island to the new Chek Lap Kok Airport), and ending at the twin silver towers of the **Shun Tak Centre**, home of the **Macau Ferry Terminal,** and the beginning of Western District.

Before the Macau Ferry Terminal, another walkway crosses Connaught Road into the **Hang Seng Bank Building** and continues over Des Voeux Road to the top floor of Central Market. At the end of that walkway you'll find the world's longest covered outdoor escalator (800 m or 2,620ft) running above street level up Cochrane Street, across Hollywood Road, up Shelley Street to Robinson Road in the Mid-Levels, then making its final ascent to Conduit Road. The escalator is only one-way though, going down in the mornings until around 10:00 to 10:30 AM then up until 10:00 PM. Travel time is around 20 minutes.

Chinatown

Veteran residents of Hong Kong still chuckle now and then over an American visitor who once hit town for the first time and immediately asked: "Where's the Chinatown?" But there is, in fact, a "Chinese" neighborhood, Western District, beyond the Shun Tak Centre, known as that not for its particularly traditional Chinese character but because very few foreigners have moved into it over the years.

Hong Kong's earliest land surveys and maps named it "Chinatown" because it was where the first hordes of immigrant Cantonese, flooding across from the mainland, set up their mat shed homes and shops. Although the burgeoning office development in Central is now pushing into it, with

more and more companies attracted by the lower rents, it is still a district in which much of the old Chinese character has survived.

Its stores are strictly Chinese, many of them selling Chinese provisions, rice, tea, herbal medicines, clothing and textiles and practical arts and crafts that are definitely not on sale just for tourist mantel-pieces, and they've retained a great deal of their traditional style and decor — old swishing ceiling fans and inner gloom while the modernized boutiques of Central glitter with decorative chrome and plate glass.

Of all the retail and residential districts of Hong Kong Island it is the most inscrutable, and well worth exploring. The open, heaped wooden barrels of Western's rice stores and strange and odorous dried animal organs and vegetation of its herbal medicine shops squat below packed tenements from which pet finches twitter and sing from rattan cages hung outside the windows. In the provisions stores, amid a planned chaos of dried foodstuffs and mounds of fresh fruit, you can still see fresh eggs being checked against naked light bulbs to ensure they're not fertilized, and "Thousand Year Eggs" being unearthed from their chemical burial mounds where they've been cured in alkaline ash for not a thousand years but maybe a few hundred days, turning their whites

ABOVE Cross-harbor ferry passes high-tech façade of the Victoria Hotel and Shun Tak Centre.

brown and yolks green, and their taste slightly metallic and very tart.

The residents of Western District reflect the character of the area itself — conservative, traditional in pursuit and taste, clinging with great dignity to that which the heady and progressive pace of change in Hong Kong has allowed them to salvage from their 5,000-year-old culture. But it won't remain that way forever. Already, the district's skyline is sprouting commercial offices, and along its harborfront one of the newest major reclamation schemes is about to mushroom with new development, matching the growth of the remarkable **Macau Ferry Terminal,** with its shopping mall and huge jetfoil pens — looking for all the world like a space age German U-boat depot. Opposite here, on the corner of Connaught Road and Morrison Street you'll find **Western Market**, a reconstructed 1858 Edwardian building, selling mainly souvenirs and fabrics, along with a Chinese restaurant on the top floor. Nearby in Man Wa Lane there are rows of stalls selling traditional soapstone chops, or seals. If you want them to, the craftsmen will translate your name into Chinese characters and engrave it on the seal. They make interesting souvenirs and are not expensive. From there wend your way through the streets and alleys of shops selling anything from batteries, electrical products and cheap clothing to funeral offerings, snakes, herbal medicines and teas and one-man printer stalls — where a business card or the like can be set up quickly in movable type and printed on a hand-operated platen press — until you reach "Cat Street" flea-market and antique shops and Man Mo Temple at the end of Hollywood Road.

Man and Mo

The 1840s **Man Mo Temple,** with its ornate green tiled roof, bell tower, smoke tower and main hall of prayer, is dedicated to the God of Civil Servants, Man Cheong, and a famous second century warrior, Kwan Kung, or Mo, since deified as the God of War, and guardian deity of pawnshops and curio dealers for good measure.

In typical Chinese fashion, the temple celebrates war, peace and commerce, and is a sacred place for Buddhists and Taoists alike — a prime example of the cultural exchange, or mutual "borrowing" of each other's gods, that made it possible for both religions to exist in harmony rather than confront each other in China. Being on the edge of Western District, Man Mo is a "working" place of worship, not a tourist attraction, and this has to be kept in mind when you're visiting.

In the main palace, you'll find huge incense coils hanging from the ceiling, each one donated by a worshiper and, as they smolder and smoke for anything up to two weeks, symbolically broadcasting prayers and pleas to the gods. As for the deities themselves, garish, richly costumed and blackened images of Man and Mo sit together on the main altar, and in front of them their tools of trade — a pen for Man, the scholarly deity, and an executioner's sword for Kwan Kung, symbolic of his own execution in the fierce intrigues of his time. "Years ago, the sword of every public executioner used to be kept in the local Kwan Kung temple," says *Temples*, by Joyce Savidge (Hong Kong Government Publications), one of the most informative and brightly illustrated guides to the territory's temple trail. "After an execution the presiding magistrate would always call at the temple to worship — and to make sure that the ghost of the criminal didn't follow him home."

MID-LEVELS

From Man Mo Temple, you can pop into one of Hong Kong's newest museums: the **Museum of Medical Sciences** (2549-5123. This is one of the first museums in the world to compare traditional Chinese and Western approaches to medicine. It's housed in the former Old Pathological Institute, an historic red brick building at 2 Caine Lane, Mid-Levels, just up Ladder Street from Man Mo Temple. Alternatively, continue up Hollywood Road or more antiques and curios. Here you can either break your journey and go back down to the shops in Queen's Road Central or hop on the escalator for a Mid-Levels tour. If you decide on the latter, as you go up the stretch from Caine Road to

HONG KONG ISLAND

Kowloon

Tsimshatsui

Cross-Harbour Tunnel

Junk Bay

Lei Tue Mun

Victoria

Harbour

Central District

Victoria

Causeway Bay

North Point

Tai Koo Shing

Shaukeiwan

Chai Wan

Cape Collinson

Big Wave Bay

Shek O

Mt Davis

Peak District

▲ Victoria Peak

Pok Fu Lam

▲ Mt Kellett

Happy Valley

Tai Hang

Jardine's Lookout ▲

▲ Mt Parker

Mt Collinson

D'Aguilar Peak

Aberdeen Country Park

Aberdeen Reservoir

Wong Chuk Hang

▲ Mt Nicholson

Wongneichong Gap

Tai Tam Reservoirs

Tai Tam Country Park

Tai Tam Road

Wah Fu

Aberdeen

Ap Lei Chau

Ocean Park

Deep Water Bay

Repulse Bay Road

Repulse Bay

Middle Island

Chung Hom Wan

Chung Hom Kok

East Lamma Channel

Lamma Island

Yung Shue Wan

N
W E
S

0   1   2Km

0   0.6   1.2 miles

Mosque Street you'll see on your left the old Jamia Mosque with its striking green-and-white minaret. Reaching Robinson Road, a short walk west takes you to Ohel Leah Synagogue, now integrated into a massive high-rise residential development. Built in 1902, it's the only surviving synagogue in Hong Kong, and China. Services are held daily, and for more information (2801-5442. Back on the escalator, take the last stretch to Conduit Road.

At this point you have two choices — walk directly back down the steps running alongside the escalator to Central, or walk east to the start of Conduit Road to a path that will take you straight into the Zoological and Botanical Gardens, with its elegant pink flamingos, Mandarin ducks, peacocks and other exotic birds, along with orangutans, gibbons and other animals. In the early mornings the gardens are a popular meeting place for people practicing *tai chi*, the ancient, disciplined ballet-like series of martial and breathing exercises that tone up the mental and physical constitution. From the gardens you'll get a good view of the former Government House directly below. Once the official residence of the British Governor, the building was erected in 1855 and features an interesting tile-roofed tower added for observation by the Japanese occupation forces when they seized Hong Kong in World War II.

AROUND CENTRAL DISTRICT

Exiting out of the gardens, walk down Garden Road to St John's Cathedral, a beautiful old church built in the late 1840s and constructed in the shape of a cross from bricks brought from Canton (Guangzhou). It combines early English, Gothic and Norman architecture. Services are held daily. For information (2523-4157. Through the church grounds, Battery Path leads you back down to Queen's Road Central where you're within easy striking distance of shops, hotels, Lan Kwai Fong, the trams and the MTR, and Statue Square. Around this

roughly ornamental pedestrian mall stand the two most striking contrasts of tradition and the twenty-first century Hong Kong — the Hongkong Bank and the Legislative Council Building.

"Beam me up, Scottie... ."
On one side of Statue Square, the arched colonial stone architecture of the Legislative Council Building (formerly the Supreme Court) recalls the days of drum tattoos and musketry, cabin trunks and tuxedos, the reign of the great ocean liners and flying boats, gin slings and fox-trots and all the other trappings and trimmings of the "white man's burden." And right across Chater Road, parked like a visitor from outer space between the headquarters of Standard Chartered Bank and the old Bank of China, stands the incredible, futuristic new headquarters of the Hongkong Bank (more popularly known by its traditional name, the Hongkong and Shanghai Banking Corporation).

There's nothing quite like this astonishing edifice of high-tech industrial architecture anywhere in Asia, and probably anywhere else in the world, and nothing else has aroused the sort of passions that still reverberate through the Hong Kong business community. Some people consider it aesthetically imprudent and even downright ugly, and certainly not the sort of image that a banking institution as traditional as the Hongkong and Shanghai should project. Personally, I take my hat off to the Hongkong Bank for breaking so radically with tradition. It's a courageous design, and every bit as brilliant as that other most controversial post-war architectural project, the Sydney Opera House in Australia. Every time I look at it, I'm reminded of the creative ingenuity that went into the sets of the industrial space colonies in Sean Connery's thrilling science fiction movie, *Outland*.

As you stand and study it, or beam yourself up the escalators into its glassed bowels, you can almost imagine the stairways retracting behind you — the rocket engines whining and dust swirling prior to T-minus 00.00.00 and lift-off. It then takes only a slight further stretch of the mind to consider that all this radicalism is simply a supreme

The twenty-first century Hong Kong — striking contrasts of colonial Legislative Council Building in front of the Statue Square and Hongkong Bank, the new Bank of China Building and Lippo Centre.

act of prudence on the Hongkong Bank's part, and quite in keeping with the Hong Kong tradition of hedging all bets — it's obviously designed to pack up and blast off to another safe tax haven should there be any real threat to free profit-making now that Beijing has taken over.

Next door to the bank, on the 11th floor of the old Bank of China Building you'll find the **Tsui Museum of Art** (2868-2688, displaying more than 2,000 pieces of Chinese antiquities including ceramics, bronze and carved wood and ivory furniture. Heading east to the meeting point of Queensway and Garden Road, you can study China's answer to the symbolic power of the Hongkong Bank's headquarters — the **Bank of China's** own gigantic 70-story 315-m-(1,033-ft)-high landmark with a soaring cubist-style design close to the existing limit of science fiction imagination. Nearby, the colonaded facade of the **Lippo Centre** and the sheer gargantuan size of **Pacific Place** are there to remind us all that Hong Kong is still a thriving international financial hub, despite 1997's change of ownership.

Down on the waterfront, **Edinburgh Place** looks almost dumpy and mundane in comparison with the Hongkong Bank. Nearby, you'll find the stately **City Hall,** the venue for much of Hong Kong's regular cultural activity.

Tea and Tapestry
In Hong Kong Park on Cotton Tree Drive you'll find **Flagstaff House,** a renovated 1940s colonial building with a distinct Greek neoclassic-style to it. Formerly home of the Commander of the British Forces, the building now houses the **Museum of Teaware** (2869-0690, featuring exhibitions of Chinese tea, porcelain and pots and much of the tea-making equipage from the latter centuries of this 5,000-year-old culture.

For more Chinese relics, the Hong Kong **University Museum & Art Gallery** (2859-2114 on Bonham Road, has an interesting exhibition of Yuan dynasty bronzeware, artifacts from the Warring States and Indian Buddhist sculptures. To get there take bus

N° 3 from Edinburgh Place, or N° 23 from Causeway Bay.

For more walking jaunts, HKTA sells an excellent booklet called *Central and Western District Walking Tour.* It tells you where to go to find the best shopping and eating, most interesting streets, main tourist attractions and facilities and has accompanying illustrations and a map.

TO THE PEAK

A short stroll up Garden Road to Lower Albert Road — just past St John's Cathedral — will take you to **St John's Building** on the other side of the road where, at its base, you'll find the lower terminal of what is quaintly referred to as the "funicular railway" the cable-operated Peak Tram (alternatively, you can take the free, topless double-decker bus from Star Ferry). Climbing smoothly up a rather disturbingly sheer series of hillsides, so sheer in some places that you have to stand at a 45-degree angle to move from your seat, it'll take you 397 m (1,323 ft) up the 554 m (1,817 ft) **Victoria Peak** that dominates Hong Kong Island — and to one of the most breathtaking views anywhere in the world. (See TOP SPOTS for more on the tram).

In the more official colonial days gone by, The Peak was strictly for the folks who lived on the hill, the measure of one's business or bureaucratic success being how close you could reside to the top. It's still Hong Kong's paramount status symbol, and so too are the fine, comparatively sprawling mansions and homes that nestle in the folds of the upper slopes and right along its highest ridges — despite the simply beastly spring and early summer weather when the humidity blankets much of it in impenetrable cloud.

In 1995, the old Peak Tower was torn down and replaced the following year by a somewhat controversial, HK$400 million seven-story complex in the shape of an upturned bowl, designed by British architect, Terry Farrell. This new **Peak Tower** contains not only the tram terminus but also a major entertainment centre, including restaurants and shops, a Dragon Train computer-operated ride through Hong Kong's history, a

Panoramic view of Hong Kong Island and Kowloon from the Peak.

motion-simulated Peak Explorer ride and a branch of the popular Ripley's Believe It or Not! Museum (see FAMILY FUN page 52 for details).

Adjacent is the ultramodern **Peak Galleria**, housing the chic **Café Deco Bar & Grill**, up-market shops, an indoor fountain and an underground car park. Miraculously, **Peak Café**, which was originally built as a sedan chair shelter in 1901, still stands, but only because there was such a public protest against developers' plans to replace it.

From the terminus a pathway (Lugard and Harlech roads) circles the peak like a collar, and a one-hour stroll gives you dramatic panoramic views of the entire harbor and its twin urban beehives, along with the islands of Lantau, Cheung Chau and Lamma. Another path (Mt Austin Road) takes you right up to the summit for an even more dramatic 360-degree view, and on a clear day you'll be able to see the islands in the south and the mountains in the New Territories.

WANCHAI AND CAUSEWAY BAY

This crowded, high-rise tourist corridor begins on the eastern side of the Admiralty and Pacific Place complexes where the glassed edges of the business citadel soften into the glowing crimson and gold of Wanchai's neon-packed entertainment district. As with all other urban areas of Hong Kong, getting there is easy — you can take the MTR from Central or Admiralty, and take a look at the world's biggest and most crowded connecting underground concourse at the same time, or you can take a taxi from the Star Ferry, approaching Wanchai along the harborfront motorway, Harcourt Road, or you can allow yourself another of Hong Kong's traditional and slightly more sedate experiences and go there by tram.

For a flat fee of HK$1.20 these grinding, rumbling double-decker antiques shuttle back and forth all day and late into the night right along the northern corridor of Hong Kong Island, linking its western and eastern extremities from Kennedy Town in the west, through Central, Wanchai, Causeway Bay and Taikoo Shing and Shaukeiwan in the

east. While they labor and clang their way through the dense urban traffic above ground, the MTR streaks along virtually the same route below. A few years ago the 93-year-old system was earmarked for the chop, but they're such faithful work horses, still carrying many thousands of passengers a day, and they're such an abiding symbol of Hong Kong, that the planners backed down in the face of the fierce public protest that was bound to follow.

Starting at Wanchai's waterfront, at the beginning of Harbour Road, you'll find the **Hong Kong Academy for Performing Arts** and the **Hong Kong Arts Centre.** Most cultural events are held in the evenings, but during the day the Arts Centre in particular has regular art exhibitions. Opposite, an entire block houses the integrated **Hong Kong Convention Centre,** the **Grand Hyatt Hotel** and the **New World Hotel.** The Hong Kong Convention Centre's dramatic new Extension out into the harbor is now one of the most eye-catching features of Hong Kong's harborfront and skyline, with a distinctive sculptural curved roof inspired by the image of a seabird soaring into the sky. Finished just in time to host the Change of Sovereignty Ceremony on June 30, 1997, the 155,000 sq m (1.67 million sq ft) Extension is purpose-built for meetings, conventions and special events and has a Grand Foyer whose 30-m- (100-ft)-high glass wall drop gives spectacular 180-degree panoramic views of the harbor.

Across the street from there you can't miss one of Asia's tallest buildings, the massive 78-story **Central Plaza.** Further along **Harbour Road** you can call in to **Causeway Centre** to the **Museum of Chinese Historical Relics (** 2827-4692, which has a collection of Chinese paintings and handicrafts; and if you have time to sit down for a few hours, there are two movie theaters in the vicinity, **Columbia Classic** and **Cine Art.**

From here several overpasses will take you across Gloucester Road and into Wanchai — to its nightclubs, bars, Chinese stores and restaurants, open markets and crowded alfresco food stalls and shops. At

OPPOSITE: Wanchai: Hong Kong Academy for Performing Arts and the Hong Kong Arts Centre with Central Plaza in the background.

the beginning of Queen's Road East, just past Pacific Place, you'll find rows of shops that specialize in rosewood and mahogany furniture, along with carved camphor chests. Further along, of historical interest there's the **Hung Shing (Tai Wong) Temple,** where locals go to have their fortunes told, and the quaint **Wanchai Post Office,** which was built in 1912, and now serves as an Environmental Resources Centre (2893-2856, open daily except Wednesdays from 10 AM to 5 PM. Towering behind these two small images of Hong Kong's past life is the

66-story **Hopewell Centre** with its breathtaking scenic elevator ride and eye-in-the sky revolving restaurant.

On your way to Causeway Bay, a nice detour is to take the tram around Happy Valley to view the district's prime attraction, the **Happy Valley Racecourse** which, like its bigger and more modern sister track over in Shatin, is the one of the most popular places in Hong Kong.

The main reason for going to Causeway Bay is, of course, to shop, both day and night, in the boutiques and giant Japanese department stores. But, there are a few other attrac-

Garish pavilions, sculptures and other attractions at Aw Boon Haw (formerly Tiger Balm) Gardens in Causeway Bay.

tions — on the waterfront in a small garden opposite the Excelsior Hotel and World Trade Centre, you can actually watch the firing of the famous Noon Day Gun, whose origin to this day is still being disputed. Nearby, the **Causeway Bay Typhoon Shelter** houses junks and sampans alongside the luxury craft of the Hong Kong Yacht Club.

To the east of the Excelsior Hotel, the recently revamped Victoria Park will introduce you to legions of early morning *tai chi* devotees and, in the late afternoons and evenings, older residents taking their prized caged birds for walkies. During the Chinese New Year and Mid-Autumn festivals the place is packed with thousands of people celebrating the occasions. If you're in an energetic frame of mind, the park has a jogging track, swimming pools and tennis courts. To the east of the park, at the beginning of Tin Hau Temple Road, the seventeenth-century **Tin Hau Temple** is well worth a visit, along with the recently restored octagonal **Lin Fa Temple** on Lin Fa Street.

From here, go up to Tai Hang Road to where you'll see a large white pagoda standing in the shadow of monolithic housing estates. This is the famed **Tiger Balm Gardens,** now renovated and renamed **Aw Boon Haw Gardens** in memory of its 1935 founder, a flamboyant Chinese multi-millionaire who came up with the recipe for the renowned balm that cures everything from a headache to a rattlesnake bite. The "garden" is grotesque but fascinating, full of grottoes, pagodas and colorful statues of mythical Chinese figures and animals. One particular tableau depicts Judgment and Hell, where saints and miscreants alike are judged on their earthly behavior. For the unlucky ones, the punishments are awful — tongues torn out, bodies sawn in half, and a host of other gruesome consequences.

Heading east from Causeway Bay, the MTR or trams will carry you to **Taikoo Shing** housing development in Quarry Bay, where the four Cityplaza towers offer bargain and up-market shopping in air-conditioned comfort and convenience, and a whirl or two around the ice-skating rink if you so desire. Further down the line you'll reach **Shaukeiwan,** once a pirate lair, now the home of one of Hong Kong's biggest

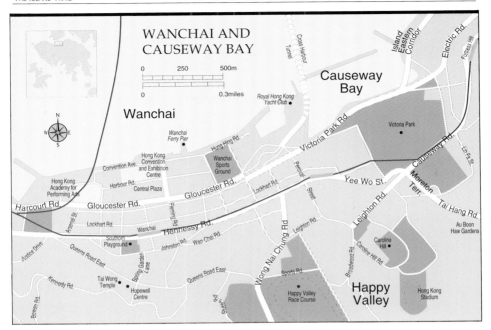

fishing fleets. Here, at the end of Shaukei-wan Main Street by the waterfront, you'll find **Tam Kung Temple**, whose deity is a locally-inspired God of Weather and Good Health and which plays an extravagantly colorful central role in the annual Tam Kung, Tin Hau and Buddha's Birthday festivals.

What distinguishes Tam Kung from other gods is his age — he's said to have been only 12 years old when people began worshipping him — and in a tradition that's quite quaint (though actually has nothing to do with his tender years) his crimson and gilded image is carried from the temple only for the opening of his birthday celebrations, then hustled back inside. Continuing on the MTR, two stops past Shaukeiwan will take you to the end of the line, Chai Wan, where an old Hakka village at 14 Kut Shing Street has been converted into the **Law Uk Folk Museum** (2896-7006.

THE ISLAND TRAIL

From Central District, the main tourist route leads over or through the island's central mountain spine to Aberdeen, Repulse Bay and Stanley. They're easy to get to — if you're not on an organized hotel tour you can take the N° 6 bus from the Central

Terminal at Exchange Square to Repulse Bay and Stanley, crossing the mountain through Wongneichong Gap and passing the garden swathe of the Hong Kong Cricket Club along the way. Or you can take a more scenic route on the airconditioned express bus, also from Exchange Square, via the Aberdeen Tunnel and Deep Water Bay. For Aberdeen itself, N° 7 and N° 70.

Aberdeen is still the most fascinating fishing and boat-people haven in Hong Kong with thousands of fisherfolk still living on a small clutter of surviving junks and their successors, new-style bullet-nosed trawlers. Along the waterfront, you'll be approached by very aggressive old ladies wanting to give you a personal sampan tour through the junks and to the floating restaurants for an outrageous fee. If you say no to their HK$300 offer and walk away they'll quickly chase after you, haggling all the way until they reluctantly agree to around HK$50 per person (for about half an hour's ride).

The town itself has been modernized, with new boutiques and shopping centers replacing much of the old Chinese retail and ship's chandler's sections, but there are still a few places of historical interest such as the 1851 **Tin Hau Temple** on Aberdeen

Reservoir Road and the **Hung Hsing Shrine** on the corner of Aberdeen Old Main Street and Aberdeen Main Road.

The island of **Ap Lei Chau**, once a quiet fishing community reached by sampan, is now connected to the mainland by a long soaring bridge and has been developed into another enormous housing estate. But here and there you'll still find fishing families tending their nets, baskets of fresh fish being hauled and slopped ashore and, all the way along the waterfront, boats being built and repaired.

lic seats, an Atoll Reef (the largest in the world), a Wave Cove with simulated waves and a most contented population of seals and other ocean life, dolphin and killer whale shows at the Ocean Theatre, an aviary, a Dinosaur Discovery Trail and a children's adventure playground.

Middle Kingdom takes you through 5,000 years of Chinese history, along with arts and crafts demonstrations, theater and Cantonese opera.

Water World is adjacent to Ocean Park with its own entrance and features giant

Just south of Aberdeen stands the pride of Hong Kong's cultural and recreational circuit, **Ocean Park/Middle Kingdom** (2552-0291 and **Water World** (2555-6055, a huge playground and marine entertainment complex built into a sharply rising coastal headland. Ocean Park was financed with a trickle of funds from the spillover of the Hong Kong Jockey Club's vast gambling profits and, like Hong Kong itself, it is in a constant state of growth.

At last count it included an outdoor escalator and cable car system linking its lowland and headland amenities, several roller coasters set dramatically on the edge of the headland, more funfair rides, a Film Fantasia-Simulator Ride containing 100 hydrau-

water slides, wave pool and more pools. It's open in summer from June to September.

All three are easily reached from Central by a special Citybus from Admiralty MTR station or, excluding Sundays and Public Holidays, a N° 6 minibus from Star Ferry.

From Ocean Park, the road winds through Deep Water Bay, one of Hong Kong's most attractive small beaches, and to the nine-hole **Hong Kong Golf Club.** From there the route continues to **Repulse Bay** — its beach and high-cost luxury condominiums.

OPPOSITE: Aberdeen and its famous floating restaurant looking out across the marine club. Scenic gondolas ABOVE glide past ornamental pagoda at Ocean Park.

The most commanding view of Repulse Bay is from the restaurant and sweeping lawns of **The Verandah**, the elegant surviving relic of the old Repulse Bay Hotel. It's not just a place for afternoon tea and candle-lit suppers, though it's expensive, even by Hong Kong standards, but also a popular place for young newly weds to have their photos taken on their wedding day. But most of the action takes place on the beach — which has been extended to more than twice its original size and in high-summer is absolutely packed with bathers,

especially at weekends — at the eastern-end complex which features two huge statues of **Kwun Yum** and **Tin Hau** standing protectively over the beach, children's playground, McDonald's and other fast-food outlets, barbecue facilities and a flea market selling souvenirs, sportswear, ladies' clothes and so on. Past the **Seaview Chinese Restaurant** at the other end of the beach, you can walk along the seafront to Deep Water Bay. Beyond Repulse Bay the road twists and turns southeast to Stanley, one of Hong Kong's oldest settlements but best known for its clamorous tourist market.

Buddhist statues ABOVE LEFT at Repulse Bay. Lavish fireworks display ABOVE RIGHT illuminates the night sky over Victoria Harbour.

Until quite recently, Stanley was a picturesque fishing village. Today, Stanley Bay is being reclaimed, the tin-roofed fishermen's and squatter's shanties are being torn down to be replaced with yet more luxury highrises and the villagers will have to find somewhere else to live. For a reminder of what Stanley used to be you can visit the **Tin Hau Temple**, at the far end of the market, and the old colonial-style Police Station, now a historical monument. Also of interest, the military cemetery opposite St Stephen's Beach.

THE HARBOR

The visual excitement of hundreds of ships of all sizes and shapes churning the water in every direction with the backdrop of Hong Kong's famous skyline is probably one of the most vivid of all the pleasant memories visitors have of Hong Kong.

The simplest way to enjoy the harbor is to take the relaxing seven-minute ride on the famous **Star Ferry** between Hong Kong Island and Tsimshatsui on the Kowloon Peninsula. Or join the one-hour Star Ferry harbor cruise operated by the **MP Tours** (2118-6235. Similar scheduled harbor cruises on gaily decorated Chinese junks, some

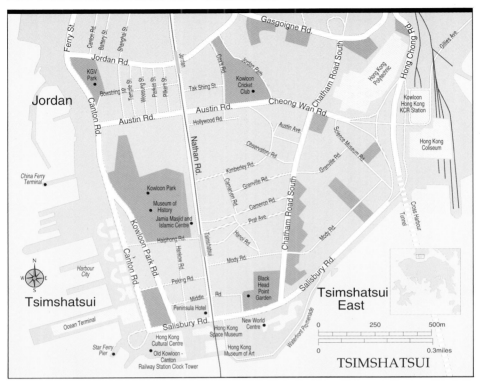

Jordan

China Ferry
Terminal

Harbour
City

Tsimshatsui

Kowloon Park

Museum of
History

Jamia Masjid and
Islamic Centre

KGV
Park

Kowloon
Cricket
Club

Kowloon
Hong Kong
KCR Station

Hong Kong
Coliseum

Tsimshatsui
East

Ocean Terminal

Star Ferry
Pier

Peninsula Hotel

Black
Head
Point
Garden

New World
Centre

Hong Kong
Space Museum

Hong Kong
Cultural Centre

Old Kowloon -
Canton
Railway Station Clock Tower

Hong Kong
Museum of Art

0   250   500m

0   0.3miles

TSIMSHATSUI

taking in dinner cruises around Hong Kong Island, are operated by **Hong Kong Watertours** (2367-1970. Details of these cruises are available at HKTA, most hotel tour desks or from Watertours' boarding piers next to the Star Ferry on both sides of the harbor. See TAKING A TOUR, page 110, for more information about these daytime and dinner cruises.

The Hong Kong Ferry Company (2542-3081 also operates a wide range of services, and the ones to the outlying islands in particular provide an inexpensive alternative to the organized harbor cruises.

KOWLOON

TSIMSHATSUI

Kowloon and Tsimshatsui, the main tourist dormitory, shopping district and playground, have none of the dramatic beauty of Hong Kong Island but make up for it with excitement. To stand at night in the crowded Middle Road, behind the Penin-

sula Hotel, or Peking or Canton roads, is to be almost overwhelmed by the blaze of neon light, a kind of frozen fireworks display of rich colors and a kaleidoscopic clash of ornate signs.

As Central District does, Tsimshatsui starts at the Star Ferry terminal, with the added convenience of an HKTA bureau on the concourse offering advice, maps and booklets on all aspects of tourism in Hong Kong, along with fairly classy souvenirs.

From there, three routes lead into the heart of this people-packed high-rise funland — you can head up the escalator into the mammoth **Harbour City** complex of shops, restaurants and hotels, or you can stroll along the harbor promenade all the way to Tsimshatsui East to more hotels, shopping plazas, nightclubs and restaurants, or walk directly along Salisbury Road and pay your respects to the Grand Duchess of tourism in Hong Kong, the lady who's virtually seen it all, the **Peninsula Hotel.**

Built in 1928, the Peninsula reigned supreme as the center of high society life in

Hong Kong through to the late 1970s, and even had the dubious distinction of being the headquarters of the Japanese military administration during the occupation in World War II. It's seen some of the most distinguished and most flamboyant names of the twentieth century come and go, and even today it's a place where you can play "Place the Face" in its ornate and renowned Lobby, trying to recall the name of the features that just passed you by, and what they were doing when you last saw them on TV.

The Peninsula's columned architecture has survived with much dignity the latter-day explosion of steel and glass in Tsimshatsui, but only just. In the 1970s, after a proposal to tear the old dowager down was quashed, the rooms and suites were renovated and redesigned to update the establishment without harming the outside frills. But even then, one of her greatest devotees, the ill-fated Harold Holt, Prime Minister of Australia, arrived to stay one day after the face-lift and immediately remarked: "You've changed the pub!" Today, the lobby has been renovated again and a 30-story tower of luxury rooms connected to the hotel has been added.

To my mind, any outing in Tsimshatsui should start with morning coffee mid the columns, crisp linen and heavy silver tableware, soaring ceiling, potted plants and equally crisp and precise service staff of the **Peninsula Lobby.**

If you begin your walk at the seafront promenade by Star Ferry, you can study another contrast of tradition and tearaway progress in Hong Kong, the old Kowloon-Canton Railway Station's **Clock Tower,** preserved after much public protest and beside it the **Hong Kong Cultural Centre.** Within the complex there's the world-class **Hong Kong Museum of Art** (2734-2167, which has a superb collection of oil paintings, lithographs of old Hong Kong along with other exhibitions of Chinese fine art and historical pictures, etc. Next door the domed **Space Museum** has one of the most advanced planetariums in the world, and features a sky theater with computerized projection which is so vivid that you actually feel as though you're journeying through outer space. There are performances in English,

but only on certain days and at certain times, so it is best to check with the museum beforehand (2734-2722.

Heading along the waterfront you can take a leisurely stroll to the end of the promenade to **Hung Hom** — the building that you'll see looking like an upturned pyramid is the **Hong Kong Coliseum.** Next to this is the Kowloon–Canton Railway Terminus (KCR), where the suburban trains serve Kowloon and the New Territories centers up to the border with China, and the expresses go right through to Guangzhou

(Canton), the jump-off point for almost the entire China trail.

This walk is a must at night, when Hong Kong is lit up, and especially when there's a full, rising moon; and it's a dazzling, romantic sight that I never get tired of.

Alternatively, you can take the pedestrian bridge just past the **New World Centre** across Salisbury Road to the shopping and hotel district of Tsimshatsui East comprising of **Regal Kowloon, Grand Stanford Harbour View, Shangri-La, Nikko** and **Royal Garden** with its scenic inside elevators. Also located here is the **Hong Kong Science Museum** (2732-3232, which has around 500 exhibits, more than half of them "hands-on," at 2 Science Museum Road. This high-tech playground is every bit as interesting as the one you may have visited in Toronto,

OPPOSITE: Modern futuristic entrance to a shopping plaza in Tsimshatsui East. The clock tower ABOVE of the colonial Kowloon–Canton Railway Station managed to survive after much protest. Behind it is the Hong Kong Cultural Centre.

Canada — complete with robots, a flight simulator, satellite weather shows, animated skeletons of everything from the human DNA structure to dinosaurs, virtual reality demonstrations, various scientific exhibits and, hanging above it all, Cathay Pacific's first aircraft, a DC-3 called "Betsy."

From Tsimshatsui East you can head west back to Tsimshatsui via Granville Road, stopping at **Kowloon Park** on Nathan Road for a much deserved break. The park has extensive sports and recreation facili-

with the bird-fanciers who bring their caged birds here to air them, show them off, compare them with other birds and listen to their song. Some of the finches, thrushes and more exotic lovebirds and parakeets change hands at up to HK$1,000 each, and the passion with which they're regarded by the Chinese — in Hong Kong and indeed throughout China — can be seen in the elegant wicker and bamboo cages, some of which cost HK$10,000 alone, and the delicate little ceramic water and seed pots.

ties — restaurants, an indoor heated Olympic swimming pool, games hall, playground, aviary, Chinese Garden, bird lake and other ponds and gardens. You'll also find the **Museum of History** (2367-1124, where relics of Hong Kong are on display, and the **Jamia Masjid and Islamic Centre,** which was built in 1984 for the Muslims in Hong Kong. Guided tours can be arranged, but by appointment only. Ring (2724-0095 for details.

Also, it's another ideal place to watch *tai chi* exercises in the morning, along

If you're visiting the park on a Sunday, you'll see local amateur musicians put on a variety show, free of charge, from 2:00 to 5:00 PM.

AROUND KOWLOON

Getting There

All of these areas are easily reached by MTR. For those interested in just wandering around Yaumatei and Mongkok on foot, checkout HKTA's *Yaumatei Walking Tour* booklet.

Yaumatei

As previously mentioned, one of the most popular places to visit at night is **Temple**

The minaret of the Kowloon Mosque LEFT in Nathan Road. Corinthian columns RIGHT decorate shopping mall.

Street, not only for bargain shopping but to watch the street theater of Chinese opera, fortune tellers and street dentists. Close by, on the corner of **Nathan Road** and **Public Square Street**, but best visited during the day, you'll find **Tin Hau Temple**, a complex of four temples originally built in the late 1870s but refurbished in 1972 after a fire destroyed the roof and rafters. Two blocks west, at the junction of Kansu Street and Battery Street, the **Jade Market** sprawls its precious wares right across the side-walks everyday from 10:00 AM until around 3:30 PM. But as I've already advised, unless you know all about jade, that is jadeite or nephrite, be careful about buying as there are many other stones which look just like jade.

Mongkok

In **Yuen Po Street**, near the Mongkok Stadium (Prince Edward MTR station is closest), you'll find a whole lane devoted to bird shops, and you may even witness a "bird-fight" in which two prized warblers, put together in a cage, will try to bully each other into submission — without actually touching each other.

Shamshuipo

Further down the MTR line at **Cheung Sha Wan,** a five-minute walk from the station will take you to an area of street markets which cluster around one of Hong Kong's proudest but often neglected cultural sites, **Lei Cheng Uk** (2386-2863 on **Tonkin Street** in Lei Cheng UK resettlement estate. This museum marks the site of a Han dynasty tomb dating from the years 206 BC to 220 AD. When the vault was discovered in 1955 some pottery and bronzeware were found inside.

Wong Tai Sin

The **Wong Tai Sin Temple** located on Lung Cheung Road near the MTR station of the same name, is dedicated to the deity who's become the patron saint of horse-race punters. Glittering in the midst of high-rises, it was built in 1973 on the site of an original place of worship, its most treasured relic being a portrait of Wong Tai Sin brought to Hong Kong from China's

southern Guangdong province 70 years ago.

What makes the temple particularly fascinating is a surrounding cluster of stalls selling joss sticks, colorful paper offerings and souvenir paper windmills — which the Chinese believe will blow away bad luck — and a nearby arcade full of soothsayers and palmists. It's here, along with the Man Mo Temple in Central District, that you can have your own fortune told in the traditional way by shaking the *chim*, a bamboo canister full of tapers, each of which has a number in Chinese on it. You shake and shake until one detaches itself, and its number is written on a scrap of paper. You take this to one of the soothsayers nearby.

You can put the powers of Wong Tai Sin to the test by shaking out two numbers, the race and the runner, and taking them along to the nearest off-course betting shop. You never know.

WHERE TO STAY

Central District, once almost exclusively Hong Kong's business district, has now developed to incorporate exciting new shopping centers, good restaurants and some fabulous new hotels. Accommodation here is invariably expensive, even by Hong Kong standards.

Wanchai and, bordering it to the east, **Causeway Bay** were traditionally the nightlife areas of Hong Kong. Today, business is booming and so is consumerism. There is now a fine choice of exclusive and affordable hotels, including some for budget travelers.

The **Kowloon peninsula** and, in particular, **Tsimshatsui** was the growth area of the 1970s and 80s, while **Tsimshatsui East**, on the harborfront has evolved more recently. There is a veritable choice of accommodation here to suit all budgets.

HONG KONG ISLAND

Very expensive (US$350 to US$450)
Conrad (2521-3838 FAX 2521-3888, Pacific Place, 88 Queensway, Central. One of the three modern hotels which define the very-

upmarket Pacific Place and tower above Central. The elliptical 61-story Conrad has 513 rooms, with spectacular views over the harbor or Peak. Its Italian Nicholini's and Cantonese restaurants are among Hong Kong's best dining venues.

Furama Hong Kong (2525-5111 FAX 2845-9339, 1 Connaught Road Central. Long time landmark on the Island's north shore, this 515-room hotel is superbly placed for business or leisure. It has four restaurants including a fine Japanese one.

Grand Hyatt (2588-1234 FAX 2802-0677, 1 Harbour Road, Wanchai. With its hallmark Hyatt lobby, dramatic and ornate, this 572-room hotel fronts onto the harbor and abuts the Hong Kong Convention an Exhibition Centre. Of its eight restaurants, Grissini's continues to be one of the finest Italian restaurants out of Italy, and One Harbour View is consistently one of the best garden-style Cantonese restaurant in Hong Kong.

Island Shangri-La (2877-3838 FAX 2521-8742, Pacific Place, 88 Queensway, Central. The second of the three Pacific Place hotels, this sheath-like hotel affords visitors spectacular harbor views. Owned and managed by Shangri-La International, it has won countless awards since opening some six years ago. Summer Palace Cantonese restaurant is one of the Island's tops.

J.W. Marriott (2810-8366 FAX 2845-0737, Pacific Place, 88 Queensway, Central. The third of Pacific Place's luxury hotels, the Marriott has a distinctive American feel. Its California-cuisine café and coffeeshops bring American traditions to the heart of Hong Kong. But don't miss its Man Ho Chinese restaurant, either.

Mandarin Oriental (2522-0111 FAX 2810-6190, 5 Connaught Road Central. For years, THE address on Hong Kong. The Mandarin Oriental's understated elegance is for those who prefer a traditional hotel, and old-world sophistication. Part of the award winning Oriental group, it is consistently voted amongst the world's best. Its Pierrot and Man Wah restaurants are by-words in fine dining while its central location couldn't be better.

Ritz-Carlton (2877-6666 FAX 2877-6778, 3 Connaught Road, Central. One of Hong Kong's few boutique hotels, The Ritz-Carlton is able to combine, seemingly effortlessly, luxury with a personal touch. The hotel boasts four fine restaurants (vodka-lovers check out Cossacks bar) and an prime location, just a minute from Star Ferry. It has 216 rooms.

Expensive (US$250 to $350)

Century Hong Kong (2598-8888 FAX 2598-8866, 238 Jaffe Road, Wanchai. One of the newer (and more affordable) hotels in Wanchai, the 516-room Century is well positioned for business, shopping and nightlife. It is connected to the Hong Kong Convention and Exhibition Centre by a covered walkway. Its Lao Chin Hing Shanghainese restaurants has earned a fine reputation among connoisseurs.

Charterhouse (2833-5566 FAX 2833-5888, 209-219 Wanchai Road, Wanchai. A 270-room boutique hotel, The Charterhouse offers five-star comfort in a personalized environment. Good location.

Excelsior (2894-8888 FAX 2895-6459, 281 Gloucester Road, Causeway Bay. Part of the prestigious Oriental group of hotels, the large, 885-room Excelsior offers luxury at a marginally more affordable prices. Ask for a room overlooking the harbor (the hotel's just in front of the celebrated Noon Day Gun site). Renowned shopping arcade. Good restaurants and popular Dickens Bar, favorite with both visitors and locals.

Luk Kwok (2866-2166 FAX 2866-2622, 272 Gloucester Road, Wanchai. Comfortably small, the 196-room Luk Kwok hotel is just minutes from the Convention and Exhibition Centre and well placed for business or leisure travelers.

Park Lane (2890-3355 FAX 2576-7853, 310 Gloucester Road, Causeway Bay. 798 rooms, many overlooking the harbor or Victoria Park, the Park Lane occupies a prime position in Causeway Bay.

Moderate (US$150 to $250)

Empire Hotel (2866-9111 FAX 2861-3121, 33 Hennessy Road, Wanchai. This 345-rooms hotel, located in the heart of Hong Kong's entertainment district, is just five minutes from the Convention and Exhibition Centre.

Grand Plaza (2886-0011 FAX 2886-1738, 2 Kornhill Road, Quarry Bay. 248 rooms, modern hotel built with clean lines. Next to Tai Koo MTR. An interesting and less busy alternative to downtown hotels.

Newton Hotel (2807-2333 FAX 2807-1221, 218 Electric Road, North Point. Modern white block of 362 rooms. International and Chinese (northern style) cuisine.

The Wesley (2866-6688 FAX 2866-6633, 22 Hennessy Road, Wanchai. In the midst of Wanchai, this 251-room hotel is also not far from the Convention and Exhibition Centre.

The Wharney Hotel Hong Kong (2861-1000 FAX 2865-6023, 61 Lockhart Road, Wanchai. 332 rooms in the commercial part of Wanchai. Cantonese and international restaurants.

Average (US$80 to $150)
Garden View International YWCA (2877-3737 FAX 2845-6263, Macdonnell Road, Central. 130 rooms, good location. Essential to book this YMCA.

KOWLOON

Very expensive (US$350 to US$450)
Hong Kong Renaissance (2375-1133 FAX 2375-6611, 8 Peking Road, Tsimshatsui. The 19-story, 500-room hotel — in the heart of Kowloon, managed by Renaissance Hotels International — is an ideal choice for tourists, businessmen and those who want to explore the best shops. The Capriccio is reputed for its fine Italian cuisine. Fancy whipping up a visual masterpiece while waiting for a first class meal? The Bostonian offers you paper and wax crayons to give credence to your creativity!

Hotel Nikko (2739-1111 FAX 2311-3122, 72 Mody Road, Tsimshatsui East. Overlooking Victoria Harbour, this medium sized, slightly more personal 262-room hotel operated by Nikko (from Japan) has a fine location for either business or leisure. Les Célébrités, the hotel's French restaurant, with its belle-époque ambiance, is noted as one of Hong Kong's finest. So, too, is its Japanese restaurant Sagano, known for great sushi.

Kowloon Shangri-La (2721-2111 FAX 2723-8686, 64 Mody Road, Tsimshatsui East. Sister hotel to the Island Shangri-La, and just as luxurious with views toward Hong Kong Island. Shangri-La sophistication and chic from the first step in its opulent lobby. Great Japanese cuisine and ambiance in the Nadaman. Shang Palace is excellent (though not cheap) for *dim sum*. French cuisine in the ultra smart and intimate Margaux restaurant. On top floor the Napa bring new wave California to Kowloon. Just minutes away from some of Tsimshatsui's best shops and nightlife.

New World (2369-4111 FAX 2369-9387, New World Centre, 22 Salisbury Road, Tsimshatsui. Next to the Regent, this modern yet stately 543-room hotel has great harbor views and is just a few minutes walk from either Nathan Road or the glitzy shopping malls of East Tsimshatsui. Operated by Kong Kong's own New World Hotels International (part of Renaissance Hotels Intl.) it has one of the best positions in Kowloon. Excellent Chinese cuisine in its Dynasty restaurant.

Peninsula (2366-6251 FAX 2722-4170, Salisbury Road, Tsimshatsui. The colonial grand dame of hostelry has been the recipient of accolades for decades. With the addition of a new tower equipped with helipad, the 300-guestroom Peninsula is striding towards the millennia in style and sophistication. Award winning hotel and extraordinary restaurants (the ultra modern Felix, designed by Philippe Starch is the newest one in the hotel, its Gaddi's restaurant has had an envious reputation for over 40 years). The Peninsula lobby is, if nothing else, *the* place to people watch in Hong Kong.

The Regent (2721-1211 FAX 2739-4546, 18 Salisbury Road, Tsimshatsui. In a class of its own, The Regent has simply, stunning views of Victoria Harbour from many of its 602 rooms. Fabulous 13-m (43-ft) glass walled lobby which backs onto the spacious promenade on the east side of Tsimshatsui. Great restaurants (Plume, Lai Ching Heen), new Club Shanghai nightclub evoking Shanghai in 1920s and fine rooms.

Royal Garden (2721-5215 FAX 2369-9976, 69 Mody Road, Tsimshatsui East. With its dramatic lobby and 422 guestrooms, this hotel is in a prime position for shoppers and business travelers alike. Sabatini's is one of the finest Italian restaurants in town. Check out its Roman-inspired year-round swimming pool on the top floor.

Sheraton Hong Kong Hotel & Towers (2369-1111 FAX 2739-8707, 20 Nathan Road, Tsimshatsui. One of the more established luxury hotels in Hong Kong, the 798-room Sheraton has a good location near the harbor, opposite the Space Museum at the start of the "Golden Mile". It has good American restaurants including New Orleans cuisine. Its art deco Someplace Else in the basement is one of Kowloon's buzziest night scenes.

Expensive (US$250 to $350)

Grand Stanford Harbour View (2721-5161 FAX 2732-2233, 70 Mody Road, Tsimshatsui East. Four restaurants, three bars. Managed by the classy Inter-Continental group, the 579-room Grand Stanford has, as its name implies, sweeping harbor views (towards Wanchai).

Holiday Inn Golden Mile (2369-3111 FAX 2369-8016, 46-52 Nathan Road, Tsimshatsui. Long time landmark on Nathan Road, the Holiday Inn has been upgraded and renovated. Hardly a better address for ardent shoppers. 600 comfortable rooms, the Loon Yuen Cantonese restaurant and the ever popular Delicatessen Corner make it an affordable choice.

The Hongkong (2113-0088 FAX 2113-0011, Harbour City, 3 Canton Road, Tsimshatsui. Part of the vast Harbour City shopping and commercial complex, and one of the three Marco Polo hotels here, the 665-room Hongkong Hotel is fabulously placed for travel anywhere in Hong Kong. Noted for its Unicorn Cantonese Restaurant, Tai Pan Grill and its popular Chinese restaurant offering Chiu Chow cuisine.

The Marco Polo (2113-0888 FAX 2113-0022, Harbour City, Canton Road. Flagship of the luxury Marco Polo group of hotels, this 440-room property is right in the midst of Kowloon's designer shopping.

The Prince (2113-1888 FAX 2113-0066, Harbour City, Canton Road, Tsimshatsui. A medium-sized hotel, the 396-room Prince (also a member of Marco Polo group of hotels) is part of the huge Harbour City

commercial and shopping complex. With a good location and facilities, it is another affordable luxury hotel.

Ramada (2311-1100 FAX 2311-6000, 73 Chatham Road South, 75 Tsimshatsui. Operated by the Ramada group of hotels this 205-room hotel is in a quieter part of town yet easily accessible.

Regal Airport (2718-0333 FAX 2718-4111, Sa Pa Road, Kowloon City. Part of the expanding Regal group of hotels, the Regal Airport is just three minutes from the Kai Tak terminals and 15 minutes from Kowloon. Ideal for overnighting, this 389-room luxury hotel has also a fine Chiu Chow restaurant.

Regal Kowloon (2722-1818 FAX 2369-6950, 71 Mody Road, Tsimshatsui East. A sister hotel to the Regal Airport, the 592-room Regal Kowloon has a good location in a shopping area just off Nathan Road. Le Restaurant de France is noted for fine French cuisine.

Moderate (US$150 to $250)

Eaton (2782-1818 FAX 2782-5563, Nathan Road, Yaumatei. 468 rooms, this hotel is just beyond the top end of the Golden Mile (Jordan St, MTR) and good option in the quieter part of Nathan Road.

Grand Tower (2789-0011 FAX 2789-0945, 627-641 Nathan Road, Mongkok. An impressive glassy tower block. 549 rooms at the top end of Nathan Road, next to Mongkok MTR.

Imperial (2366-2201 FAX 2311-2360, 30 Nathan Road, Tsimshatsui. A great location in the heart of Kowloon. 222 rooms.

Kimberley (2723-3888 FAX 2723-1318, 28 Kimberley Road, Tsimshatsui. In the older part of Tsimshatsui. 456 rooms. Very near airport.

Kowloon (2369-8698 FAX 2739-9811, 19 Nathan Road, Tsimshatsui. Managed by the Peninsula group, this 736-room glass wall of a hotel is at the top end of moderate. However, great position at bottom end of Nathan Road. The Pizzeria is its popular north Italian restaurant. Also good *dim sum* in the Wan Loong Court.

Metropole (2761-1711 FAX 2761-0769, 75 Waterloo Road, Yaumatei. Located between Mongkok and Yaumatei, the 487-room Metropole is slightly out of the center. Portuguese restaurant.

The Salisbury YMCA (2369-2211 FAX 2739-9315, 41 Salisbury Road, Tsimshatsui. A really upmarket YMCA. It has 380 rooms, including some dormitories. Invariably heavily booked (for its affordable prices, excellent location), so reservation well ahead is advisable.

Average (US$80 to $150)

Caritas Bianchi Lodge (2388-1111 FAX 2770-6666, 94 Cliff Road, Yaumatei. 90 rooms,

matei. Stone's throw from MTR. 50 rooms. Good value.

Chungking House (2366-5362 FAX 2721-3570, Block A, 4/F, Chung King Mansions, 40 Nathan Road, Tsimshatsui. Convenient for shoppings at Tsimshatsui. Probably the most respectable (HKTA approved) of the Chung King Mansions hostels.

Holy Carpenter Guest House (2362-0301 FAX 2362-2193, 1 Dyer Avenue, Hung Hom. Only 14 rooms and very affordable. Bit out on a limb but worth it if you're on a tight budget.

quieter part of Yaumatei and near the MTR station.

Caritas Lodge (2339-3777 FAX 2338-2864, 134 Boundary Street. No frill accommodation at affordable rates.

Hong Kong YWCA Anne Black Guest House (2713-9211 FAX 2761-1269, 5 Man Fuk Road, Waterloo Hill Road, Mongkok. Basic and affordable.

YMCA International House (2771-9111 FAX 2388-5926, 23 Waterloo Road, Yaumatei. Good location and fair prices. Near the Yaumatei MTR station.

Inexpensive (below US$80)

Booth Lodge (The Salvation Army) (277-9266 FAX 2385-1140, 11 Wing Sing Lane, Yau-

STB Hostel (2710-9199 FAX 2385-0153, 2/F Great Eastern Mansion, 255-261 Reclamation Street, Mongkok. Only 27 rooms. Basic and very inexpensive by Hong Kong standards.

Huge hotels like the Regent ABOVE have sprung up in Tsimshatsui East, an tourist city built on land reclaimed from Victoria Harbour on the eastern shores of the Kowloon Peninsula.

The New Territories

SHATIN

The Wong Tai Sin Temple comes under enormous worship pressure in the autumn and winter months when the horses are running at the huge Shatin Racecourse, first major stop on the trail through the New Territories. The racetrack's size and technological grandeur have already been dealt with — see page 164. Shatin is also the home of the huge **New Town Plaza,** a good spot for luxury bargain shopping, featuring the Yohan department store with its vast basement food art, and indoor computer-controlled musical fountain, an outdoor amphitheater for cultural shows and orchestral concerts, a mini-golf course, children's playground and tennis courts.

An even more spectacular local facility is the **Hong Kong Sports Institute** (2681-6888 near the racecourse, a giant Olympic-standard complex that includes a 250-m (850-ft) velodrome, athletics field, "energy room" full of weightlifting equipment, a hall for table tennis and fencing, a 25-sq m (30-sq yard) training pool, 12 squash courts, a judo hall, indoor sports hall with room for two tennis courts or eight badminton courts, a huge gymnasium, 15 outdoor tennis courts, and restaurants and snack bars. It's the pride of Hong Kong's sporting world, described by the President of the International Olympic Committee as the best he'd seen in 130 countries, and it's open everyday for visitors from 8:00 AM to 10:00 PM. The trouble is, you can't use it. Most of its facilities are booked out by major multi-nationals and corporations in Hong Kong.

One place you'll have no trouble visiting and spending some time in is the remarkable **Ten Thousand Buddhas Monastery** behind the Shatin Railway Station. It takes a half an hour to get to it, climbing 431 steps, but it's worth the effort. In the main hall you'll find not 10,000 but 12,800 Buddha images lining the walls, and the human effigy of the temple's founding abbot, Yuet Kai, preserved and covered with gold leaf in a glass showcase. Along with large gilded Buddhas which preside over the main altar, there are also tall decorated images of the 18 *lohans*, the disciples of Sakyamuni Buddha. You'll also find a fierce mounted image of Mo, or Kwan Kung, the God of War, standing guard in one of the halls, along with the God of Wisdom riding a huge blue lion and the Goddess of Mercy, Guan Yin. In **Tai Wai**, just west of **Shatin,** there's an interesting walled village called **Tsang Tai Uk,** which was built as a stronghold by the Tsang clan in 1859, and a few minutes walk away, near Tai Wai KCR station, the Taoist **Che Kung Temple,** dedicated to a deified general credited with saving the area from a plague.

Shatin is also the home of the **Chinese University,** which has a superb collection of more than a thousand Chinese paintings and calligraphy, 300 Han and pre-Han bronze seals and 400 jade flower carvings in its **Art Gallery** (2609-7416.

There is a major hotel in Shatin, the **Regal Riverside** (2649-7878 FAX 2637-4748, Tai Chung Kiu Road, Shatin which offers an alternative panorama to staying in Tsimshatsui or on Hong Kong island and is only 15 minutes from Kai Tak Airport. See listings at the end of this chapter for more information.

GETTING THERE

To reach Tsang Tai Uk, take the KCR to Tai Wai station. From there, the monastery is the next stop down the line at Shatin and the stop after that will take you to the **Shatin Racecourse** at Fo Tan.

TSUEN WAN

From Shatin, the New Territories trail leads to the **Chuk Lam Shim Yuen Monastery** at Tsuen Wan, also known as the "Bamboo Forest Monastery" because it was first established in a bamboo mat shed in 1927. Now an ornate, sprawling temple with a sweeping, curved and tiled roof, it houses three of the biggest images of Hong Kong. Another venue of interest is the **Sam Tung Uk Museum** (2411-2001, on Kwu Uk Kane, which features relics and a re-created traditional

Hong Kong imports most of its food from China but many of the fresh market vegetables found locally are grown on New Territories plots as seen OPPOSITE.

village of the most colorful of the Chinese clans in the New Territories, the Hakkas, who migrated into southern China from the north several centuries ago. You'll see the Hakka women all over the New Territories, distinctive for their wide-brimmed and fringed black hats, and on the construction sites in the urban areas, where they've made it a tradition to work as laborers. A short taxi ride from the MTR station will take you to **Lo Wai Village** and to the **Yuen Yuen Institute,** a temple complex dedicated to Buddhism, Taoism and Confucianism. Vegetarian food is available.

GETTING THERE

Tsuen Wan is easily reached by MTR.

TUEN MUN

In the center of Tuen Mun's high-rise housing estates you'll reach two of the most interesting places of worship in Hong Kong, the **Ching Chung Koon Temple** at Tuen Mun and the **Miu Fat Monastery** at nearby Castle Peak. Ching Chung Koon is a purely Taoist temple, also known as the "Temple of Green Pines," and packed with garish images and altar guardians that were carved in Beijing 300 years ago. It's dedicated to Liu Tung Bun, one of the Taoist Eight Immortals, legendary beings who have been deified as superior human spirits, or fairies, and have the power to become invisible and bring the dead back to life.

Among Ching Chung Koon's other treasures are its famous bonsai collection, a series of lanterns, more than 200 years old, which once decorated the Imperial Palace in Beijing, a 1,000-year-old jade seal and a library of 3,872 books covering 4,000 years of Taoist history. The temple is also a sanctuary for old people without homes or families, who live in a building in the grounds and are supported by visitors' donations.

At Castle Peak's Miu Fat Monastery you're confronted by what could, without irreverence, be called Buddhism Inc. It's a huge, multi-storied temple, packed on most

OPPOSITE Sunrise over New Territories fish farms.

days with worshipers and virtually lined throughout with thousands of small Buddha images and niches paid for by the faithful to gain merit and to keep the establishment in the style to which it has become accustomed. And that style, judging from its latest renovations, is considerably up-market.

Miu Fat has many treasures, including beautiful gilded images of the Three Precious Buddhas on the altar in the main temple — the founding Sakyamuni Buddha flanked by the Lord of the Western Paradise, the Chinese Buddhist version of Nirvana,

GETTING THERE

From Hong Kong Island, take the Tuen Mun hoverferry from Pier 5 in Central; from Kowloon, take the MTR to Tsuen Wan, then bus N° 66M, or bus 68X from the Jordan Road terminus. From Tuen Mun the Light Rail Transit (LRT) will take you to both destinations; to reach Ching Chung Koon Temple alight at Ching Chung station and to reach Miu Fat Monastery go to Lam Tei station.

and the Healing Buddha. There's also a large vegetarian restaurant where the lunch menu is as good as any in Hong Kong. Going from the old to the new, the **Gold Coast Hotel (** 2452-8888, Castle Peak Road, Castle Peak Bay, has to be seen to be believed and like everything else in Hong Kong it's big. Situated on the coast in 40.5 hectares of landscaped gardens, the HK$600 million, 18-story, 450-room luxury resort's facilities include fine restaurants, a spa, adult and children's swimming pool, chip and putt golf and driving range, water-sports, squash and tennis courts, fitness center, disco, business center and conference facilities. The hotel also has its own hoverferry service from Central and Tsimshatsui East.

YUEN LONG

For another look at traditional Chinese life, the **Kun Ting Study Hall** and **Tang Ancestral Hall** in Ping Shan, just west of Yuen Long. The ancestral hall is one of the largest in the New Territories, with three halls and two internal courtyards, and today is still used by the Tang clan. The study hall was built around 1870 mainly for education and ancestral worship. Nearby, you'll find the ancient, hexagonal **Tsui Shing Lau Pagoda**, first built in the fourteenth century to ward off evil spirits. Somewhat diminished in size from seven stories to three, the pagoda used to rise up out of a rustic swathe of duck farms and rice paddies — today most of the farms have disappeared and the pagoda is now dwarfed by high-rises.

East of Yuen Long, **Kam Tin Walled Village**, or **Kat Hing Wai**, has all the character, sights and smells of Old China although its inhabitants now get so many tourists they not unreasonably 'request' a donation (around HK$5) when you enter and a fee for posing for photographs. Surrounded by high brick walls and a moat, the village was built in the 1600s by the Tang clan, and it was obviously fortified as protection

GETTING THERE

From Hong Kong Island, take the Tuen Mun hoverferry from Pier N° 5 in Central, then the LRT to Ping Shan station. From there the ancestral hall is about a 30-minute walk along Ping Ha Road so if you see a taxi, grab it. If you're coming from Kowloon, it would be best to take the MTR to Tsuen Wan station then bus N° 68M to Yuen Long. You can also catch bus N° 68X from the Jordan Road terminus but the journey is quite long, taking

both against the pirates who operated from Hong Kong and Kowloon and warring factions in this, a peripheral southern area which has always lain far beyond the centers of imperial authority to the north. There was also a "walled" city in urban Kowloon, near the old Kai Tak Airport, but it was established for a far different reason. It was left exempt from the colonial lease on the New Territories to provide a safe haven, or diplomatic quarters, where Chinese Government officials could reside and conduct business as ambassadors to the colony. Until the early 90s, when it was completely demolished and the site transformed into a park, it was home to more than 50,000 people.

about one and a half hours. Once in Yuen Long, take the LRT to Ping Shan station, or go by taxi. To reach the walled village, take bus N° 64K from Yuen Long to Tai Po (it passes Kam Tin en route) or a taxi.

LAU FAU SHAN

On the edge of Deep Bay and the western border with China, and right next to the huge new township of Tin Shui Wai, **Lau Fau Shan** is an interesting little fishing settlement which has been the center of the oyster

OPPOSITE AND ABOVE Oyster shells festoon the waterfront and streets of Lau Fau Shan in the New Territories.

farming industry in Hong Kong for many years: the entire township is built on discarded oyster shells. It's a dying industry these days because of the increasing pollution in Deep Bay; previously, most of the oysters were exported or turned into oyster sauce. There are still some popular seafood restaurants here, though.

GETTING THERE

From Yuen Long, take bus N° 655, or take a taxi.

you'll reach **Lok Ma Chau** lookout point, which for more than three decades was the closest most foreigners were able to get to China. Along with the Lo Wu Bridge to the east, it was the point where tour groups could mount observation towers and look across rice paddies, duck farms and the Zhenzhen River and boast later that they actually saw "Red China." Nowadays, of course, it's not the ducks and paddy fields you notice so much as the towering skyscrapers of Shenzhen's Special Economic Zone — and with the China door wide open

THE BORDER AREAS

Further north at Santin there are more ancestral halls, **Man Lun-Fung** and **Man Shek Tong,** along with a stately traditional Chinese official's house, **Tai Fu Tai,** which has been beautifully restored. Built in 1865 by the Man clan, the mansion is decorated with wood carvings, murals and terracotta figures. It's now the highlight on the HKTA Heritage Tour (see TAKING A TOUR, page 110 for details). Just beyond San Tin

to tourism, you can get a visa in 24 hours and see the real thing.

Heading east you'll arrive at **Fanling,** on the main KCR railway line, once just a farming community but now a booming town. But despite its progress, Fanling has still managed to retain some of its past which can be seen at **Luen Wo Market** a traditional rural market with stalls selling dried fish and mushrooms, 1,000-year-old eggs, herbal medicines, beancurd, gold fish and paper offerings. You'll also find the recently restored **Tang Chung Ling Ancestral Hall,** which is believed to have been constructed in 1525.

In Fanling itself, you can visit the famous **Po Sang Yuen Bee Farm,** which

ABOVE: Surrounding "moat" of village near China border. OPPOSITE :Campers at the Sai Kung Peninsula.

produces the most exquisite honey and invigorating honey drinks. The farm is near the KCR station and to arrange a visit (2669-5840.

A short taxi ride from the town center, the **Hong Kong Golf Club** has three championship courses, which are open to visitors, but on weekdays only. For more details see SPORTING SPREE, page 32.

For naturalists, the **Luk Keng bird sanctuary** at Starling Inlet in the far northeast of the New Territories combines a study of egrets and herons, and their breeding season from March to September, with another vantage point for views of China. Some wonderful walks in the nearby Plover Cove area, and sights in Tai Po including the Tai Po Railway Museum are described in THE OPEN ROAD, page 36–37.

To get even closer to the border, you can carry on to **Sha Tau Kok** at the mouth of the bay, but again, you can just as easily get a bus or train to the Shenzhen Special Economic Zone or the train to Guangzhou and spend a couple of days in China itself instead of peeking over the back fence. See SHORT BREAKS, page 74, for information on how to go alone or with a tour.

GETTING THERE

To get to Lok Ma Chau, take a taxi from Sheung Shui KCR station. San Tin and Tai Fu Tai are also best reached by taxi from either Sheung Shui or Yuen Long. Luk Keng Bird Sanctuary isn't as difficult to get to as you would expect — from Fanling KCR station minibus N° 56K takes you right there.

SAI KUNG PENINSULA

There's one other interesting place to visit on the "other side" and that's **Hebe Haven** and **Sai Kung,** where a cluster of old villages around the shallow bay are rapidly being transformed into marine resorts. If you feel like taking a rest from the shopping plazas and packed streets of the urban tourist districts, or feel the need to lay back and get your feet up after your New Territories tour, you'll find relative tranquillity, windsurfing and other watersports, blazing sunsets,

interesting fishing communities, wonderful hiking in the Country Parks and a pleasant place to stay — the Beach Resort(2791-1068, Lot 1780 DD221, Tai Mong Tsui Road, Sai Kung, which has its own beach, swimming pool and recreational amenities. Take a taxi from Sai Kung town to get here.

GETTING THERE

From Choi Hung MTR station in Kowloon bus N° 92 or minibus N° 1 goes to Sai Kung town via Hebe Haven.

CLEAR WATER PENINSULA

Clear Water Bay is another quite dramatic area of beaches, Country Parks and fishing communities, along with the **Tin Hau Temple** in **Joss House Bay.** The temple, which has been restored a number of times, is thought to have been built in the thirteenth century, toward the end of the Song (Sung) dynasty.

If you happen to be in Hong Kong for the Tin Hau Festival, held each year to celebrate the birthday of Tin Hau (Goddess of the Sea), on the 23rd day of the third lunar month that is, April or May — then head for Joss House Bay where you'll see thousands of fisherfolk

in festively decorated boats paying their respects to the goddess.

GETTING THERE

From Choi Hung MTR station take bus N° 91 to the entrance of the Clearwater Bay Golf Club. From there follow the signposts to the temple.

THE TOUR TRAIL

For those who don't want the hassle of public transport, the HKTA and several private tour operators (see TAKING A TOUR for details) offer a number of New Territories tours to most of the sights already mentioned. The HKTA Land Between Tour, for example, takes in such attractions as the **Bamboo Forest Monastery** near Tsuen Wan, Tai Mo Shan mountain, the fish and duck farms of Shek Kong, the golf club at Fanling, Luen Wo market, the bird sanctuary at Luk Keng, Plover Cove Reservoir, a fishing village in Tolo Harbour, Tai Po, the Chinese University and Shatin.

It's an interesting tour and quite reasonably priced at HK$365 for adults and HK$315 for children, considering the distance it covers. But it's also becoming increasingly difficult to promote and sustain as rural adventure with the amount of new development that's going on throughout the area. In many places, especially around the gigantic New Towns, the old rustic paddy life is scarred by major construction, new roads and drainage systems, and some of the traditional tranquillity can only be glimpsed through convoys of huge dump-trucks and their clouds of exhaust. But then, development is as much a matter of pride in Hong Kong as the lingering tradition and antiquity.

WHERE TO STAY

The **New Territories**, once seemingly remote from central Hong Kong, are now just a hoverferry or MTR ride away. Capitalizing on this, there are interesting options for visitors to Hong Kong who would like to combine fine accommodation with a more leisurely environment.

Expensive (US$250 to $350)
Regal Riverside (2649-7878 FAX 2637-4748, Tai Chung Kiu Road, Shatin. A hive of activity during race days, this large 830 room hotel offers Asian and international cuisines. The Seafood Restaurant is particularly good for Cantonese seafood. It's just a stone's throw from the Shing Mun river and only 15 minutes from Kai Tak Airport.

Moderate (US$150 to US$250)
Gold Coast Hotel (2452-8888 FAX 2440-7783, 1 Castle Peak Road, Castle Peak Bay, Tuen Mun. The first hotel to bring resort-style luxury into the New Territories, the 450 room Gold Coast Hotel is a veritable beachside hotel designed in the form of a pyramid. Man-made beaches, good sports facilities and a marina are part of the attractions. Cantonese restaurant and coffeeshop. Easily accessible from Central (by hover-ferry) or from Tsuen Wan MTR, this inexpensive yet luxurious hotel facing Lantau island, provides an interesting alternative to city hotels.

Fish traps adorn the foreshores of Po Toi O Bay in the New Territories.

The
Outlying
Islands
and
Macau

THE OUTLYING ISLANDS

For some reason, Lantau, Lamma and Cheung Chau are called the Outlying Islands. But they're not as outlying as the name suggests since they can be clearly seen from Hong Kong and Kowloon and are not more than one-hour away by ferry.

Lantau and Lamma islands, in particular, offer beautiful countryside for walking and hiking, as well as old temples and interesting fishing villages, an area of Hong Kong that most tourists don't even know exists.

Ferries and hoverferries to Lantau, Peng Chau and Cheung Chau leave from Pier 6 and Pier 7 in Central, west of Star Ferry.

LANTAU

Lantau is, in fact, a whole new Hong Kong. It's nearly twice the size of Hong Kong Island, and for the time being (until the Chek Lap Kok International Airport takes over completely from Kai Tak) quite undeveloped, offering magnificent hiking, camping, fishing and other recreational pursuits. It also features a colossal Buddha statue, monasteries, temples, a fort and even has a small tea plantation. The island broods just beyond the urban jungle of Hong Kong — dark and silent and huge and almost mysterious at night, a rustic green rolling switchback of hills in the day's sun.

The ferries from Central take you to **Silvermine Bay,** also known by its Chinese name, Mui Wo, or "Five Petal," the island's major township. It's named after a silver mine which once operated north of the town. The town has a fairly upmarket hotel, the **Silvermine Beach Hotel (** 2984-8295 and also has an indoor sports centre with swimming pool and squash courts.

But the prime reason for visiting Lantau is to visit the beautiful **Po Lin ("Precious Lotus") Buddhist Monastery,** which lies on the high Ngong Ping Plateau close to Lantau Peak. To get there you take a bus from Silvermine Bay, passing the **Shek Pik Reservoir.** Po Lin was first established in 1905 by a group of reclusive Buddhist monks, and the present temple complex dates back to 1927. It's the most important Buddhist

center in Hong Kong, and once every three years it attracts hundreds of novice monks from all over Asia for special study and prayer. The main temple features three magnificent bronze Buddha images — Sakyamuni, the Healing Buddha and the Lord of the Western Paradise; and an even more spectacular one — the "world's largest" outdoor bronze Buddha statue (34 m or 114 ft high and weighing 250 tonnes) which, on a clear day, can be see from as far away as Macau — stands by the monastery. Vegetarian food is available.

At the nearby **Tea Gardens (** 2985-5161 — Hong Kong's only commercial tea plantation — you can stop off for a cup of Chinese tea, or even stay overnight in one of their (very basic) bungalows if you wish and spend the next day watching the picking and processing of several varieties of tea. From Silvermine Bay you can also go by bus to the northwestern shoreline of the island, to **Tai O,** a small fishing and market town which for more than a century was the center of the salt-panning industry in Hong

OPPOSITE AND ABOVE: Two faces of Lantau Island — twice the size of Hong Kong Island and only marginally settled and developed, Lantau so far has remained one of the territory's main area of open-air recreation.

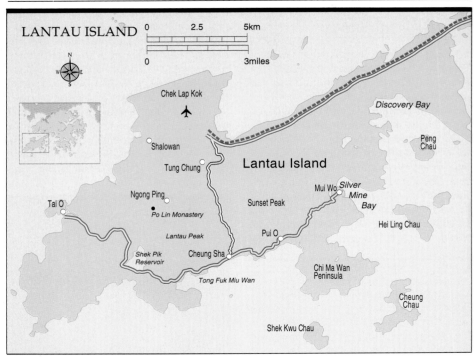

LANTAU ISLAND

Chek Lap Kok

Discovery Bay

Peng Chau

Shalowan

Tung Chung

Lantau Island

Mui Wo Silver Mine Bay

Tai O

Ngong Ping

Sunset Peak

Hei Ling Chau

Po Lin Monastery

Lantau Peak

Pui O

Shek Pik Reservoir

Cheung Sha

Chi Ma Wan Peninsula

Cheung Chau

Tong Fuk Miu Wan

Shek Kwu Chau

Kong. Now, it's more famous for its seafood restaurants, which cluster along the waterfront, and its fisherfolk huts on stilts above the muddy estuary. It also has an eighteenth century **Kwan Tai Temple**, dedicated to the God of War and Righteousness, a deified general who lived in the Three Kingdoms Period (220–265 AD) and is remembered for his crusades against injustice and corruption. Two other temples have recently been renovated, **Han Wong**, overlooking the bay, and **Kwan Yum** just outside the village. There's also a direct ferry service to Tai O from Central District during the weekends and on Public Holidays only which calls in at a small coastal village, Sha Lo Wan, along the way.

Another route from Silvermine Bay takes you to the foot of **Sunset Peak**, a 869 m (2,851 ft) mountain which offers blissful solitude and rest for those who find the clamor of Hong Kong too much to take. It's an arduous three-hour climb to the peak, up a winding path that leads through woodlands and misty meadows, but once there you stand close to clouds, enjoying cool breezes and panoramic views of Lantau Island and a great deal of the rest of the

territory. You can camp up there, and awake in the mornings to the clang of cow-bells among a herd of dairy cattle that feed on the lush hilltop grasses. You'll also find a series of old stone huts that various companies and community groups rent for employees and members who need a break from it all.

Down below, in the village of **Pui O**, you can round off your Sunset Peak expedition with a meal and bottle of wine in one of Hong Kong's most unusual and most popular "outlying" restaurants. If you alight from the bus near the Pui O village school and walk up the hill that rises from the right hand side of the road you'll find **Charlie's** (2984-8329, which offers quite a remarkable menu that ranges from Cantonese food to fish and chips, to curries and even to lemon pancakes, with an outstanding wine list that also includes champagne, port and liqueurs. It's closed all day Wednesdays and lunchtime on Tuesdays unless prior bookings are made.

Another hoverferry and high-speed ferry service goes from Star Ferry in Central District to the **Discovery Bay** residential resort on the northeastern coastline of Lantau. It's a new executive-class dormitory of high-rise blocks and two- and three-story beachfront condominiums with a sweeping man-made beach where you can rent a windsurfer or sailing dinghy for the day or just sit and broil in the sun. It also has 27-hole top-class golf course; for more details see SPORTING SPREE, page 32.

Behind Discovery Bay a path leads up and over the steep mountainsides to another of Lantau's main cultural attractions, the **Trappist Monastery of our Lady of Liesse.** Built in 1956 by Cistercian monks, the monastery supports itself through a dairy farm at Yuen Long which provides fresh milk to some of Hong Kong's major hotels. It welcomes visitors, and offers cheap accommodation at about HK$150 a day — for inquiries (2987-6292. And it offers peace, too — there are signs at the entrance which appeal for "No Radios" and "Silence." Another way to reach the monastery is to go to Peng Chau island on the Silvermine Bay ferry (but make sure it's the one going via Peng Chau) from Central, and then crossing by small motorized boat, or *kaido*, to the hillside on which the monastery stands. If you have time in Peng Chau, take a wander — the island has a 200-year-old Tin Hau Temple and shops selling hand-painted porcelain.

Lastly, as an extreme contrast to the Trappist Monastery, you might want to see Lantau's claim to engineering fame these days: the site of Hong Kong's new **Chek Lap Kok Airport slated to open 1998.** One of the world's largest construction projects, the vast 1,248-hectare (3,083-acre) island site (about the same size as Hong Kong's Kowloon peninsula) is constructed largely from reclaimed land. The original Chek Lap Kok island that once stood off Tung Chung on Lantau's northern coast was levelled and in one of the world's largest reclamation operations, the surrounding waters were filled in to form a new man-made island, nearly six kilometers long and three and a half kilometers wide at its broadest point.

The new airport (which will initially open with one runway only) is designed to handle 35 million passengers a year and three million tonnes of air cargo annually. A second runway and associated facilities will open by the end of 1998.

LAMMA ISLAND

Ap Lei Chau
Luk Chau Wan
East Lamma Channel
Aplipai
Yung Shue Wan
Luk Chau Island
Power Station
Hung Shing Ye Beach
Ha Mei Wan
Picnic Bay
Lo So Shing
Sok Kwu Wan
Tang O
Mt. Stenhouse

To link the airport with downtown Kowloon and Hong Kong Island, 34 km (21 miles) of expressways and tunnels and a new high speed Airport Railway have also been built, as well as a third cross-harbor tunnel (Western Harbour Tunnel) and the world's longest road/rail suspension bridge, Tsing-Ma. Of course, if you've flown into Hong Kong when the airport is opened, you'll have seen and experienced it all at first hand. Otherwise, you can take a bus from Mui Wo to Tung Chung and gaze in wonder at the sight across the water. For more information about the airport project, you can also check out the Airport Authority's Internet website at http://www.hkairport.com.

LAMMA ISLAND

Lamma Island is the closest of Hong Kong's other islands, and again it's largely undeveloped — except for the Hong Kong Electric Power Station on the northwest waterfront — and still nods sleepily in a rustic atmosphere of small villages and fishing havens. The ferries go to two destinations, Yung Shue Wan, or "Banyan Tree Bay" in the north near the power plant, and **Sok Kwu Wan** which lies in the island's narrow central spine.

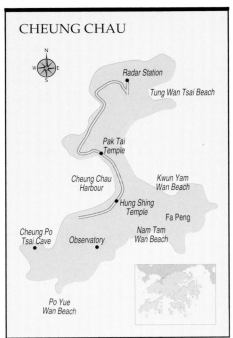

CHEUNG CHAU

Radar Station

Tung Wan Tsai Beach

Pak Tai
Temple

Cheung Chau
Harbour

Kwun Yam
Wan Beach

Hung Shing
Temple

Fa Peng

Cheung Po
Tsai Cave

Observatory

Nam Tam
Wan Beach

Po Yue
Wan Beach

Lamma features several good beaches, many countryside walks, including a strenuous climb up its main peak, Mount Stenhouse, interesting village life and two Tin Hau temples, one in each major town. But it's famous above all for its seafood restaurants which virtually line the waterfront in both Yung Shue Wan and Sok Kwu Wan. Those in Sok Kwu Wan are probably the most popular because the environment is more pleasant — a bay filled with fish-traps rather than the distant stacks of the power station. At weekends, tourists and local residents flock there to pack the covered alfresco eating places, feasting off deep-fried spiced crab, prawns, mussels, oysters and prawns. Yung Shue Wan also has a lively expatriate community, many bars and restaurants.

CHEUNG CHAU

Cheung Chau, a 2.4-square-kilometer (just under one square mile) dumbbell-shaped island close to Lantau, is one of the most densely populated of the outlying islands. Many of its 40,000 inhabitants commute to

Cheung Chau, a confortable 50-minute ride by air-conditioned ferry from Hong Kong Island, is one of the most densely populated outlying islands.

Hong Kong Island to work. Cheung Chau has a crowded and popular huddle of seafood restaurants on the main waterfront, or Praya. There's also a huge fishing and trading fleet, including many junks, that sits off the promenade. At the boat-building yard you'll see as you enter the harbor, traditional fishing junks, elegant teak and yakal pleasure junks were once constructed, in a confusion of crowded slipways. Nowadays, the yard mostly just does repairs and the occasional building of a new fishing trawler.

urbanized main island and Kowloon. But all that peace and quiet pace explodes each April or early May during the week-long **Bun Festival** (see THE BUN FESTIVAL page 82), held to appease the spirits of victims of a plague which swept Cheung Chau in the late 1880s. As huge towers loaded with buns loom over the island's most famous cultural monument, the Pak Tai Temple to the east of the Praya, parades, lion dances and processions clash, bang and howl along the waterfront day after day, highlighted by children in ornate traditional costumes supported by

Cheung Chau was once a thriving port, watering place and market town for junks plying the South China Coast to and from Macau, and had a busy, well-developed society long before Hong Kong itself was settled. Much of that society remains — clans and trade guilds still dominate the island's industrious but carefully-paced fishing and business life.

For some years the island has been a place of retreat for foreign writers, photographers and other "media types" anxious for a more relaxed lifestyle than that of the

children harnessed on tall poles so that they seem to be floating over the mêlée. An altar near the Pak Tai Temple bears giant papier-mâché effigies of the God of the Earth, God of the Mountains and the black-faced Lord of the Ghosts. Throughout the festival, no meat is eaten on the island, so the restaurant fare is strictly vegetarian.

At other times, the car-free center of Cheung Chau is a place for strolling, especially through the market stalls and narrow streets of the waterfront area, where you'll find small factories and workshops engaged in traditional arts and crafts. Its main temples are quite dramatic — the **Pak Tai Temple,** built in 1783, features images of its supreme deity, the Spirit of the North, also

ABOVE: For centuries boat-building has been one of the traditional occupations for the villagers in the outlying islands. OPPOSITE: The Macau Grand Prix — a major annual event.

known as the Supreme Emperor of the Dark Heaven and Protector of all Seafarers, along with the attendant gods Thousand Mile Eye and Favorable Wind Ear.

A sampan ride from the Praya to Sai Wan will take you to a **Tin Hau Temple** and the **Cave of Cheung Po Tsai,** a notorious pirate who once menaced the seas from Cheung Chau. Inland from the Praya there's another small temple, the **Kwan Kung Pavilion,** dedicated to the martial god, Mo, of the Man Mo Temple on Hong Kong Island. The Kwun Yum Temple, to the east of the pavilion, com-

MACAU

Visitors staying on the Hong Kong Island side of Hong Kong are ideally placed for an excursion into another high-living east-meets-west world, that of Macau.

No visit to Hong Kong is really complete without a day-trip or overnighter comparing its fast-paced urban hustle with the relative permanent siesta that exists on its Portuguese-administered sister enclave to the west, Macau and its two islands, Taipa and

memorates Guan Yin, the Goddess of Mercy, and the Kwai Yuen Monastery is a small and remote place of worship to the south.

At weekends, especially during the summer, Cheung Chau is packed with local holiday-makers who come here to swim, laze on the beach, eat seafood at the many restaurants along the Praya, or go windsurfing. The **Cheung Chau Windsurfing Centre** (2981-8316, just past the Warwick Hotel on Tung Wan Beach, is where local Cheung Chau girl, Lee Lai Shan — who won Hong Kong's first Gold Medal in the 1996 Olympics — first learnt to windsurf. You can rent equipment here and have a go yourself, or just sit at the Centre's open-air café and watch other Olympic hopefuls.

Coloane, which are linked to the city by two bridges and a causeway. And no visit is really complete either without a fling or two at Macau's principal industry and source of income, its casinos.

Macau arose as a trading port for foreigners on the South China Coast long before Hong Kong, and was established by Portuguese traders and missionaries in 1557. Its trading power gave way to that of Canton (Guangzhou) and the other Treaty Ports opened up by the British in China, and was eventually eclipsed by the phenomenal growth of Hong Kong, leaving this tiny mainland enclave with a lot to show in the way of culture, especially its Roman Catholic churches and cathedrals, but not much

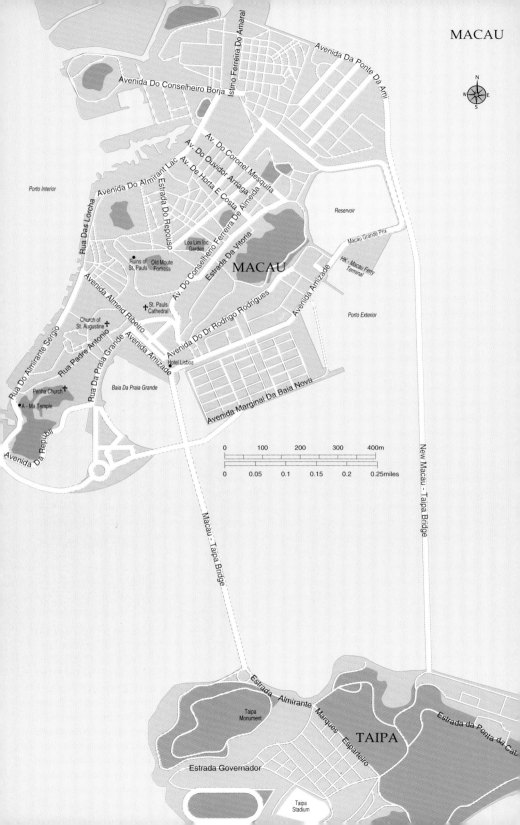

else. Nowadays it's a fascinating blend of Cantonese joss and quite seedy Portuguese colonial authority — along with the annual roar and high-octane odors of its most celebrated European contribution, the **Macau Grand Prix** and a burgeoning holiday resort, offering high-class hotels and a great deal of gambling and nightlife to go with them. It's also in a frenzy of development: a very modern, much larger ferry terminal has already been built, office towers, apartment blocks, hotels and banks have sprouted up, and an international airport on Taipa, along with a four-lane bridge into the city, has recently opened. But most ambitious of all is the amazing reclamation going on in Praia Grande Bay where a city surrounding two artificial lakes, for a population of around 60,000, is about to emerge, increasing Macau's land space by 20 percent. The area will contain office and residential towers, hotels, parks and a tree-lined promenade.

Macau returns to Chinese sovereignty in 1999, and since there are few political conflicts between Macau and China the handover is likely to pass with a great deal less fuss than it did in Hong Kong.

TOURIST INFORMATION

For information contact **Macau Government Tourist Office** ((853) 315566 FAX (853) 510104, at 9 Largo do Senado, Macau. In Hong Kong they're located at 336 Shun Tak Centre, 200 Connaught Road (2857-2287. Or try their website at http://turismo.macau.gov.mo.

Macau's currency is patacas but Hong Kong money is freely circulated. HK$100 = $102.30 patacas, or about eight patacas = US$1.

GETTING THERE

To get there you can go by high-speed jetfoil or hydrofoil, jetcat or steamer from the Macau Ferry Terminal on the western harborfront of Hong Kong Island, or from the China Ferry Terminal in Canton Road, Tsimshatsui. The trip by jetfoil takes about one hour and the fare is HK$132 one way (HK$143 at weekends). Helicopters also leave from the ferry terminal but will set you

back HK$1,206 (one way) during the week and HK$1,310 at weekends. The opening of Macau's International Airport in 1995 means you can now also arrive by air: there are currently services from Lisbon, Taipei, Singapore, Seoul, Bangkok, Beijing, Shanghai, and several other mainland Chinese cities, many served by Macau's own airline, Air Macau (396-5555.

You're going "overseas," from Chinese to Portuguese sovereignty, so don't forget your passport.

WHAT TO SEE

Macau is so small that it's a place for walking, bicycling, or tooling around comfortably in its own form of individual tourist transport, a Mini-Moke. They rent at around HK$450 a day (HK$500 a day on weekends), and you can book them in Macau at **Happy Mokes** ((853) 831212, or through **Avis Rent-a-Car** ((853) 336789 FAX 314112 in Macau and in Hong Kong at (2576-683 FAX 2895-0371.

The sightseeing is interesting if for nothing else than the fact that you're studying another example of two alien cultures that have managed to live fairly peacefully alongside each other for centuries. You can see it in the contrast of Buddhist and Taoist temples and Roman Catholic churches, and in the accommodation that the two societies have reached on philosophy and lifestyle — the bustling grab-happy Cantonese character snoozing beneath the trees along the *praia* during the afternoon siesta. In a few of the older shopping streets of the downtown area, you're also taking a look at Hong Kong, say, 20 years ago, before it began leaping towards the twenty-first century.

There are many temples, most of them Buddhist and ornately decorated, headed by the **A-Ma Temple** at Barra Point, from which Macau derives its name, A-Ma Gau or Bay of A-Ma. It's dedicated to a peasant girl who miraculously survived a violent storm on her way to Guangzhou in the early sixteenth century, and subsequently reappeared in Macau as a goddess. The monastery features several images of her, along with Buddhist and Taoist statues, and a model of an ancient war-junk.

Another fascinating temple is **Kun Iam Tong,** on the Avenida do Coronel Mesquita, dedicated to the Goddess of Mercy and featuring the deity herself costumed in embroidered silk and flanked by 18 Buddha images. There are also images of the Three Precious Buddhas in pavilions and halls placed among elaborately landscaped gardens and fountains.

Among the many churches, **St Paul's,** built in 1602, is the most prominent one — the remains of its towering stone façade and grand staircase on Rua de Sao Paulo is one of the most popular tourist symbols of Macau. The Cathedral on Largo de Sto.

Agostinho, re-built in 1937, features magnificent stained-glass windows and is the focal point of Macau's principal religious events, especially the huge parades and masses of Easter. The **Chapel of St Francis Xavier** on the island of Coloane rates a special visit because of its baroque cream and white, oval-windowed architecture and its relics of the disastrous attempt to Christianize Japan — a crusade which ended with the massacre of hundreds of foreign and Japanese missionaries, priests and followers in 1597 and 1637.

Also well worth visiting is the **Macau Maritime Museum**, opposite the A-Ma temple, which concentrates on Portuguese and Chinese maritime links past and present. It's open from 10 AM to 5:30 PM daily

The busy town square in front of the city hall in the centre of Macau.

to engage in the strictly Chinese passion for betting on two flies strolling up a wall.

The Lisboa is the biggest, most popular and busiest casino, and the only place in Macau where roulette is still played. There are eight other casinos, including the **Macau Palace** floating casino, the **Kam Pek**, the **Jai Alai** (near the Yaohan Department Store and ferry terminal) and deluxe casinos in the **Mandarin Oriental** and **Hyatt Regency**.

You'll find the main Chinese games are roulette, *fan tan*, blackjack and big and small (*dai siu*). The ranks of slot machines are left to the bread-and-butter punters, Japanese tour groups and other visiting foreigners. Unless you're an experienced gambler and know how to slide onto the tables and control your bets, stay out of it and just watch. If you want to take your chances with the slot machines, be prepared to blow a couple of hundred Hong Kong dollars and then withdraw. Their payouts are sparse, and even when you win big there's nothing like the promotional celebration you get in Atlantic City or Las Vegas.

A Hong Kong journalist and his wife hit an incredible HK$1.8 million jackpot in the Lisboa, and wouldn't have known it if they'd been distracted and hadn't actually watched the five red sirens fall into place. There were no bells, flashing lights or sirens. Then, before they'd even been given their check, members of a local triad, or underworld gang, approached them and told them it would cost them half the jackpot to leave Macau. They bravely refused, but ended up handing over HK$100,000 for "protection and security." The wife and children left for Hong Kong that night. The journalist crept quietly out of the hotel the next morning. "Here I was, a big winner," he told a friend later. "And I had to slink out of the Lisboa feeling like a thief!"

except Tuesdays. Racing fans may prefer the **Grand Prix Museum** in the Tourist Activity Centre near the ferry terminal, open daily from 10 AM to 6 PM.

CASINOS

But of all that Macau has to offer, nothing stirs the blood more than its main tourist attraction, the casinos. And nothing can clean you out quicker if you catch the gambling fever. It's as well to accept and appreciate beforehand that the casinos are not there to make tourists happy. Their main customers, and overwhelmingly so, are the Hong Kong Chinese taxi drivers, amahs, laborers, office workers and largely working-class family groups that flood to Macau

GREYHOUND AND HORSE RACING

For more gambling, Greyhound races are held year-round at the **Canidrome** ((853) 574413, Avenida General Castelo Branco, near the border, on Tuesdays, Thursdays and weekends from 8 PM, and horseracing at the **Macau Jockey Club** on Taipa island, mid-week and at weekends from June to

September. For information ((853) 863-1317 or 821188.

RECREATION AND NIGHT LIFE

Aside from sports facilities at the hotels, you can go horse riding at the **Macau Horse Riding Centre** ((853) 328303, Hac Sa, Coloane, ten-pin bowling and ice skating at the **Future Bright Amusement Park** ((853) 989-2318, Praca de Luis Camoes, and wind-surfing at **Cheoc Van** and **Hac Sa** beaches. Also at **Hac Sa**, a sports and recreation complex features an Olympic-size swimming pool, mini golf course, tennis courts, children's playground and roller skating. The **Westin Resort Games Centre**, also at Hac Sa on Coloane, has billiards, table tennis, board games and table soccer.

Most up-market hotels have discos — the **Green Parrot** at the Hyatt is a popular place for the young and not-so-young swingers and the Presidente has nightly cabaret and dancing in the **Skylight Disco and Nightclub.** If you want a touch of the more exotic, the Lisboa features the famous **Crazy Paris Show,** a nude revue which is quite exciting if your tastes run to Miss Green's School for Dance and Deportment for Semi-Naked Young Ladies.

WHERE TO STAY

When you arrive in Macau you're left in no doubt as to why you've been attracted there — the double roofs of the giant **Hotel Lisboa**, the biggest casino in town, are shaped like the hubs of roulette wheels. If you're there purely for gambling, the Lisboa is probably the place to stay — but it's one vast betting machine, with everything centered on its gaming floors, and there's very little charm or culture to go with it. If you stay there, the hotel bluntly demands a deposit, or your credit card, before they'll hand over the key, just in case you find yourself a little down on your luck the next day.

At the **Mandarin Oriental,** the rooms are a little bigger and more comfortable, the whole atmosphere a little more relaxed and pleasant, and it has its own small casino on the first floor. Out on Taipa Island, the one that lies on the other end of the sweeping

coathanger bridge from downtown Macau, the **Hyatt Regency** is a family resort with swimming pool, squash and tennis courts and games room. On the southeastern end of Coloane island, overlooking Hac Sa beach, you'll find another resort, the luxurious eight-story 208-room **Westin Resort,** stunningly terraced up the mountainside. Sports facilities include one heated indoor and two outdoor swimming pools, eight tennis courts, two squash courts, lawn bowling, health club and access to the **Macau Golf and Country Club**. Around the other side of the island, the **Pousada de Coloane**, has a beautiful location near the beach, with some rooms with balconies overlooking the sea, but it's quite shabby and rundown, which is a shame.

One of my favorite hotels is the old colonial-style **Bela Vista**, which lies west above the Praia Grande waterfront. Once very run down, and the best deal in town, it's now been restored to its former glory and is now the most expensive hotel in Macau. If the price frightens you, at least pop in for a look and sit a while and have an early evening drink on its veranda — it's very romantic. The hotel has gone through several incarnations, serving as a school, a haven for refugees, a hostel and a canteen for British servicemen. And it's recently been announced that after Macau is handed back to China, the Bela Vista will change roles yet again and become a Portuguese consular office.

Not all hotels are five-star, and accommodation such as Portuguese-style inns and villas are available. If you intend to go at the weekend rates are higher and a reservation is a must. During the week, most hotels will give a discount. The Macau Government Tourist Office produces a detailed hotel brochure with an indication of their rates and facilities, a selection as follows:

Expensive (from US$150)
Bela Vista ((853) 965333 FAX (853) 965588, Hong Kong booking (2881-1688.
Hyatt Regency ((853) 831234 FAX (853) 830195, Hong Kong booking (2559-0168.
Mandarin Oriental ((853) 567-8888 FAX (853) 594589, Hong Kong booking (2881-1688.
Pousada de Sao Tiago ((853) 378111 FAX (853) 552170, a hotel with character built

in an old fort. Hong Kong booking (2739-1216.

Ritz ((853) 339955 FAX (853) 317826, Hong Kong booking (2540-6333.

Westin Resort ((853) 87 111 FAX (853) 871122, Hong Kong booking (2803-2015.

Medium (from US$80)

Holiday Inn ((853) 783333 FAX (853) 782321, Hong Kong booking (2736-6855, has its own, small casino.

Hotel Lisboa ((853) 377666 FAX (853) 567193, Hong Kong booking (2559-1028.

New Century ((853) 831111 FAX (853) 832222, Hong Kong booking (2581-9863.

New World Emperor ((853) 781888 FAX (853) 782287, Hong Kong booking (2724-4622.

Presidente ((853) 553888 FAX (853) 552735, Hong Kong booking (2857-1533.

Inexpensive (below US$80)

Guia ((853) 513888 FAX (853) 559822.

Mondial ((853) 566866 FAX (853) 514083, Hong Kong booking (2540-8180.

Pousada de Coloane ((853) 882143 FAX (853) 882251, Hong Kong booking (2540-8180.

The mixture of colonial Portuguese and Chinese architecture ABOVE give Macau its special east–west flavor.

Sintra ((853) 710111 FAX (853) 566-7749, Hong Kong booking (2546-6944.

WHERE TO EAT

Macau is a great place for eating and drinking — Portuguese wine is still incredibly cheap — and restaurants are everywhere. For Portuguese and Macanese food such as African chicken, Portuguese sausages, green vegetable soup, king prawns, Macau sole and double doses of olive oil, on Coloane try the famous **Fernando's** ((853) 328264 at Hac Sa beach and, by the entrance to Coloane Park, **Balichao** ((853) 870098. On Taipa, **Pinocchio's** ((853) 827128, and **A Petisquera** ((853) 825254 at 15A Rua de Sao Joao. For exquisite aesthetic surroundings don't miss **Clube Militar de Macau** ((853) 714009 on the mainland at Avenida da Praia Grande 795; and the restaurant in the **Bela Vista** ((853) 965333.

FROM MACAU TO CHINA

As with Hong Kong, Macau has had a special tourist allure over the past 30 years — its position right on the border with China. Now, of course, you don't go there to peek over at PLA border guards and their checkpoints, you can go across by bus on a 10-hour HK$960-a-head day-tour of Zhongshan in the Zhuhai Special Economic Zone, and go from there if you wish right through to Guangzhou. And if you want to do something completely different, you can book into China's "first golf course and country club", the **Zhongshan Hot Spring Resort** a half an hour from the border, and bang your way around the pseudo Scottish links fairways in between tennis, spa bathing, local sightseeing or just relaxing in the club's traditionally-landscaped water gardens. There's also the **Lakewood Golf Club** Zhuhai's newest deluxe resort, which includes a 27-hole golf course and a Formula One—standard racing track which hosted China's first international racing event in November 1996.

For details on trips into China, see SHORT BREAKS on page 74, or contact a reputable travel agent such as China International Travel Service in Hong Kong (2853-3888.

Travelers'
Tips

VISAS

At the time of going to press, there have been few changes to visa regulations since Hong Kong became a Special Administrative Region of China in July 1997. The only major change is a reduction in the period of time — from 12 months to six months — that British citizens can stay in Hong Kong without the need of a visa. Like other foreign nationals, British citizens will also now have to obtain a visa if they want to work, study or settle in Hong Kong. The Hong Kong Immigration Department will continue to process and approve applications for visas from those that require them. The only difference will be that Chinese rather than British consulate offices will accept the applications.

Commonwealth citizens and citizens of Canada, Australia, New Zealand and of most European countries can stay three months with no visa. Americans are allowed one-month visa-free permits. All visitors must have a valid passport, and must fill out a landing card, either on the plane to Hong Kong or on arrival there, to be presented at the immigration counter. All residents of Hong Kong are required to carry an identity card and visitors are advised to carry their passport or some other identification with a photo at all times.

CUSTOMS

Hong Kong is a free port, but that doesn't mean you can bring in anything you like. The usual strict restrictions on firearms, dangerous items, drugs and what have you apply here as elsewhere, and as far as duty-free goods are concerned you can carry in a one-liter bottle of alcohol, 200 cigarettes (or 50 cigars or 250 gm of tobacco), 60 milliliters of perfume and 250 milliliters of toilet water.

HEALTH

Unless you've been in an infected area in the previous 14 days you won't need a cholera certificate, or any other vaccination stamp. Hong Kong itself has very high health and hygiene standards — you can safely drink the water — but the high summer temperatures and humidity can cause skin and fungal problems, called "Hong Kong Foot," if you stay for any length of time. On a short visit, with your tolerance for tropical germs quite low, it's advisable to stay away from cooked food stalls.

COMMUNICATIONS

Hong Kong has a very efficient telephone system, and local calls are free if they're made from a private phone. Some hotels charge for local calls, however, and there are also public phones that cost HK$1 a call. Most hotels have International Direct Dialing (IDD). Cardphones for both local and IDD calls are located at some 500 sites and operate on stored-value phonecards available at most Telecom CSL shops, Hong Kong Telecom Service Centres and HKTA and other public locations in three denominations: HK$50, HK$100 and HK$250. There are also Creditcardphones and Coinphones for local and IDD calls. For more details call International Customer Services on 10013. If you want to connect directly with your country's operator you can use the Home Direct service by using the relevant dial access number from any phone or at the touch of a button from dedicated Home Direct phones at the airport, Ocean Terminal and other major tourist areas.

For directory inquiries dial (1081.

TRANSPORTATION

AIRPORT BUS SERVICE

Until the new Chek Lap Kok Airport opens in mid-1998 you'll arrive at Kai Tak Airport in Kowloon. There are currently three air-conditioned Airbus coach services, operated by Kowloon Motor Bus (KMB) company, which feed travelers cheaply from Kai Tak to Taikoo Shing, Tsimshatsui, Causeway Bay and Central District, calling at most major hotels along the way. The A1 service does a shuttle service to and from Tsimshatsui for a flat fare of HK$12; A2 (HK$19) covers Central District, terminating at the Macau Ferry Terminal; A3 (HK$19) serves Causeway Bay; and A5 (HK$19) Taikoo Shing. The service operates at 15- to 20-minute intervals from around 7:00 AM till midnight. In addition, there's the A20 service, operated by the China Motor Bus (CMB) company, which runs to and from Central (HK$19) via the three hotels in Pacific Place. Once the new Chek Lap Kok Airport opens, there will be services operated by KMB and Citybus to both Kowloon and Hong Kong Island destinations. Citybus will run four Airbus services: the A21 to Kowloon KCR station; the A11 to Causeway Bay; the A12 to Sai Wan Ho Ferry Pier; and the A22 to Lam Tin MTR station (fares not available at time of writing). KMB will provide Airbus services to Tsuen Wan (HK$17) and Shatin (HK$20) and conventional bus services to Tuen Mun, Tai Po, Kwai Fong MTR and Tin Shui Wai.

AIRPORT RAILWAY

An additional line, the Airport Railway, will open in mid-1998 linking Hong Kong's new airport at Chek Lap Kok with Kowloon and Hong Kong Island. The railway will provide two separate services: a fast passenger link to the airport, called the Airport Express, and a domestic service called the Lantau Line linking Central with west Kowloon, Tsing Yi and Tung Chung (the new town opposite Chek Lap Kok). The Airport Express will whisk passengers between the airport and the new Hong Kong Central station (near the Exchange Square) in 23 minutes with just two stations en route — Kowloon and Tsing Yi.

The new Lantau Line will interchange with the existing MTR's Tsuen Wan line at Lai King (located four stops before Tsuen Wan) and provide an alternative, speedier route to Central (eight-and-a-half minutes compared with the present 23 minutes traveling time on the Tsuen Wan Line).

MTR (UNDERGROUND)

The Mass Transit Railway (MTR) operates three lines: one on Hong Kong Island, between Sheung Wan in Western District and Chaiwan in the east, which passes through Central District, Wanchai, Causeway Bay, North Point, Quarry Bay, Taikoo Shing and Shaukeiwan. The second line shoots across the harbor to Tsimshatsui, though Yaumatei, Mongkok, Shamshuipo and Laichikok to as far as Tsuen Wan in western Kowloon. The third line connects eastern Hong Kong with eastern Kowloon, and from Quarry Bay crosses the harbor to Lam Tin, continuing northwest through Kwun Tong, Choi Hung, Wong Tai Sin and Kowloon Tong and then south to Mongkok and Yaumatei.

MTR trains run from 6:00 AM to 1:00 AM, every two minutes during rush hour. For more information (2750-0170 or you can collect an MTR handbook, free of charge, from any MTR ticket office.

KCR (OVERGROUND)

From Hung Hom, the Kowloon-Canton Railway (KCR) runs through Kowloon and the New Territories, with access to such places as Mongkok, Shatin, Taipo, Fanling and Sheung Shui, to Lowu at the Chinese border. But unless you have a China visa, Sheung Shui is the last stop as Lowu is a restricted area. MTR tickets can be used on the KCR, which connects with the MTR at Kowloon Tong. Trains run from 5:35 AM to 12:25 AM about every six minutes. For enquiries (2602-7799.

LRT (OVERGROUND)

The Light Rail Transit (LRT) operates in the western New Territories between Tuen Mun ferry pier and Yuen Long. The LRT has a number of lines, which can be a bit confusing, so be sure to study the route map before getting on any train. For information (2468-7788.

TAXIS

Taxis are plentiful, and reasonably cheap, on both sides of the harbor, with urban taxis operating on a HK$14.50 flagfall for the first two kilometers and HK$1.30 for each 200 meters thereafter and rural taxis on a HK$12.50 flagfall and HK$1.20 for each

200 meters thereafter. There are a growing number of orderly taxi ranks in Central, Tsimshatsui and other major centers, but otherwise it's everyone for himself at the kerbsides — and I've yet to meet any visiting Westerner who can outsmart a Cantonese when it comes to hailing and grabbing one. The worst times to try to get a cab are around 4 PM each day, when the fleets change drivers, and on race days. If you cross the harbor you must pay an extra HK$20 for the Cross Harbour Tunnel fee — it's actually $10 each way, the driver gets to

west of Exchange Square on the island and the Star Ferry in Tsimshatsui. Fares are cheap, but you must have the exact fare. There are also mini-buses that dart in and out of the mainstream transport, picking passengers up wherever they're hailed, rather like taxis, and feeding awkward or distant destinations. Maxi-cabs, a green and yellow version of these "service" vehicles, provide direct access to distinct points — the Star Ferry terminal in Central to the Mid-Levels, Aberdeen and Ocean Park, for example.

keep the extra HK$10 for his return toll. The toll for the new Lantau Link is expected to be about HK$100.

Aside from the occasional young hot-rodder, the drivers are quite expert and most speak a little English. If you're not happy with their service there's a police hotline that you can call — (2527-7177 but remember to note the taxi number or your complaint cannot be investigated.

BUSES

Public buses are also plentiful, both on the island and in Kowloon, and the HKTA provides timetables and information on routes. The main bus terminals are just

For more information on routes, fares and other enquiries, call Kowloon Motor Bus Company (KMB) (2745-4466, and for the Hong Kong Island, China Motor Bus Company (CMB) (2565-8556 and Citybus (2736-3888.

FERRIES

The Star Ferry (2366-2576 shuttles back and forth between Central District and Tsimshatsui for HK$2 first class from 6:30 AM to 11:30 PM. In addition, there is also a service between Central District and Hung Hom via Whampoa Garden and another between Central District and Wanchai. If you want to reach the outlying islands and Tuen Mun in the New Territories, the Hong Kong Ferry Company (2542-3081 operates from a group of piers in Central district on Hong Kong Island, just west of the General Post Office and Star Ferry. There's also a hover-ferry service between Central and Tsimshatsui East, departing from Queen's Pier, in front of City Hall.

TRAMS

For the cheapest scenic land transport, there is little to beat the 93-year-old tram service that runs from Kennedy Town in Western District right through the heart of Central, Wanchai and Causeway Bay and then heads east into the re-developing centers of North Point, Quarry Bay and Shaukeiwan. The fare is cheap and all it costs is HK$1.60. But don't use them if you're trying to get somewhere in a hurry — they're slow. Trams run along this route from 6:00 AM to 1 AM.

PEAK TRAM

On Hong Kong Island the Peak Tram runs from 7:00 AM to midnight, every 10 minutes, from its lower terminus on Garden Road in Central, taking about eight minutes to reach The Peak Terminus 397 m (1,324 ft) up ictoria Peak. Each way the fare for adults is HK$15, but if you buy a return ticket HK$23. Children pay HK$4 each (or HK$7 return). From Star Ferry a free, open-air double-decker shuttle-bus service runs to the 7:00 PM.

RICKSHAW

What was once the cheapest form of travel in Hong Kong, the rickshaw, is today one of the most expensive. Now all but phased out, they're there mainly for tourist snapshots, and for a short run around the block. Negotiate first — if you're lucky, you just might be able to get a photo for HK$50 and a ride for HK$100. But be warned: these drivers are aggressive and greedy.

HELICOPTER

Helicopters can be chartered for sightseeing and for more details and prices contact

Heliservices (2802-0200, Fenwick Street Pier Heliport, Central. For flights to Macau, East Asia Helicopters (2859-3359.

CAR RENTAL

Chauffeur-driven cars are widely used in Hong Kong. Most major hotels have limousines available for guests, or you can call Avis Rent-a-Car (2576-6831. For those thinking of self-driving, I suggest you forget it — street parking spaces are few and far between, and car parks are nearly always full.

MEDIA

NEWSPAPERS

A number of English-language dailies are printed here — the *South China Morning Post, Hongkong Standard, USA Today International*, the *Asian Wall Street Journal* and the *International Herald Tribune*. For weekly regional news, *Asiaweek* and the *Far Eastern Economic Review* are a good bet.

Hong Kong's lifestyle is fast-paced, whether it's public transport OPPOSITE or the insatiable need to keep up with trends through the wealth of printed media which floods the newstands daily ABOVE.

TELEVISION

Satellite television seems to expand by the day and for the moment there are about five channels including Star TV's Star Plus, MTV, and Prime Sports. There are also about 20 Cable TV channels including ESPN1 (an American sports network), BBC, CNN1 and CNBC Asia. Some hotels feature HKTA's Explore Hong Kong and The Hongkong Channel's video guides.

RADIO

The main English-language radio stations are the Radio Television Hong Kong's (RTHK) British-style Radio 3 AM/FM, Radio 4 AM/FM (classical music) and Radio 6 AM (BBC World Service Relay); Commercial Radio's Quote AM, which sounds like a British Station trying to go West Coast; and Metro Plus AM and FM Select.

LANGUAGE

The language of 98 percent of the Hong Kong population is, of course, Chinese, and the dialect is Cantonese. It's completely different in tone and vocabulary to the national tongue of China itself, Mandarin. But before you begin rushing for English-Chinese phrase books and dictionaries, rest assured that most Chinese who you'll come into direct contact with as a tourist in Hong Kong will speak reasonable or fluent English. In the streets there are special English-speaking Chinese police officers, identified by a red flash under the numbers on their shoulders.

CURRENCY

The Hong Kong dollar is linked to the American dollar (HK$7.8 = US$1) and its banknotes come in denominations of $1,000, 500, 100, 50, 20 and 10. Don't be confused by the different designs — they are issued by the three major banks, the Hongkong Bank, the Standard Chartered and the Bank of China. There are also silver coins in $5, $2 and $1 denominations, and bronze coins for 50¢, 20¢ and 10¢. Most banks are open Mondays to Fridays from around 9:00 AM to 4:30 PM, and on Saturdays till 12:30 PM.

If you want to change your currency, generally speaking, the banks give the best exchange rates. You'll find that the hotel desks and the shop-front money-changers charge a commission.

TIPPING

Most major restaurants include a 10 percent service charge in the check — and expect to keep some of the change. Elsewhere, my advice is to tip everyone from bellboys to toilet attendants if they offer a genuine service, but not more than HK$5. Also, add a dollar to the meter fare to keep the taxi drivers happy.

ELECTRICITY

All electrical appliances in Hong Kong work on 200/220 volts, 50 cycles, and American appliances and plugs need transformers and adapters. Most hotels provide shaver adapters.

DEPARTURE

At the airport, remember to have enough money left to pay the airport tax of HK$100 for adults and children 12 years and above (free for those younger than 12 years) when you check in to leave.

ACCOMMODATION

Hong Kong's hotels are among the best and most luxurious in the world, and their rates are among the highest, too. But other options do exist. Despite the wealth of smart hotels, there is a choice of accommodation with prices ranging from five-star right down to hostel class, catering both for the "discerning" and budget traveler. The HKTA provides a comprehensive list of properties that they endorse, including a range of less expensive hotels, guesthouses and hostels. Details from any HKTA office or from their Internet website.

With fast and efficient cross harbor connections, it makes little difference which side of Victoria Harbour you opt to stay on. Indeed, as the outer islands develop and high speed sea transport becomes the norm between the isles and the heart of town, nothing is very far anymore in Hong Kong.

Accommodation on Hong Kong island and in the Kowloon peninsula are listed under WHERE TO STAY page 205; for the New Territories, refer to WHERE TO STAY page 221; for Macau, see WHERE TO STAY page 233.

TOURS AND TOURIST INFORMATION

The **Hong Kong Tourist Association (HKTA)** will provide advice, and books, on shopping, sightseeing, culture, dining and entertainment. They also advise visitors to shop and eat only in places that display their sign — all HKTA members are required to give value for money, an accurate representation of products sold and a reliable and polite service. HKTA also publish loads of other books, maps and brochures, some in different languages, *Hong Kong This Week, The Official Hong Kong Guide*, guides on walking tours, shopping, dining and entertainment. HKTA offer many interesting tours (or will put you directly in touch the tour company) — Sunset and Dinner Cruises, Cocktail Cruises, a Family Insight Tour, Hong Kong City Tour with Lunch, Aberdeen Sampan Tour, Aberdeen and Islands Lunch Cruise, Kowloon and the New Territories Tour, to name but a few, along with their Sports and Recreation Tour, Heritage and Land Between Tours and a Come Horse-racing Tour. See the SPECIAL INTERESTS and TAKING A TOUR sections for more information.

The trams and Star ferries are also available for tours or private charter. Harbor journeys range from a an Afternoon Chinese Tea Cruise to a Sundown Cocktail Cruise and a Harbour Lights Dinner Cruise. Tram Tours, from daytime to dinner excursions,

are on a special open-top antique tram. All tours include drinks on board, a souvenir, lucky draw and entertainment. For private hire, the tram takes in three routes starting from the depot in Western: Causeway Bay-Happy Valley and back (two hours); North Point and back (two hours); and North Point-Happy Valley (three hours). For more details — MP Tours (2118-6241, or call into their Star Ferry booking counters, at Star Ferry on both sides of the harbor.

Tourist Information
For any general tourist information call (2807-6177 (multilingual).

For tours (2807-6390 Mondays to Saturdays; (2807-6177 Sundays.

For 24-hour INFOFAX information menu (facsimile information service — English only): in Hong Kong dial 90060 771128 on a facsimile machine, or, from overseas, (852) 177-1128. Local calls cost HK$2/minute 8 AM to 9 PM, HK$1/minute at all other times; overseas calls are based on the international direct-dial rate.

Or you can visit the HKTA's award-winning Wonder Net web site at http://www.hkta.org for the latest information on Hong Kong, including the most current tour prices and lists of travel agents and tour operators in Hong Kong. You can also contact HKTA.

You'll find HKTA's Tourist Information and Gift Centres at the following locations:

HKTA offices on Hong Kong Island
Jardine House HKTA, Shop 8, Basement, 1 Connaught Place, Central, Hong Kong. Open 9 AM to 6 PM, Mondays to Fridays; 9 AM to 1 PM Saturdays; closed Sundays and public holidays.
HKTA Head Office: 9-11/F, Citicorp Centre, 18 Whitfield Road, North Point, Hong Kong (2807-6543 FAX 2806-0303, E-mail: hktahk@hkta.org

Kowloon
Star Ferry Concourse, Tsimshatsui. Open 8 AM to 6 PM, Mondays to Fridays; 9 AM to 5 PM weekends and public holidays.
Hong Kong International Airport HKTA (on arrival only). Open 8 AM to 10.30 PM daily.

HKTA Oversea offices

HKTA has 16 offices worldwide and a selection of addresses follow:

Beijing ((8610) 6465-1603 FAX 6465-1605, C211A Office Building, Beijing Lufthansa Centre, 50 Liangmaqiao Road, Chaoyang District, Beijing 100016, People's Republic of China.

Australia ((02) 9283-3083 FAX (02) 9283-3383, E-mail: hktasyd@hkta.org, Level 4, Hong Kong House, 80 Druitt Street, Sydney, NSW 2000.

Canada ((416) 366-2389 FAX (416) 366-1098, E-mail: hktayyz@hkta.org, 3/F Hong Kong Trade Centre, 9 Temperance Street, Toronto, Ontario M5H 1Y6.

France (01 47 20 39 54 FAX 01 47 23 09 65, E-mail: hktapar@hkta.org, Escalier C, 8ème étage, 53 rue François 1er, 75008 Paris

Germany ((069) 95 91 29-0 FAX (069) 597 80 50, E-mail: hktafra@hkta.org, Humboldt Strasse 94, D-60318 Frankfurt/Main.

Italy ((396) 688 013 36 FAX (396) 687-3644, E-mail:hktarom@hkta.org, Via Monte dei Cenci 20, 00186 Roma.

Singapore ((65) 336-5800 FAX (65) 336-5811, E-mail: hktasin@hkta.org, 9 Temasek Boulevard, #34-03 Suntec Tower Two, Singapore 038989.

Spain ((343) 414-1794 FAX (343) 201-8657, E-mail: hktabcn@hkta.org, Pau Casals 4, 08021 Barcelona.

United Kingdom ((0171) 930-4775 FAX (0171) 930-4777, E-mail: hktalon @hkta.org, 3/F, 125 Pall Mall, London.

United States of America ((212) 869-5008/9 FAX (212) 730-2605, E-mail: hktanyc@hkta.org, 5/F, 590 Fifth Avenue, New York, NY; ((310) 208-4582 FAX (310) 208-1869, E-mail: hktalax@hkta.org, Internet:http://www.hkta.org/usa, Suite 1220, 10940 Wilshire Boulevard, Los Angeles, CA 90024-3915; ((630) 575-2828 FAX (630) 575-2829, E-mail: hktachi@hkta.org, Suite 200, 610 Enterprise Drive, Oak Brook, IL 60521.

EVENTS AND ENTERTAINMENT LISTINGS

In addition to the free publications offered by the HKTA, which give you basic information about what's going on, there are a couple of other publications (both free) with refreshingly opinionated reviews and listings.

The monthly *bc Magazine* (2976-0876, has comprehensive listings of entertainment, bars, clubs and restaurants. It's website is at http://www.netvigator.com/bconline.

The weekly *HK Magazine* (2850-5065, has restaurant and entertainment listings and reviews as well as features and a classified section. You can pick it up at restaurants, bars, bookshops and cultural centres all over Hong Kong, for instance the Fringe Club, the Go Down, Mad Dogs, Times Bookshop, Hong Kong Book Centre (all in Central); The Arts Centre, BB's Bar and Brasserie, Delaney's (all in Wanchai); Cultural Centre Bookshop, Hard Rock Café, Swindon's Books (in Tsimshatsui).

Another website offering an entertainment guide to Hong Kong can be found at: http://www.webhk.com.

CONSULATES & COMMISSIONS

There are at least 89 Consulates and Commissions in Hong Kong and contact numbers for some of the major ones follow:

Australia (2827-8881 FAX 2827-6583
Belgium (2524-3111 FAX 2868-5997
Canada (2810-4321 FAX 2810-6736
Denmark (2827-8101 FAX 2827-4555
Finland (2525-5385 FAX 2810-1232
France (2529-4351 FAX 2866-9693
Germany (2529-8855 FAX 2865-2033
Greece (2774-1682 FAX 2334-2738
Italy (2522-0033 FAX 2845-9678
Luxembourg (2877-1018 FAX 2869-6623
Netherlands (2522-5127 FAX 2868-5388
New Zealand (2877-4488 FAX 2845-2915
Portugal (2802-2587 FAX 2845-7944
Singapore (2527-2212 FAX 2861-3595
Spain (2525-3041 FAX 2877-2407
Sweden (2521-1212 FAX 2596-0308
Switzerland (2522-7147 FAX 2845-2619
United Kingdom (2901-3111 FAX 2901-3066
United States of America (2523-9011 FAX 2845-1598

Bibliography

Bilingual Hong Kong Guide Book (Hong Kong Street Map), Universal Publications, 1997 edition.

Hong Kong 1997 & Beyond, FAR EASTERN ECONOMIC REVIEW, Hong Kong, 1997.

Hong Kong Guidemaps, Hong Kong, Universal Publications Ltd, 1987.

DANA GOETZ *Hong Kong Factory Bargains*, Hong Kong, Delta Dragon Publications, 1987.

DEREK KEMP *Twelve Hong Kong Walks*, Hong Kong, Oxford University Press, 1985.

EDWARD STOKES, *Hong Kong's Wild Places*, 1996.

FRENA BLOOMFIELD, *The Occult World of Hong Kong*, Hong Kong, Hong Kong Publishing Company, 1980.

JOAN REID AHRENI/RUTH LOR MALLOY, *Hong Kong Gems and Jewelry*, Hong Kong, Delta Dragon Publications, 1986.

JOHN WARNER, *Fragrant Harbour*, Hong Kong, John Warner Publications, 1986.

LYNN PAN, *The New Chinese Revolution*, London, Hamish Hamilton, 1987.

MARK ROBERTI, *The Fall of Hong Kong*, John Wiley & Sons, 1996.

MARTIN WILLIAMS ET AL, *The Green Dragon, Hong Kong's Living Environment*, Green Dragon Publishing, Hong Kong, 1994.

PETER CHANCELLOR *Shades of Hong Kong*, London, International Fine Arts Publications, 1983.

PETER WESLEY-SMITH, *Unequal Treaty — 1898-1997*, Hong Kong, Oxford University Press,

RICHARD HUGHES *Borrowed Place, Borrowed Time*, London, André Deutsch, 1976.

SUSAN JEFFREY, *Drummond's Hong Kong Guide to Art & Antique Dealers*, Hong Kong, Drummond's, 1986.

SUSAN THOMAS SCHNEIDER, *Born to Shop — Hong Kong*, New York, Bantam Books, 1986.

T.C. LAI, *Chinese Painting — Its Mystic Essence*, Hong Kong, Swindon Book Company, 1974.

T. K. GHOSE *The Banking System of Hong Kong*, Singapore, Butterworth, 1987.

TIM CAREW, *The Fall of Hong Kong*, London, Pan Books, 1976.

Photo Credits

Quick Reference A–Z Guide
to Places and Topics of Interest with Listed Accommodation, Restaurants and Useful Telephone Numbers